Collins Revisio[n]

D1102963

New GCSE English

✔ For GCSE English from 2010

Foundation

Written by Sarah Darragh
Series Edited by Keith Brindle

Revision Guide Contents

Exam Practice Workbook Contents

Understanding and producing non-fiction texts

References

For more details on Section A and Section B of the exam, see:

pages 6–7
for Section A

pages 52–53
for Section B

Exam paper

- Your examination is worth 40% of your overall GCSE grade.
- The exam is two hours long and has two sections: **Section A: Understanding non-fiction texts** and **Section B: Producing non-fiction texts**. Each of these sections is worth an equal 20% of your overall GCSE grade.
- Section A tests your **Reading** skills
- Section B tests your **Writing** skills
- You have to answer **all the questions** on the exam paper.

The remaining 60% of the GCSE is split between Controlled Assessment tasks in Speaking and Listening, Reading and Writing.

The skills you are assessed on

When the examiners mark your answers, they are looking for certain skills. These are summarised in the four **Assessment Objectives**. This book supports all the assessment objectives for Reading and Writing.

The reading skills you are assessed on

In **Section A** of the exam, you need to show that you can:

- **demonstrate an understanding of the texts' purpose and audience.**
  This means explaining the content, audience and the purpose of the text: what a writer says and is suggesting.
- **select evidence from the texts to use in your answers.**
  This means picking appropriate quotations to use to support the points you make.
- **make comparisons between the texts.**
  This means explaining the ways in which a text is similar to, or different from, another text. You need to refer to examples when you compare.
- **evaluate how effective the text is.**
  This means explaining how well you think the text does its job – how well it appeals to the audience it is intended for, and the purpose it is intended for.
- **understand the techniques that writers use.**
  This means writing about the language and the ways the words and presentational features have been used.
- **understand the ways in which the texts are organised and presented on the page.**
  This means writing about the position and appearance of pictures and text elements on the page and how they relate.

The writing skills you are assessed on

In **Section B** of the exam, you need to show that you can:

- **communicate clearly, effectively and imaginatively.**
  This means writing so that the reader understands what you are saying and is interested in it.

- **demonstrate a clear idea of the purpose and audience.**
  This means being able to write in a particular form (e.g. a letter or a newspaper article) and for a particular audience (e.g. for older people).
- **organise your writing.**
  This means using sentences and paragraphs, and giving your writing structure.
- **use a range of interesting words and sentence structures.**
  This means using varied vocabulary, techniques such as repetition and contrast, and different types of sentence for different effects.
- **punctuate and spell accurately.**
  This means using a range of punctuation, such as question marks and semi-colons as well as full stops and commas, and showing that you can spell accurately.

GCSE English and English Language at a glance

GCSE English/English Language

Examination paper	40% of total marks
2 hours • Section A: Understanding non-fiction texts 20% • Section B: Producing non-fiction texts 20%	

Speaking and Listening	20% of total marks
3 assessments Presentation Discussing and listening Adopting a role	

English Controlled Assessments	English Language Controlled Assessments
2 assessments	3 assessments
Literary Reading	Extended Reading
20% of final marks	15% of final marks
Producing Creative Texts	Creative Writing
20% of final marks	15% of final marks
	Spoken Language Study
	10% of final marks

Understanding non-fiction texts

Examiner's tip

No marks are awarded for spelling, punctuation or grammar in Section A. The examiners are looking for how well you **understand** the texts. Focus on your Reading skills, not your Writing skills, in this section.

Section A: Understanding non-fiction texts

- **Section A** of your English exam will assess your **Reading skills**.
- You will be given **three media/non-fiction texts** to read. You will be asked **five** questions. One of the questions will ask you to **compare** the presentation of two of the texts with each other.
- You will have an hour to complete this section, and must answer **all** the questions.

The texts

- The texts you will be given will be media and non-fiction texts. This means any type of text which has been written for a **non-literary purpose**: leaflets, articles, reports, biography and travel writing are all examples of this type of text.
- Each text will have a clear **form**, **purpose** and **audience**.
- There might also be a connection between the texts: possibly a thematic similarity such as 'healthy eating' or 'transport'.
- However, there will be clear differences between the texts in terms of the form, audience and purpose, allowing to **compare** the way they have been presented.

The exam paper – Section A

Foundation Tier
Section A: Reading
Answer all questions.
You are advised to spend about one hour on this section.

Read **Source 1**, *Mattie is a hero,* a newspaper report, and answer the question below.

1 Give four reasons from the article that show that Mattie is a hero. *(4 marks)*

2 What did Lucy Downes think of Mattie? *(4 marks)*

Now read **Source 2**, an article from a travel magazine entitled *How the Eskimos survive,* and answer the question below.

3 Find four things which make the writer respect the Eskimo way of life and explain why they impress her. *(8 marks)*

Now read **Source 3**, *Real Heroes,* an extract from a biography about a family that lived through an earthquake, and answer the following question.

4 How has the writer, John Hallett, used language to make us sympathise with:
- Oliver
- Melanie?

(12 marks)

Now look again at all three **Sources**. They have each been presented to attract the interest of the reader.

5 You are going to compare the presentational features of two of the texts. Choose two of the **Sources** and compare them, using these headings:
- pictures and headings
- other presentational features

(12 marks)

The skills you will be assessed on in Section A

The questions that you will be asked in Section A are based on Assessment Objectives. Some questions will test more than one objective, but within the Section as a whole you will be assessed on your ability to achieve the following:

Assessment Objective	What this means in detail
Read and understand texts	You will need to be able to understand what the text is about. Can you identify the **form**, the **purpose** and the **audience**?
pages 10–37	
Select material appropriate to purpose	You will need to be able to find some **evidence** from the text to use in your answers. Can you use **quotation**?
pages 12–13	
Collate material from different sources, making comparisons and cross-references as appropriate	You will need to be able to **select** the parts of the texts that will support your ideas. Can you **compare** the texts with each other using appropriately selected material?
pages 46–47	
Explain and evaluate how writers use linguistic, grammatical, structural and presentational features to achieve effects and engage and influence the reader, supporting comments with detailed textual references	You will need to be able to write about the **effects** of the words that have been used. Can you identify things about the **presentational features** and **layout** of the texts and comment on the effects of these?
pages 38–51	

Kinds of non-fiction texts

Key points

- Section A of your examination will ask you to read **three non-fiction texts** that you will not have seen before.
- You will complete **five questions** on these three texts.

The skills tested

- There will be at least one question based on each text in the first four questions. Then the fifth question will ask you to compare two of the texts. These fourth and fifth questions are worth more marks.
- The five questions you will be asked will test your ability to:
  - find information (this is **information retrieval**) (4 marks)
  - write about what is being **suggested** or **inferred** (4 marks)
  - **find evidence** and say **what it is suggesting** (8 marks)
  - write about **language** (12 marks)
  - compare the **presentational features** used in texts (12 marks)
- All four of the Assessment Objectives are tested through this part of the exam.

What to expect from the texts

- This exam is assessing your ability to read and understand non-fiction.
- A **non-fiction text** is based on **facts, events, reality** and **point of view**. So, for example, an extract from a novel, a short story or a poem would **not** come up on this exam paper.

REMEMBER

The word **media** means 'method of communication'. If you think about the purpose of newspapers, web pages, leaflets, magazines, their primary purpose is to **communicate with an audience**.

What is a non-fiction text?

- Non-fiction falls into two broad areas: media texts and general non-fiction.
- Types of **media text** include: newspaper and magazine articles, advertisements, reviews, editorials, web pages, obituaries, advice sheets or leaflets. A media text will come from a **media source** – for example, a newspaper, a magazine or a web page.
- A **general non-fiction texts** might not be from a media source but will still be based on **fact rather than fiction** – for example, extracts from biographies, letters, instructions, or reports.

Analysing text types

- There are a number of different text types within media and non-fiction. Each is targeted at a particular audience and is written for a particular purpose.
- Each text type uses particular devices – language, layout and presentational features – to achieve its purpose and to reach its target audience effectively.

Examiner's tip

As you answer the questions, focus on **how** the writer has used language or layout and/or presentational features to achieve their purpose. It is never enough to just identify the features themselves.

How to 'read' a non-fiction text

- To be successful in your exam, you need to focus clearly on what the writer wants to achieve and the methods used – in other words, the Why, What and How of the text.
  - **Why** has it been written? What is its purpose?
  - **What** is the writer's message, or what are the messages? What does the writer want us to think?
  - **How** has the writer used language, layout and presentation to achieve their purpose?

- Each examination question will tell you the **form** of each non-fiction text. A typical instruction might look like this:

  'Read **Item 1**, '*The Beauty of Cornwall*', which is an extract from a travel guide to Great Britain.'

Read texts efficiently

- The first time you read the exam texts, you will probably be 'skimming and scanning' – in other words, getting a general sense of what the text is about.
- When you are getting ready to answer the question, however, you need to read in a more careful, efficient way. You will gain better marks if you comment on the use of precise parts of the text – words and phrases – with clear supporting evidence. It is really important to be *specific* rather than make generalised statements.
- One of the five exam questions will ask you to find particular pieces of information (**information retrieval**). This is designed specifically to assess your ability to *read and understand the text and select appropriate evidence*. This type of question might ask you to 'find 3 examples' or 'what you learn/discover about' a particular subject from the text. However, don't forget, **all** of the exam questions are asking you to show your ability to select relevant information and to support your comments with direct reference to the text.

Allocating the exam time

- If you spend the first **5–10** minutes reading through the questions and the three texts, you can then divide up the rest of the hour according to how many marks each question is worth. It works out at around 5 minutes each for Questions 1 and 2, 10 minutes for Question 3 and 15 minutes each for Questions 4 and 5. Remember, this exam is testing your **reading ability** so devoting some time to reading the texts at the start is extremely important.
- It is also a good idea to leave **five** minutes at the end of your exam to check through your work.

Examiner's tip

- It is really worth spending at least five minutes reading the three texts before you start answering your questions. Remember, this exam is testing your **reading** ability so using some time to read the texts is very important.
- It is also a good idea to leave **five** minutes at the end of your hour to check through your work.

REMEMBER

Allow about 5 minutes for Questions 1 and 2 and 10 minutes for Question 3. Allow yourself more time to answer Questions 4 and 5 which are worth more marks than the other questions. So spend 10–15 minutes on each of these.

Purpose and audience

Key points

- Every text has a **purpose** and an **audience**. Good writing has a clear audience and purpose in mind.
- In your exam you will be provided with a range of different text types to read. The purpose and audience are key to your understanding of these texts.

Examiner's tip

When looking at a text, try to work out if it has more than one purpose. For example, a leaflet for a local attraction will give lots of information but its main purpose is to persuade people to visit.

Purpose

Here are some general, common purposes to writing with which you are probably familiar:

Inform	Explain	Entertain	Advise
Describe	Argue	Persuade	Review

When you write about the text, you are likely to mention the purpose and the audience; this demonstrates your engagement with the text. If you understand the purpose of the text it is much easier to identify why the writer has used particular techniques to achieve that purpose.

Look at this response to a text from a TV listings magazine:

The writer's purpose is mainly to persuade viewers to watch the programme. The facts about the appearance of the, 'long-awaited return to our screens of Robbie Williams', are surrounded by language designed to attract a large audience, 'eagerly-anticipated final', 'the nation on the edge of its seat'.

Makes early reference to the purpose and audience of the text

Good linking of audience and purpose to the key language features that are used.

Use of direct evidence as support for points made

Audience

When you are considering audience, think carefully about:

- Who is the intended **target audience**? A particular age-group, interest group, group in society?
- What is the intended effect of the text on the target audience?

The writer will have chosen these features to appeal to the target audience:

- The **presentation** of the text – the use of colour, pictures, diagrams, font style/size
- The **language** used – level of difficulty and variety of vocabulary and sentence structure
- The **content** and **style** of the text.

REMEMBER

Form is often linked to **purpose**: for example, a newspaper report is more likely to be to inform and explain than to persuade.

Writing about purpose and audience

Read the article opposite from a national newspaper and the student's notes on these questions:

- Who is the audience and what is the purpose of this text?
- How is the language chosen appropriate for the purpose and audience?

School Puts Slang on Curriculum!!

'Slang is sabotaging the way we speak' say critics. Some people want it banned altogether. However, a London school has recently added to the furore over the way slang is being increasingly used in daily life, by offering a course on slang to its A-Level students. In addition to studying Chaucer, Beowolf and Shakespeare, students will be learning about street-talk and studying 'wigging'.

'Slang has always been part of the way we speak', says a spokesperson from the school. 'It is fascinating for students to learn about the history and heritage of slang – it enables them to use language in a much more powerful, manipulative way'. However, another school is so concerned about the ways in which their students speak that it has banned 'street talk' from the corridors and classrooms. 'Young people need to learn about appropriateness and register in their communication with others – to allow the sloppy, often disrespectful forms of non-standard English to develop is having a direct negative influence on their ability to communicate in a range of situations.'

"studying 'wigging'!"

Here are one student's notes in response to the questions on page 10.

Notes
Audience: general adult – 'sabotaging' and 'appropriateness' are quite high-level vocabulary choices.
Tone: impersonal style – no direct opinions from the writer, but two opposing opinions are used within the article to give two different points of view.
Purpose: on the surface informative, although the use of exclamation marks in the headline and pull quote suggests that the writer assumes the reader will not approve of the decision to teach slang.

Examiner's tip

Inferring meaning, or 'reading between the lines', is an important reading skill. Two of the questions in your reading exam will ask you to infer meaning from the texts. For example, these notes show that you can infer from the exclamation marks in the headline that the writer thinks the idea is ridiculous. This is what is being suggested.

(See pages 42–43 for more on Inference.)

Analysing a range of features

Reading involves de-coding meaning from everything on the page, not just from the words. This might include:

- The use of colour, fonts, images
- The position or layout of particular features or information
- Headlines, sub-headings

Task

Develop the student's notes above into a response about the newspaper report. How does the report appeal to its target audience and fulfil its purpose?
Write about how language is used.

Selecting and using information

Key points

- Section A of your examination will ask you to read and answer questions on some **unseen non-fiction** texts. You are assessed on your ability to read and understand the text.
- It is vital to read each question carefully to see exactly what it requires and then to select relevant information from the text to use in your answer.

Selecting information

- Find key words or phrases in the question that indicate what to look for in the text and where to look for it. For example:
  - What are *five of the different things* you can do while on holiday in...
  - Find *three pieces of evidence* to support the writer's view that...
  - In the *final paragraph* of the article what is being suggested by...

Read the following question and then the text which from a biographical article about Cheryl Cole (Tweedy).

Find four examples of events in Cheryl Cole's early media career.

Cheryl Ann Tweedy has spent nearly her entire life in the limelight. Born June 30, 1983, in Newcastle upon Tyne, England, Cheryl began her modeling career at the tender age of 6 when she won the prestigious World Star of Future Modeling competition. And she didn't stop there. In the years that followed, she was named 'Best Looking Girl of Newcastle,' 'Most Attractive Girl' at the Metro Square, and she starred in a string of popular commercials seen throughout the British Isles.

'Chezza,' as she's known in the media, won another competition of sorts, at the age of 16, when she beat out thousands of other young women to earn a place at the Royal Ballet Summer School in London. Despite her success as a dancer, Cheryl's true love was singing and she longed for the opportunity to show off her dazzling vocal prowess.

Compare your four examples with the ones on page 98.

Examiner's tip

Reading the question before reading the text can save time, as then you will be reading it with real **purpose**.

Examiner's tip

Don't just copy text – use your own words to maximise your marks.

Using textual references

- To support the points you make in your answers, you need to **refer directly to the text**. This means using relevant references – often quotations.
- By using quotations you show that you are interpreting meaning from the text and have a **full understanding** of it.
- However, using textual reference is not the same as 'copying out'. You will not have much time to respond to each question, so your use of evidence needs to be **short** and **snappy**. So avoid long quotes.

Examiner's tip

In the exam, it helps to underline the important information.

How to quote

There are two ways to use a quotation:

- **Embedded quotes** are shorter quotations which are identified with quotation marks but are placed in the middle of your own sentence.
- **Longer quotes** may be a whole phrase or even a sentence (as long as it is not too long!). If you are using longer quotations, place a colon at the end of your comment. Then start a new line and indent the quotation.

Task

Read this extract from a tourist guide and then have a look at how a Grade C student has used evidence in their answer. They have been asked to comment on how the writer uses language to make the area seem attractive to tourists.
Find examples of both embedded quotes and longer quotes in the response.

Wicken Fen

Wicken Fen is an amazing place. It has existed for thousands of years and has an abundance of wildlife. It is an area of land that is wet and beautiful. You can imagine yourself in the past, listening to the sound of the wind in the reeds and the birds calling. You hear the warblers and other wildfowl and the buzz of so many insects.

There are boardwalks, so you can get close to the flowering meadows and grasses and see the animals: voles, otters… Or, even more exciting, you can journey out on a traditional boat and spend the day watching and marvelling.

The writer uses adjectives to make the area seem attractive. There are words like 'amazing' and 'beautiful', which seem absolute, as if this is as good as it could get. There is even some onomatopoeia, with the 'buzz of so many insects'. It is trying to make the reader think they are actually there.

To make it seem packed with animals, we are given the list with an ellipsis at the end, as though there are too many to even mention:

'you can … see the animals: voles, otters…'

There are also words that make it seem as if things never stop ('watching and 'marvelling') – the 'ing' words make it all seem endless…

Selects appropriate words for comment

Explains the effect

Technical vocabulary

More appropriate vocabulary

Perceptive point to finish

C

Good points

- This response focuses in detail on *how* the text has been written rather than what it is about.
- The student shows that they have understood the text clearly and are using relevant pieces of evidence to support their comments.

REMEMBER

Examiners will award you marks for:

- Making a clear point
- Supporting your point with a short piece of evidence
- Commenting on how the evidence proves your point.

Perspective and point of view

Key points

- To show clear understanding through your reading, you must be able to identify and comment on the **perspective** of the text.
- This means more than just paraphrasing (putting into your own words) what the writer has already said. It means identifying the writer's **point of view** and what he/she is suggesting.
- Writing about perspective often involves analysing and commenting upon the **structure** and **language techniques** used to construct the text.

Examiner's tip

If there is a clear perspective to the writing, the writer will use structure as well as their words to make this clear. One simple way check on this is to read the **first and last paragraphs** and the **topic sentence** of each paragraph in between. These should show a consistent point of view.

Writer's perspective

- Perspective means 'attitude' or 'standpoint'. It will really help your answers if you have a clear understanding of the writer's perspective. It will be aspects of language and or the structure of a text that make the writer's perspective clear. In some instances, the presentational features will also be important.
- First of all, you will need to decide what the writer's attitude is towards the subject of their text – his or her point of view. This will also help you to clarify the purpose of the text. For example, rather than noting that a text is about the problems concerning global warming, you would identify that the writer is **supporting** the need for more action to be taken, or **asking for more research** to be done.

Read the following article from the BBC's *Panorama* website about the rise in youth crime. As you read, think about this question and use the annotations to help you.

What do you learn about the writer's feelings about this place from the way they write?

Strong statement in first sentence, makes perspective clear

Aberfeldy, a small rural town in Perthshire, in the Central Highlands of Scotland, could not have a more beautiful geographical setting but the attraction of the town ends there. The central square is the focal point of gatherings of underage 'neds' drinking Buckfast [alcohol] every night.

Point of view obvious

Drugs are rife and this is one of the nastiest, most violent little communities I have ever come across. The town has one policeman – the local 'Community Liaison Officer'. There are beatings and acts of violence on a daily basis and at weekends the streets are more dangerous than many large cities, even Glasgow. You are at serious risk after the pubs kick out on a Friday or Saturday night of being set upon by drunken louts, many of whom are under-age and high on an alcohol speed combination. There have been many serious assaults over the past year yet, although the police have been involved, there have been no prosecutions.

Use of emotive language

Use of personal pronoun to make the problem more immediate

The use of inverted commas implies the Community Liaison Officers are powerless

This is a town with serious anti-social behaviour problems which are being ignored by the authorities. The main offenders are well known to the police but there is no effort to impose ASBOs or address these issues. One police officer says he counted 92 young people in the square at 2am one Sunday morning. Is counting yobs a policing method? Maybe it's a new way to sleep off your responsibilities. The town is a disgrace.

Appears to be about the lack of police support

Sarcasm, poking fun at police

Clear criticism of police methods

Short sentence sums up the points made

Here is the beginning of one student response to the question on page 14:

The article starts by sounding as if the writer likes this place. One of the first things they say is that it has a 'beautiful geographical setting' which is a very positive description. It isn't long before this idea begins to change though. At the end of the first sentence it says: 'the attraction of the town ends there'. This suggests that the only good thing about Aberfeldy is the location and there is nothing else positive about the place.

The writer describes the town centre as a place where lots of teenagers go to drink and take drugs. The use of very negative vocabulary like 'nastiest' and 'most violent' makes it clear that this is an unpleasant place in the writer's opinion. The negative impression is reinforced by details of 'beatings' and 'acts of violence' which happen 'on a daily basis'.

The writer clearly thinks the police should be imposing ASBOs and clearing out people from the town square, so it can be a little more respectable. Indeed, the final sentence ('The town is a disgrace') sums up his attitude...

Comment on structure and organisation

Comment showing understanding of inferred meaning and writer's perspective

Supported comments on language effects

Still focused on the question

C

Investigating point of view

- Sometimes you have to look deeper for the writer's point of view. For example, news reports often include quotations from people who are connected to the story. While the writer's words seem neutral, these quotations can often voice a strong point of view that reveals the writer's real perspective.

REMEMBER

A writer's perspective can be revealed by other people's words as well as their own. Quotes from witnesses or those closely involved may be used to say the things that the writer really wants to!

Read the following newspaper report. Notice how the writer starts by stating the facts of the story and then uses other's words to give an opinion on what happened.

States fact but verb 'forced' hints at writer's viewpoint.

States fact – which bus involved

States fact – what the bus company did

A BUS driver was forced to take down tinsel from his bus – for health and safety reasons.

The number 65 bus, from Nottingham to Normanton on Soar via the QMC and Clifton, was all dressed up for Christmas with tinsel wrapped around its rails.

But Premiere Travel bus company removed the decorations, claiming it breached rules set by the Government's Vehicle and Operator Services Agency.

Susan Ludlow, of Edgware Road in Bulwell, said: "Has bureaucracy gone mad, political correctness got out of hand or is the country just becoming anti-Christmas?

"The Christmas decorations gave the bus a very festive feel and all the passengers were delighted and complimented the driver".

The verb 'claiming' hints that this is only the bus company's view

Use of quotation to provide passenger's opinion and reveal writer's perspective

Positive opinion of the bus driver's actions given through quotation – reflecting the writer's feelings about the decorations

Task

Use the annotations around the news report to help answer these questions:

- What makes the writer's viewpoint come across as neutral at first?
- Why does the bus company want the driver to remove the decorations? What word hints at the writer's perspective here?
- How is the quotation used to present the writer's perspective on the story?
- What do you think the writer's viewpoint is?

Reading reports

Key points

- A report is a particular type of **information text**.
- The **purpose** of a report is to **pass on specific information** about a particular event or issue, inquiry or investigation, so that others may **take action** using the findings of the report.
- A report is normally written for a specific **audience**.
- Reports usually follow a clear **structure**.
- The style of a report is usually **formal**, using the **third person** and **past tense**.

Types of report

Here are some examples of different sorts of report:

- A company report passing on details of a customer survey to their management committee
- A group of scientists' formal report of their findings from their research project
- A report to a school Governing Body on the findings of the Student Council's survey
- A **newspaper report**: what you are most likely to encounter in the exam.

Formal reports

Take a close look at this **formal report** and the annotations that consider its structure and style.

Sets out the details of what was required

The Student Council was asked to conduct a survey to find out exactly what our students feel about the recent changes in school policies. In particular, it was required to focus on:

- uniform
- the new school day
- lunchtime arrangements.

The work had to be completed before the end of term.

The methods used

We devised questionnaires (see Attachments A, B and C) and issued them to form tutors, so that they could be completed in pastoral time. Since the responses were all anonymous, students were asked to be honest about their opinions, but to take the survey seriously, so that a thorough analysis could be carried out. Because of other priorities, it took several weeks for all the forms to be returned but, eventually, 95% of them came back.

Begins to work through details

Percentages to emphasise the strength of feelings

The results were quite startling. Although there had been a full consultation on what new school uniform should be introduced, over 69% of students complained about it. Despite their initial enthusiasm, 45% of girls no longer liked wearing a blazer; and over 90% of boys would prefer to wear a sweatshirt. 96% of students think that school uniform should be abolished all together.

In each case, results are summarised for the reader

Although everyone likes the new school finishing time of 2.30, over 70% of students wish the lunch break could be longer, and would even consider starting school earlier, if that meant they could have an hour-long break in the middle of the day, as in the past.

Presumably the report would sum up the results and then offer suggestions for further action

Relevant detail taken from the survey throughout

The idea of a staggered lunchtime, with different year groups eating at different times, was not popular. 68% said they did not like having to wait until 1.15 for lunch and many pointed out that they had breakfast before 7 o'clock each morning, so they were unable to concentrate in the pre-lunch lessons. There was also concern about the noise, with some having lunch and others still in lessons…

REMEMBER

- Formal reports are always **factual**.
- They usually follow a **clear structure**: Introduction, Method, Results, Conclusion.
- The tone is **formal** and uses **past tense**.

This is how a student responded to the following question:

Which things were most unpopular amongst the students?

96% of students did not like the new school uniform and that was the most unpopular thing, which is natural really. Then there were lots of other things they didn't like, such as not liking blazers and wanting sweatshirts. Most students didn't like the lunchtime being short and they complained about the noise being made.

D

Good points

- The response answers the question.
- It refers to some details and outcomes from the survey.

Examiner's advice for improvement

- Add more precise details, rather than general comments.
- Make sure that all the results are included.

Another student offered this more precise answer:

The students criticised all three areas. 69% did not like the new uniform and 96% wanted to get rid of it all together. 70% wanted a longer lunchtime and almost as many (68%) were unhappy at having to have a late lunch after having breakfast early, presumably so they could get to school on time. The report also mentions criticism of the noise caused by those enjoying their lunch break, whilst others are still working, but there are no details of how many complained.

C

REMEMBER

Questions about reports may ask you to:

- Retrieve information or find evidence from a text
- Comment on the language used and, possibly, on what is being suggested
- Comment on whether the style and tone are appropriate.

Task

Comment on how the writer uses structure to present the Student Council report.

Examiner's tip

If you refer to key words and phrases from the question in your answer, it is clear to the examiner that you are keeping your focus on the question.

Newspaper reports

- News reports are usually written in an impersonal style.
- The writer will provide facts – any opinions will come from 'sources' or people whose words are being reported through direct quotation.
- How the report is written might suggest the writer's viewpoint.

Read the following news article which is from the BBC website. The annotations highlight some important features of article writing.

Choice of quote in headline indicates bias

Rage Against The Machine: 'We want to wipe the smug grin from Simon Cowell's face'

Emotive language used to engage reader interest

The hotly contested battle for the Christmas number one reached boiling point today after Rage Against The Machine told how they wanted to 'wipe the smug grin from Cowell's face.'

Article reports what has been said

The American group, which is currently set to beat Joe McElderry's single 'The Climb' to the top spot tomorrow with 'Killing In The Name', have been the subject of a powerful internet campaign against the X Factor winner's record.

Quotations from the band involved

The group's guitarist Tom Morello said of the movement: 'It's trying to save the UK pop charts from this abyss of bland mediocrity.

'I don't believe it has anything to do with Simon Cowell personally. I like that guy. He's a great entertainer. He's going to do fine with his No. 2 this Christmas. What you're seeing is real democracy.'

Phrase to introduce an element of impersonal tone

He added that the band would be donating the unexpected royalties to the homeless charity Shelter.

'We graciously extend the same invitation to Simon Cowell,' he added.

Quotation from 'other side' in order to offer a little balance to the article

McElderry is said to be furious about the rival group, and said of the track: 'It is dreadful and I hate it. How could anyone enjoy this?'

He was also pictured throwing darts at a picture of the rock band's frontman Zack de la Rocha.

Bias apparent again at the end

Morello had sympathy for the 18-year-old however: 'The campaign has nothing to do with that nice young man, and his parents are going to be proud of him when he comes second.

Task

Look again at the news report about the battle for the Christmas number one.
What is the writer's viewpoint and how is it revealed?

Reading articles

Key points

- An article from a journalistic source – a newspaper, magazine or web page – is likely to be one of the texts you are asked to consider.
- **Feature articles** tend to offer more than just information; they often provide more of a **considered view** or an **interpretation** of an event or issue.
- Exam questions on feature articles may focus on the **language** used as well as the effects of **layout** and **presentational features** or what is being suggested.

(See pages 38–39 for more on analysing presentational features.)

REMEMBER

- Show that you understand the form, purpose and audience of the text as well as the content.
- Including detailed comments on the effects of particular words and techniques will get you higher marks.

Good points

- The response focuses on the use of language, identifying particular features for one detailed comment in particular.
- The response works well towards the end, where the student extends their point in the final sentence.

Feature articles

- Whereas news reports usually have an impersonal style, feature articles may contain opinions and be written in the **first person** (I/we). They provide the writer's and others' views and interpretation, as well as information.

Read the following article which is a feature on homelessness from *The Big Issue*.

Thousands of people live rough in our public streets and parks. Rough sleepers are more likely to be attacked, abused and robbed than any other group. Yet, they are subject to harassment from the authorities and the public.

There are those who believe that the homeless people, who sleep rough, should be eliminated. They should somehow be swept from our streets and placed in unappealing hostels. Some believe they are a danger to society .... that they are thieves and murderers.

The above view is far from the truth. In fact, those who are forced to sleep rough are often the ones in danger. *Big Issue* vendor Ralph Milward was kicked to death in the quiet Dorset suburb of Westbourne. The fact that there are rough sleepers in our streets and parks is evidence of our failure as a society.

What we need to do is to deliver social care interventions that really work. We need to build bright new hostels for the unfortunate homeless. We need to give them relevant education concentrating on functional skills, so that they can, if possible, find work in the future. How much better it would be, if the homeless were housed and employed.

List of three verbs emphasises the violence

Emotive language used to reinforce point of view

Deliberate choice of verb to show detachment from homeless people

Implies that the homeless are worthless, like rubbish

Clear topic sentence stating the writer's viewpoint

Includes the reader suggesting a shared responsibility

Use of pronoun 'we' to involve the reader and suggest their need to act

Concluding sentence – presenting an unarguable vision for the future.

Here is how one student began to analyse the article in answer to this question:

How does the writer of this article use language to present their views about homelessness?

This article says that homeless people are treated very badly. It uses some strong emotional words to make the readers feel sorry for the homeless, such as 'attacked, abused and robbed'. The writer makes use of the persuasive technique 'list of three' in order to make the point about the dangers faced more powerful. Also, these words make the homeless sound like victims and are used to make the reader sympathetic and want to help...

C

Task

- Complete the response to the homeless article using the student answer as a starting point.
- You may use the information in the comment boxes around the article to help you comment on the language of the article.

Reading advertisements

Key points

- It is quite likely that you will find an advertisement, either from a magazine, web page or newspaper in Section A of your exam.
- You may need to **identify** features of presentation and/or language, and **say why** each has been used.
- If the **form** is an advert, the **purpose** will clearly be to persuade, but you will need to think carefully about the target **audience** for the advert.

Presentational features

Presentational features are essentially the way the text is set out to appear on the page. These aspects include:

- Use of images
- Use of colour
- Font style, size and colour
- Use of text – layout and organisation as well as language
- Logos, slogans, shapes

Notice how these features are used in this advert.

Big business
Not what you're aiming for?
www.graduatefutures.co.uk

How to start analysing an advert

You need to prove that you can write about *why* presentational features have been used, not just identify them.

Add to these notes which one student made in response to the advert above.

Clear focus on the effects of the image

Links the image to the overall purpose

Comments on effect created by angle of image

Evaluates features rather than just identifying them

Notes

Main image – huge towering skyscrapers viewed from below. This suggests that the person is looking up, possibly aiming high? This would link to the main idea of the advert. The image seems to be saying that aiming for 'big business' is very hard. The perspective of the photograph makes the viewer seem trapped at the bottom.

Audience and purpose – it's clearly aimed at college leavers who are looking for work – the name of the company explains this. The main text speaks straight to the reader – 'not what you're aiming for'. This makes the advert and the company seem friendly which is the overall message they appear to be selling.

Text – friendly tone, use of white writing makes the messages stand out – the tone links to the idea that working in 'big business' would be unfriendly. What this company is promoting is a smaller, more friendly working environment.

Identifying and commenting on presentational features

When looking at adverts, it is really important to focus on the effects of the images.

A typical question you may be asked could be:

Write about the ways in which this advert uses:
- **layout**
- **other presentational features.**

Use of 'commands' to appeal directly to reader

Main header text in red links to the image of footprints

Full page photo of a deserted beach – suggests lovely weather, peace and relaxation

The couple are walking towards the sunset, suggesting exploration and romance

Body text is presented with wavy borders suggesting relaxation

Footprints in the foreground – draw reader's eye into middle of image – the couple

Logo also in red placed at corner in line with footprints.

Here is how one student responded to this question. The annotations show you why it was awarded a Grade C.

Range of features examined

Interpretation

Identifies the immediate impression

<u>Layout</u>

The first thing we notice in the picture is the couple wandering off into a rich sunset. The whole advertisement is in late evening shades, which are romantic and warm. The footsteps lead us to the couple, and the way they curve into the distance suggests the lazy, relaxed mood they are in. The body of the text follows that same curve, showing everything is in harmony. The idea of footprints is reflected in the red heading, which is like the red of the sun and it connects with 'Devon' at the bottom, as if Devon is the place for a romantic walk.

Arrives at a purpose of the text

Ideas sensibly linked

C

Good points

- This is a detailed response in which the points made are supported throughout.
- The mood is central to the effect of the advertisement and to the interpretation in the response.

REMEMBER

Good readers 'read' the *whole* text, not just the words. Look at how presentational features help you to understand a text.

Task

Complete this answer on the advert by writing the section on other presentational features.

Reading leaflets

Key points

- Leaflets can serve a variety of **purposes**: to give information, to offer advice, or to persuade the reader to act or think in a particular way.
- Information usually comes in short sections in leaflets, allowing them to be read very easily.
- Presentational features such as sub-headings and bullet point lists are often used to break the information down into short pieces of text. Use of image and colour also helps convey the message.

Reading a leaflet

- When writing about leaflets in the exam, always consider the writer's main aim, and make links between this and the layout and the presentational features.
- You may also be asked to focus on the way language is used to achieve this aim and what is suggested by the language, or you may need to locate information.

Look at this leaflet from an airline company.

Here is how one student started to write about the use of **presentational features**.

The leaflet is almost all in blue, which is good because it shows it's all part of the same thing. It is also right, because it's about flying and the sky is blue. As it's about the in-flight entertainment you can get on Jet2, there are pictures showing you that. There is a man being offered an in-flight machine for watching programmes and then there are lots of pictures showing you programmes you can see. The red really grabs your attention and the £5 stands out because it is there twice. The writing is in black and white so the sections are clearer.

> True point, but obvious

> Some understanding of the use of colour

> Identifying features

> Again true, but explanations are relatively simple

D

Examiner's tip

Commenting on the effect of individual language choices and layout features is good but if you can also show how these elements work together, e.g. use of colour and image, you will gain more marks.

This improved response has more features of a Grade C:

This leaflet, from an airline company, uses presentational features to advertise a positive feature about its journeys - the entertainment provided - and persuade customers to choose this airline.

The leaflet uses colour and images to highlight its major selling features; the use of blue as the main colour makes the rest of the images stand out, as well as linking to the idea of blue skies and freedom. The blue also contrasts well with the red, which is important to the company as the red contains the main points of the leaflet: the price, the ease of use and, most importantly, the name of the airline company.

The use of photographs is limited to screen captures of the range of films/TV shows on offer, enabling them to stand out and be highlighted straight away by the reader. Also, they are designed to appeal to a wide audience, with a range of films being chosen in order to demonstrate that there are plenty of types of entertainment on offer for a wide range of people...

C

Good points

- Starts well by referring directly to the question.
- Moves beyond 'spotting' the features to comment on the effects achieved.
- Links are made to explore how the presentational features work together (though more could be added).

Writing about leaflets

Read the leaflet below. What do you notice about the way it has been presented?

Important information at the top
Black background suggests possible grim results of flu
The key purpose of the leaflet is written in capitals
Colour scheme simple – blue and white and black – and makes image stand out
SWINE FLU INFORMATION
0800 1 513 513
www.nhs.uk
www.direct.gov.uk/swineflu
IMPORTANT INFORMATION ABOUT SWINE FLU
This leaflet contains important information to help you and your family – KEEP IT SAFE
Large image showing swine flu 'germs' being sprayed into the air
Hand features large in foreground – useless in preventing germs from spreading
The words 'keep it safe' also in capitals, for emphasis

Task

Write an answer to this question:

How have presentational features been used for effect in this leaflet?

Use the annotations as a starting point.

Reading diaries and blogs

Key points

- Diaries are factual accounts, usually organised **chronologically**.
- A blog (or 'web log') is also a form of diary, but written for and read online by a wider audience.
- If a diary extract comes up in the exam, you might be asked to comment on its language features and their effects or the writer's viewpoint, as well as simple information questions.

Diaries

- Personal diaries are written in the first person and are informal in style, usually written for the writer's eye only. They include personal recollections as well as facts about daily events.

Below is an extract from the final diary entry of Captain Scott, whose famous *Discovery* expedition to the Antarctic ended in the tragic death of himself and his whole party in 1912.

Read the diary, using the annotations to help you identify the particular language features Scott uses.

Clear purpose to the diary entry – to provide an account of the expedition

Numerical list creates a factual tone

Gives a personal opinion after the list of facts

Powerful adjective amongst this factual account makes a strong impact

Emotive language used to show extreme circumstances

The causes of the disaster are not due to faulty Organisation, but to misfortune in all risks which had to be undertaken.

1. The loss of pony transport in March 1911 obliged me to start later than I had intended, and obliged the limits of stuff transported to be narrowed.
2. The weather throughout the outward journey, and especially the long gale in 83° S., stopped us.
3. The soft snow in lower reaches of glacier again reduced pace.

We fought these untoward events with a will and conquered, but it cut into our provision reserve...

Every detail of our food supplies, clothing and depots made on the interior ice-sheet and over that stretch of 700 miles to the Pole and back, worked out to perfection. The advance party would have returned to the glacier in fine form and with surplus of food, but for the astonishing failure of the man whom we had least expected to fail. Edgar Evans was thought the strongest man of the party.

The Beardmore Glacier is not difficult in fine weather, but on our return we did not get a single completely fine day; this with a sick companion enormously increased our anxieties.

As I have said elsewhere, we got into frightfully rough ice and Edgar Evans received a concussion of the brain – he died a natural death, but left us a shaken party with the season unduly advanced.

Use of first person throughout (we' more often than 'I')

Here is how a student responded to the following question about the Scott's diary extract:

What do we learn about Scott's thoughts and feelings in this diary extract?

Scott identifies all the things that have gone wrong with the expedition. He says they have been unlucky with many things such as the loss of pony transport, the weather and the soft snow. He feels they still fought hard and the planning over such things as 'our food supply, clothing and depots' was perfect. They were really put into trouble by the lack of fine weather and the fact that Edgar Evans got concussion of the brain. This, he says, is what turned them into 'a shaken party', especially when Evans died.

C

Good points

- The response includes the relevant details from the diary.
- There is an appropriate summary at the start.
- Evidence supports the idea.

Blogs

- Blogs are also written in first person and organised chronologically. Like diaries they are an 'on-going' piece of writing, added to regularly. They can seem more like someone talking than most personal diaries.
- A blog often has a wider general audience than a personal diary and its content and tone reflect this.

Read these blogs, written by Glenn Morris, the leader of an educational Arctic expedition.

Northern Lights offer a stunning midnight display

March 28th 2009

+ AUDIO MP3

Hi it's Glenn here. Here's an update. We've reached a fish camp on the way back to Iglulik and going very well now. Last night we camped on the ice very late and it was pitch black when we set up the tent.

It was absolutely astounding because I'd never seen a sight like it. The Northern Lights were just stunning like green inverted curtains shimmering over the entire sky. It was very cold and it was absolutely stunning and as well as that the stars were just numerous in this great black expanse of the Arctic winter. So it was really quite entertaining watching the Northern Lights. We should reach Iglulik all being well sometime on Saturday.

Uses first person, 'we' to include the reader – making it seem personal

Provides an 'update' or status report

Shares information with the reader on their experiences during the journey

Blizzard conditions on the way to Iglulik

March 25th 2009

+ AUDIO MP3

Hi it's Glenn. It's very late up in the Arctic. We've just set up camp. We left quite late today as last night was extremely windy and there was a ground blizzard. We left it until about 2 o'clock and packed up and set off. Nevertheless we were still travelling in what was in effect a ground blizzard — not very pleasant! It blows fine snow all over you and you get covered. Nevertheless we were vigilant and careful which is what is needed to make sure you don't get too wet, or damp or too cold. We got on fine and made good mileage on our way to Iglulik.

Offers immediate information about where they are and what they are doing – typical of a 'blog'

Creates informal 'talk-like tone by the use of punctuation

Task

Read Glenn Morris' blogs again.
Comment on the way language has been used in the blogs to:

- make the situation clear
- make the situation interesting.

REMEMBER

- Before you start writing, identify the purpose and audience of the blog or diary extract.
- Then, if the question requires it, comment on the language features that deliver that purpose to the intended audience.

Reading biography and autobiography

Key points

- **Biographies** are written *about* the person concerned and **autobiographies** are written *by* the person concerned.
- A biography will be written in **third person**, an autobiography in **first person** and their **structure** and organisation is normally in **time order**.
- Exam questions you will meet on this type of writing are likely to focus on how language is used to meet this purpose. You may also be asked to infer meaning from the extract, or to find information.

Biographical writing

- Biographical writing is a type of non-fiction text which is about the life, and possibly work, of a real person – possibly a public figure or someone who has had a significant impact on the world.
- The **purpose** of biographical writing is usually a mixture of entertaining and informing the reader.

Autobiographies

•An autobiography is the story of someone's life – or a significant part of their life – written by the person themselves.

The following extract is from Sir Robin Day's autobiography. Sir Robin used to interview politicians on television, and this is about his first ever time in front of the cameras – in the 1950s, when television was less high-tech and there were no autocues!

I was ready to go. But there was a little more delay. The lighting was causing trouble with my spectacles – reflection flashes from the lenses and shadows from the heavy hornrims. An engineer climbed up ladders to adjust the arc-lamp until the director in the control room was satisfied. It seemed to take a very long time. I began to sweat under the heat of the lights.

We had been asked to memorise our material so that we would not have to look down. They wanted to see us looking full-face into the camera. I took a final look at my notes. The phrases which last night were crisp and bright seemed limp and dull, but it was too late to make any changes.

'Are you ready?' called the floor manager. I nodded.

'Stand by.' He stood to one side of the camera, and raised his arm above his shoulder.

'Thirty seconds to go …Fifteen seconds.'

Suddenly the floor-manager jabbed his hand down towards me. A red light glowed on top of the camera. This was it.

Annotations:

- Short, dramatic sentence at the start makes the moment seem tense
- Detail brings scene to life
- Tension building – he is sweating because he's tense as well as from the heat of the lights
- Makes contrast between two sets of description
- Spoken dialogue adds variety and sense of realism
- Countdown increases tension further
- Short sentence creates dramatic ending

Examiner's tip

With autobiography, you are likely to have to look closely at the way language is used to present the person and the events they are recounting.

Here is one student's approach to this question on the extract:

How does the writer use language to engage the interest of the reader?

The passage starts with a short sentence, perhaps suggesting his worry. The mention of 'sweat' develops this emotion: the word is basic and brings us close to his feelings. He says that his phrases had seemed 'crisp and bright', which is a positive and lively expression, but then there is a contrast with 'limp and dull', which suggests lifelessness.

There is another short, abrupt sentence when the floor manager speaks: 'I nodded'. We then get a count-down, to increase the tension, and this is followed by the dramatic 'Suddenly...' and it is all finished with another short sentence to show his fear: 'This was it.'

C

Good points

- Shows clear engagement with the language of the text.
- Picks out particular language features which will gain the reader's interest.
- Uses appropriate quotes to support ideas.

Biographies

- Biographies contain events from the person's past, designed to give the reader a clear picture of what their life was like and how they have been influenced by the life they have led.
- Authors of biographies need to research a great deal into the person or **subject** they are writing about. Many biographies contain a great deal of information.

On the next page is a brief extract from a biography of John Wilson, founder of Sight Savers International.

First, read this **synopsis** (short summary) for the biography – it is the sort of synopsis often found on the back cover of a biography. Notice how much information it contains about the life and work of John Wilson.

Positive opening comment about the subject

John Wilson did more than anyone else to prevent and cure blindness, and help blind people, throughout the world between the 1940s and his death in 1999. He also made a significant contribution to the cause of disabled people in general. His achievements deserve comparison with those of other charismatic figures like Helen Keller and Albert Schweitzer.

Compares Wilson with other key figures

Examiner's tip

Although biographies and autobiographies are non-fiction texts, like many other non-fiction texts they may include 'literary' techniques. For example, the writer may use similes or metaphors to engage the interest of the reader in the same way as in fiction and poetry. Look out for examples of these when reading this type of text.

Now read this extract from John Wilson's biography.

> The day's timetable included a chemistry class. The pupils were to carry out an experiment. Wilson later described what happened:
>
> 'There was a rubber tube leading into a retort filled with water. The idea was that oxygen, when it was produced, would come bubbling up into the water. It was my turn to heat the test-tube with a Bunsen burner. I was sitting on a high stool very close to it, playing the blue flame from the Bunsen burner on to the test-tube when it suddenly exploded. The chemicals had been wrongly labelled and produced an explosive mixture. It must have been quite an explosion because they say it shattered whole rows of bottles and wrecked part of the room.'
>
> A classmate confirms this: 'There was a huge bang. We got peppered with glass. Everybody was bleeding. I got some glass in my face, but they managed to remove it.'
>
> One boy present was blinded in one eye. John Wilson was blinded in both.

Here is how one student began their analysis of how language is used for effect in this extract from John Wilson's biography.

To begin with, the expression is just matter-of-fact, as the experiment is described. It is quite 'everyday': 'There was a rubber tube...'. Then, the account begins to sound more interesting as Wilson's childishness is stressed. He was sitting on a 'high stool', as if he was not big enough to stand, and was 'playing with the blue flame'. The word 'playing' makes it all sound like a game. Of course, it all changed in an instant when it 'suddenly exploded'. This phrase is to shock the reader and bring a longer sentence to a sudden halt. After 'exploded', there is 'explosive', for emphasis, then 'explosion', almost as if there is an echo...

Identifies style

Associated vocabulary is picked out

Explanations

Sensitive point, indicating response might develop to a higher grade

C

Good points

- The student quotes specific words and phrases that are used for effect.
- First-hand accounts are commented upon.
- The use of language is analysed with some meaning being inferred.

Task

Complete the analysis of how language is used for effect in John Wilson's biography.

- Biographers often raise interesting issues about the person they are writing about. If the person is a historical figure, a biography can shed new light on their life or give fresh information.

The extract below is from a biography of the Victorian artist and poet, Dante Gabriel Rossetti. Rossetti was a member of the Pre-Raphaelite movement, which was a group of nineteenth century artists, writers and critics.

His paintings and poetry have been liked by some and disliked by others. Their popularity changes all the time. Currently, his pictures of beautiful women with long hair can be seen on all kinds of items that we buy in the shops. His poems were once highly acclaimed – not least because they were so sexual – but are now largely unread. Perhaps they are simply unfashionable.

First paragraph summarises the differences in how his artistic life is viewed

His private life also causes much discussion, even today. It was linked closely to his artistic life. He was in love with his model Elizabeth Siddal, but postponed their marriage and chased other women. In a grandly romantic gesture, he even went so far as to bury his poems in Elizabeth's coffin; but later he wanted them back, and dug them up seven years later…

Second paragraph focuses on his love life

His life cannot be separated from his work – they are both equally interesting

Elizabeth Siddal, painted by Rossetti

Task

In this extract:

- What do we learn about the admiration for Rossetti?
- What is there to suggest he should not be admired?

REMEMBER

In your exam, the first question will always ask you to find specific pieces of information. Try to use words or phrases from the text or extract to support your points when you answer this question.

Reading travel writing

Key points

- Travel writing is a particular genre of non-fiction writing. It is not to be confused with a 'guide book' – the two have differences in purpose and form.
- Travel writing tends to have a narrative element to it – often an account in **time order** of a visitor's experiences whilst travelling.
- It is usually in the **first person** as it is one person's account, from their point of view.
- Although **factual** in content, there will be an **element of bias** in travel writing – the writer will often include their opinions on their experiences within their writing.
- In exam questions it is likely to be the language of travel writing that will come up, or what the writer is suggesting.

Travel writing

- Travel writing involves describing travel experiences. It can be factual but can also give individual interpretations of the experience. The very best travel writing allows the reader to feel as though they are participating in the journey!
- Generally, the purpose of travel writing is to entertain and inform the reader whereas a guide book contains more facts and information and may also advise the reader.

Now read this extract from *Notes from a Small Island* in which American journalist, Bill Bryson, describes his first time in England.

> My first sight of England was on a foggy March night in 1973 when I arrived on the midnight ferry from Calais. For twenty minutes, the terminal area was aswarm with activity as cars and lorries poured forth, customs people did their duties, and everyone made for the London road. Then abruptly all was silence and I wandered through sleeping, low-lit streets threaded with fog, just like a Bulldog Drummond movie. It was rather wonderful having an English town all to myself.
>
> The only mildly dismaying thing was that all the hotels and guesthouses appeared to be shut up for the night. I walked as far as the rail station, thinking I'd catch a train to London, but the station, too was dark and shuttered. I was standing wondering what to do when I noticed a grey light of a television filling an upstairs window of a guesthouse across the road. Hooray, I thought, someone awake, and hastened across, planning humble apologies to the kindly owner for the lateness of my arrival and imagining a cheery conversation which included the line, 'Oh, but I couldn't possibly ask you to feed me at this hour. No, honestly – well, if you're quite sure it's no trouble, then perhaps just a roast beef sandwich and a large dill pickle with perhaps some potato salad and a bottle of beer.' The front path was pitch dark and in my eagerness and unfamiliarity with British doorways, I tripped on a step, crashing face-first into the door and sending half a dozen empty milk bottles clattering. Almost immediately the upstairs window opened.
>
> 'Who's that?' came a sharp voice.
>
> I stepped back, rubbing my nose, and peered up at a silhouette with hair curlers.
>
> 'Hello, I'm looking for a room,' I said.
>
> 'We're shut.'
>
> 'Oh.' But what about my supper?
>
> 'Try the Churchill. On the front.'
>
> 'On the front of what?' I asked, but the window was already banging closed.

A typical question you could be asked would be:

What does Bill Bryson think of England when he first arrives?

Here is one student's response.

Bill Bryson doesn't have a very good experience when he first arrives. At first it is all very busy – 'aswarm with activity' – and then it goes very quiet which makes it seem almost scary – 'abruptly all was silence'. He uses words like 'dark' and 'fog' and 'shuttered' to make England seem like it is very gloomy and not very welcoming.

When he sees the guest house he describes the light as 'grey' which doesn't sound very welcoming but it creates humour because when he imagines them welcoming him it is clearly contrasted with what actually happens when the door opens and he is not welcomed at all.

REMEMBER

- Look for different language techniques that the travel writer uses to convey information to the reader.
- Be aware of the attitudes or feelings that the travel experience causes in the writer.

I do end up feeling sorry for Bill Bryson. He was alone, late at night, in an English town with nowhere to go and nowhere to stay. He must have been feeling pretty desperate. 'The window was already banging shut,' like his hope of finding food and a room for the night.

The extract is funny because he is very hopeful and positive but he doesn't have a very good first experience at all...

C

Good points

- This extract from a response comments on the contrast of mood and atmosphere using direct quotation.
- It touches on the writer's implied message about England and the English but this could be developed.
- It recognises some of the humour in writer's portrayal of his thoughts and actions.

Read the following extract from the travel journals of George Orwell written in the 1930s. As you read the extract, what do you learn about Sheffield in the 1930s?

Had a very long and exhausting day (I am now continuing this March 4th) being shown every quarter of Sheffield on foot and by tram. I have now traversed almost the whole city. It seems to me, by daylight, one of the most appalling places I have ever seen. In whichever direction you look you see the same landscape of monstrous chimneys pouring forth smoke which is sometimes black and sometimes of a rosy tint said to be due to sulphur. You can smell the sulphur in the air all the while. All buildings are blackened within a year or two of being put up. Halting at one place I counted the factory chimneys I could see and there were 33. But it was very misty as well as smoky - there would have been many more visible on a clear day. I doubt whether there are any architecturally decent buildings in the town. The town is very hilly (said to be built on seven hills, like Rome) and everywhere streets of mean little houses blackened by smoke run up at sharp angles, paved with cobbles which are purposely set unevenly to give horses etc, a grip. At night the hilliness creates fine effects because you look across from one hillside to the other and see the lamps twinkling like stars. Huge jets of flame shoot periodically out of the roofs of the foundries* (many working night shifts at present) and show a splendid rosy colour through the smoke and steam. When you get a glimpse inside you see enormous fiery serpents of red-hot and white-hot (really lemon coloured) iron being rolled out into rails.

Negative first sentence – sets tone for the whole account

Implies that he has seen more than enough

Use of powerful 'negative' adjective

Expresses strong opinion

'Monstrous' imagery continues - creating sense of fear and danger

Language changes from highly descriptive to a more factual account

* **foundries**: places where metal is cast (shaped) using intense heat

Task

Using the following suggestions, write your answer to this question:

How does Orwell use language to show his feelings about Sheffield?

You could include:

- The effect of negative descriptive vocabulary (monstrous, slummy)
- How Orwell wants the reader to react to his description.

Reading reviews

Key points

- A review is **form** of non-fiction text which provides a **description** and an **evaluation** of an event, an object or publication such as a book or film.
- The **purpose** of a review is to provide a clear overview and an evaluative judgement or recommendation. A review is often written for a clear **audience** with a shared interest in the topic
- Reviews are often, but not always, written in **first person**.
- They tend to place their topic in context, comparing it to similar events, objects or publications. They often 'rate' the topic in terms of its appeal to the audience.
- It is likely that the focus in exam questions about reviews will be on language choices, how these link to the writer's viewpoint and with what effects. You might also be asked to find information.

REMEMBER

- The purpose of a review is to give an overall evaluation.
- Focus on the language and structure and how they are used to present a particular point of view.

Analysing reviews

- When you read a review, make sure you notice the ways in which it is structured and the way language is used to express a clear point of view.
- So one of the first things to consider when reading a review is the standpoint of the reviewer – is their view biased or unbiased?

Read this review for a video game and the annotations around it.

First sentence introduces the game

The much-loved adventure game Monkey Island set sail on a new journey earlier this year and has recently come into port with its fifth and final episode. Tales of Monkey Island follows the further adventures of Guybrush Threepwood, a pirate, as he pursues his wife, Elaine. At the same time, he has to fight his enemy, Lechuck. This tale has some amusing twists and turns. The warm-hearted love of Guybrush and Elaine is at the heart of the story and there is also humour. It's a funny game and, though it goes a bit quiet at times, the playful puzzles will keep you entertained for hours and hours and hours. Tales of Monkey Island is a lengthy adventure that is easy to enjoy and easy on your wallet. It will be loved by new gamers and veteran gamers alike.

Summarises the game's content

The writer offers personal views

Positive comments develop the opinion

Final evaluation by the writer

This next review is for a film.

After all the hype surrounding the release of *Teddy's Magic Christmas*, I must confess to feeling like the hero of the hour when I proudly presented the last-minute surprise tickets to my kids. Their almost tearful gratitude had all of us damp-eyed with festive emotion and warm with Christmas spirit. Unfortunately, this completely evaporated within the first ten minutes of this dreary, derivative and quite frankly dire excuse for a film.

The basic plot has been made clear in the advertising. Poor Teddy (voiced by new star Zak Valance) is the last remaining toy in Mr Muggins' toyshop and has to fight against the advance of high-tech gadgetry. By doing this, he can save the children of the world from cynical, plastic products and can remind us (sniff, sniff) about the magic and true meaning of Christmas.

While I'm not suggesting that films aimed at the very youngest of filmgoers absolutely have to have a believable plot-line, they surely do need to have some kind of story to carry them along, at least. Otherwise you simply don't care. Which, I'm afraid, is exactly what happened to us – we simply didn't care, because the major flaw of the film in my opinion was that Teddy had all the personality of...well...a stuffed toy!

Overall judgement: don't waste your money

Rating: ★★ *(and that's just because it's Christmas)*

Here is one response about the review writer's opinion of the film:

The writer of this review doesn't straight away tell the reader whether they liked the film or not. You have to read on to find out what their opinion is. They set the scene first which is good because it sounds like a real family going to see this film.

It is clear after reading the review that he doesn't like the film at all because he says 'unfortunately' which makes it sound like he was disappointed. He also makes it sound over the top because his children sound like they were crying when he gave them the tickets, which is silly. He uses hard words like 'dreary' to describe the film which make it sound rubbish.

D

Good points

- This response identifies the writer's overall opinion.
- It shows some understanding of *how* the review reveals the writer's feelings.

Examiner's advice for improvement

- Include mention of more of the ideas in the text.
- Examine the writer's ideas in more detail.
- Extend the analysis so that all parts of the review are included.

Examiner's tip

To help understand a reviewer's tone, read between the lines of the text, looking for implied meaning. For example, when the reviewer says of children's films 'they surely need to have some kind of story to carry them along', they are really saying that this kind of story is missing.

The first sentence of the review does not immediately let the reader know what they think of the film, though the word 'hype' might make you think it is not all that good if it needs hype. The children obviously wanted to see the film, but 'unfortunately' sets the tone for the rest. The writer describes the film as 'dreary, derivative and dire' and the alliteration makes it sound dull and depressing.

The reviewer suggests that there is not even a clear story-line ('surely need some kind of story to carry them along') and it is not 'believable'. She ends by saying she and the kids really didn't care about what happened. That was also to do with the fact that Teddy was just like a stuffed toy, rather than being a character you could engage with.

The comments at the bottom sum it all up: 'don't waste your money' and the generous rating of two stars 'just because it's Christmas'.

C

Task

Write a response to the Monkey Island game review, commenting on how the writer has used language to express their point of view.

Reading web pages

Key points

- Web pages are designed to provide, and navigate through, a lot of information.
- Web pages are usually designed according to specific conventions.
- In your exam you may be asked to comment on the language used, the organisation or the presentational features of the web page, or you might have to locate information

Reading a web page

- Reading web pages requires different kinds of reading skills to printed text. You are reading quickly, often skimming and scanning in order to find specific information on the page straight away. A web page uses particular layout conventions and presentational features to help you do this.
- Also, a web page has to be immediately appealing and accessible otherwise the reader will just skip to another site. Designers and writers take this into account when they structure and create web pages.

Look at the different features and devices used on this web page.

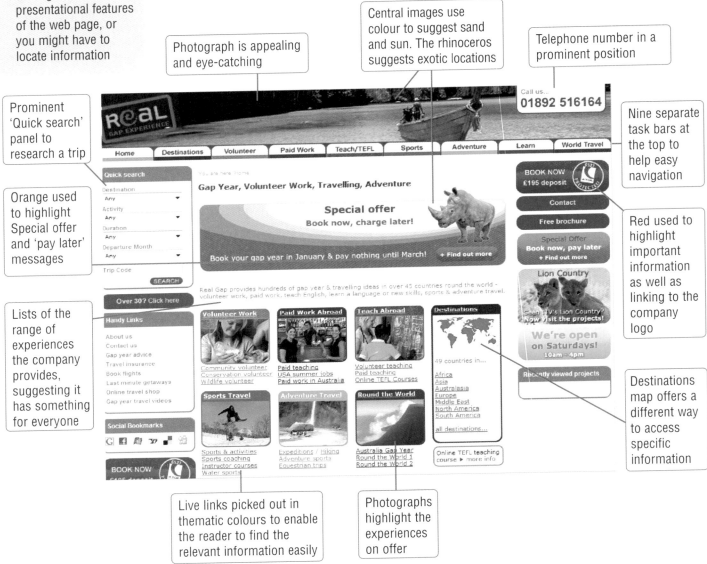

Photograph is appealing and eye-catching

Central images use colour to suggest sand and sun. The rhinoceros suggests exotic locations

Telephone number in a prominent position

Prominent 'Quick search' panel to research a trip

Nine separate task bars at the top to help easy navigation

Orange used to highlight Special offer and 'pay later' messages

Red used to highlight important information as well as linking to the company logo

Lists of the range of experiences the company provides, suggesting it has something for everyone

Destinations map offers a different way to access specific information

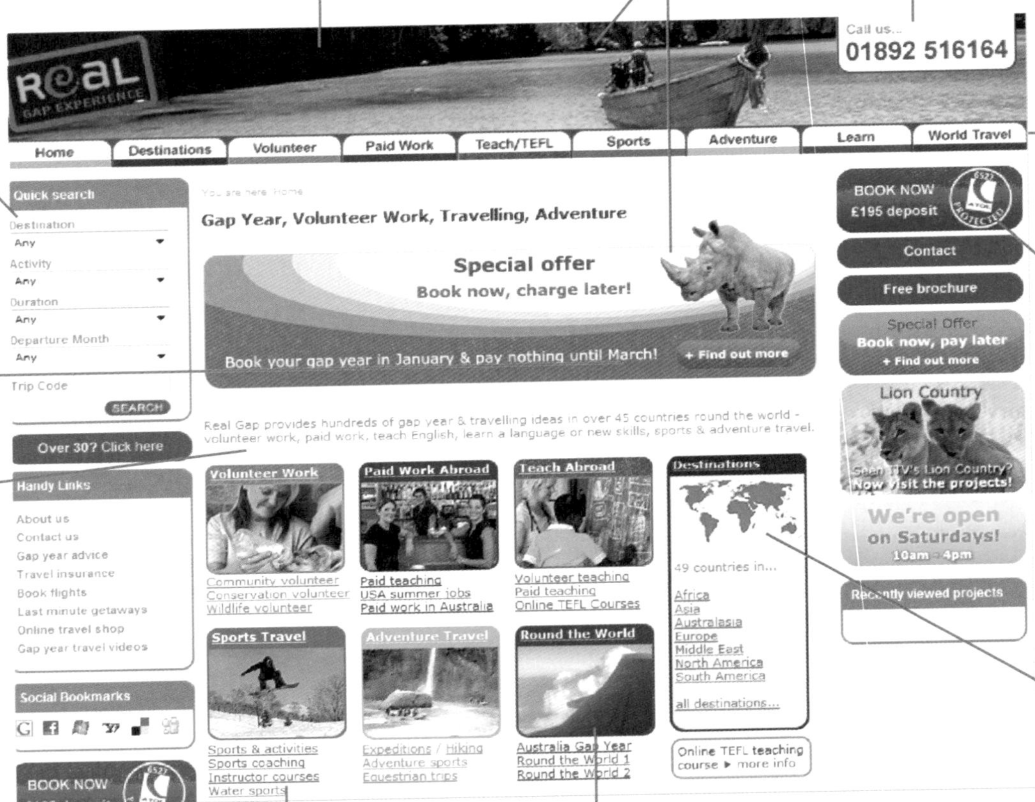

Live links picked out in thematic colours to enable the reader to find the relevant information easily

Photographs highlight the experiences on offer

Read one student's analysis of this web page, on the following page. They have responded to the question:

How does this web page use language to engage and keep the interest of its audience?

The web page sets out to appear exciting. So much of the language is there to grab the reader's attention: 'Book now' appears more than once, telling the reader what to do. Also, there are two significant exclamation marks, as if someone is full of enthusiasm when they are saying the words. And, of course, the first thing we might notice, right next to the hippo is 'Special offer', which makes it seem as if there is a sale going on, or something like that.

The language generally is intended to make it seem there are many things on offer to someone wanting to have a gap year – travel, do volunteer work or adventure abroad. There are 'hundreds of gap year and travelling ideas', which makes it all seem large and attractive. There is a list headed 'Destinations', as if you could go anywhere in the world. 'Lion Country' is given capital letters, as if that might be one of the destinations, and that sounds dangerous and will appeal to young people wanting adventure...

C

Good points

- The response identifies features on which to comment.
- There is an understanding of how the different bits of language build together into an overall impression.

Read the following example of a web page from the World Wildlife Fund's website.

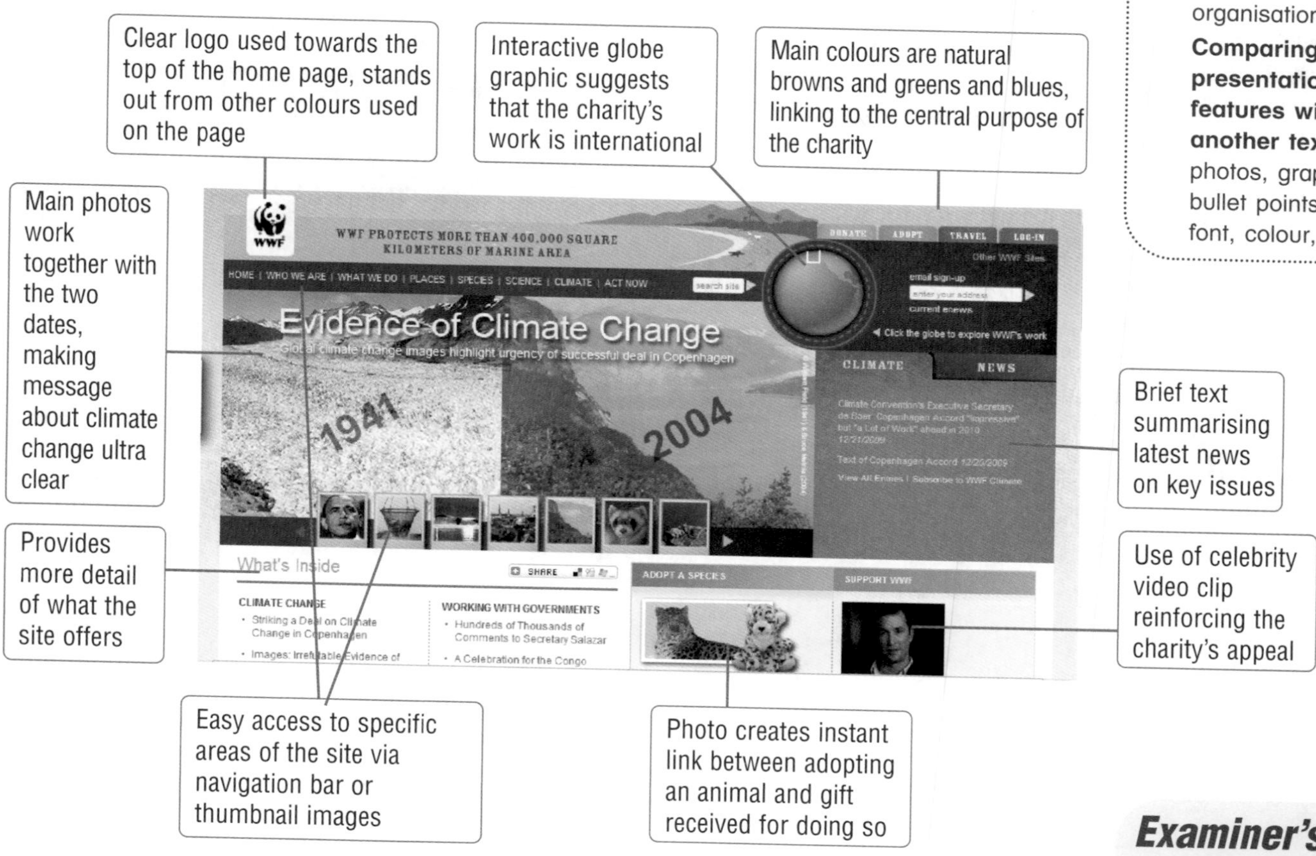
Clear logo used towards the top of the home page, stands out from other colours used on the page
Interactive globe graphic suggests that the charity's work is international
Main colours are natural browns and greens and blues, linking to the central purpose of the charity
Main photos work together with the two dates, making message about climate change ultra clear
Brief text summarising latest news on key issues
Provides more detail of what the site offers
Use of celebrity video clip reinforcing the charity's appeal
Easy access to specific areas of the site via navigation bar or thumbnail images
Photo creates instant link between adopting an animal and gift received for doing so
WWF PROTECTS MORE THAN 400,000 SQUARE KILOMETERS OF MARINE AREA
Evidence of Climate Change
1941
2004
CLIMATE
NEWS
What's Inside
CLIMATE CHANGE
WORKING WITH GOVERNMENTS
ADOPT A SPECIES
SUPPORT WWF

REMEMBER

- Questions about web pages in your exam could focus on either:

  Language: content, style and organisation, or

  Comparing their presentational features with another text: photos, graphics, bullet points, size of font, colour, etc.

Task

Compare the ways:

- pictures
- other presentational features

are used to appeal to the readers of the Real Gap Experience and WWF web pages. What are the similarities and differences in the features and their effects?

(For extra support on how to compare texts, see pages 46–47.)

Examiner's tip

When 'reading', do not think just about the actual words. Reading means 'de-coding' and can include the effect of pictures, fonts, colour, logos – in fact, any design feature can contribute to your overall 'reading' of a text.

Reading information texts

Key points

- Texts whose main **purpose** is to provide **information** come in a wide variety of **forms**: leaflets, web pages, instructional texts such as DIY guides or recipes, guide books and reference texts or texts giving hints or advice.
- The language of an information text is usually impersonal, quite direct and clearly organised.
- Most information texts will have a **target audience** in mind, even if it is a 'general adult' audience. Target audiences can be categorised by age, background, gender, interests, location, beliefs and many other factors.

REMEMBER

Target audience is the term used to describe the group of people the text is written for.

Information texts

- Information texts, like the one below, often use **subheadings** or other **clear organisational features** to guide the reader easily through the material.

Read the following information text from the Chester Zoo website and the annotations that introduce its features.

Asian Elephant

Asian Elephants are smaller than African elephants and have much smaller ears. Their backs are also more rounded than the African elephant and they have an extra toenail on each foot – four per foot in all. The tusks, which are specially adapted incisor teeth, are only found on males, although some males, especially in Sri Lanka, have no tusks. They have stout bodies and thick legs, with a thick, wrinkled, dry skin, grey to brownish in colour. The long sensitive trunk comprises of the nose and upper lip and is used to feed, plucking at grasses and passing them into the mouth. They also use the trunk to wash with and to vocalise. The trunk has a single prehensile 'finger' at its tip, unlike African elephants which have two.

Uses the present tense

Lots of information in the form of facts about Asian elephants

Subheadings divide the material, making it easy for the reader to find information

What do they eat?
Chiefly grasses, but also scrub and bark, fig leaves and some fruit. They have also been known to eat banana or rice crops if they roam into plantation areas. They eat an average of 150kg of vegetation a day and drink 80 to 100 litres of water a day.

How long do they live?
Up to 70 years

Did you know?
Elephants use infrasound to communicate, which is a sound level with a frequency too low to be detected by the human ear. It is also used by whales, alligators, giraffes, rhinoceros and hippopotamuses.

Direct question, simply worded, suggests a younger audience

Try completing the spider diagram that one student has begun below for this information text. Add brief detail from the text under each subheading.

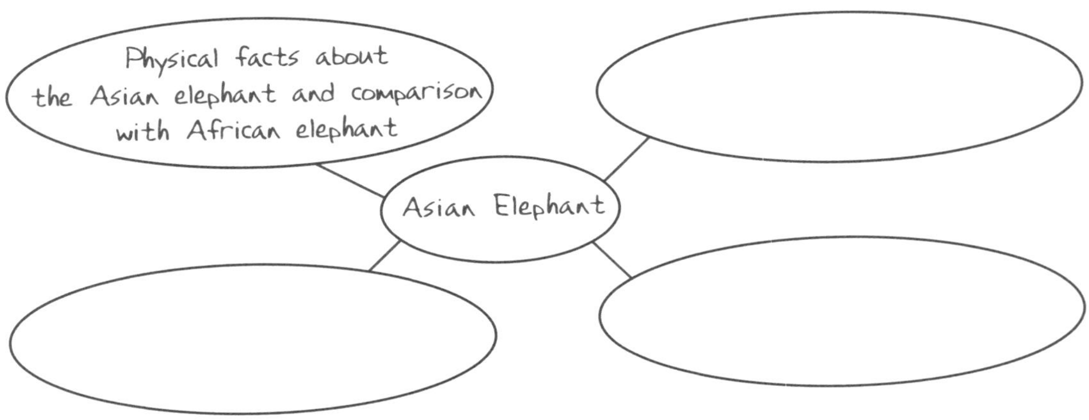

Giving more than information

- Some information texts combine presenting facts with other purposes, such as giving tips or advice. This has an influence on the language features of these texts.

For example, look at the following text from the CBBC *Newsround* website:

Worksheet: Tips for staying green

Updated 05 September 2002, 15.33

We've come up with some easy ways to help save the planet. Re-cycle glass bottles, jars, newspapers and magazines and tin cans. Save them and take them to local re-cycling centres. Re-use plastic shopping bags and envelopes, don't get new ones. Persuade your mum or dad (or whoever does the gardening) to have a compost heap. Put a brick in a plastic bag into your toilet cistern, then the toilet will use less water each time you flush. Use paper on both sides. Try and buy products that don't use much packaging. Give unwanted gifts and clothes to a charity shop. Only fill the kettle up with the amount of water you need to boil that time. Don't leave the TV or video on standby. If you get a lift to school in a car, take your mates along for the ride. Ask whoever does your washing to use the machine at 40 degrees, as this helps conserve power. Switch lights off when you're not in the room. Get a clockwork mobile phone recharger. Cycle to places! Have showers instead of baths.

Annotations:

- Use of friendly 'we' voice to give the information and advice
- Mention of 'parents' makes the age of the audience more clear
- Suggests the reader goes to school
- Hints that the reader does not do housework
- Simple sentence at the start makes the meaning clear
- 'Commands' throughout, designed to give clear advice
- Packed with detailed information
- Use of informal language to appeal to younger audience

REMEMBER

In your exam, the first question will always ask you to find specific pieces of information. This helps you to focus on some of the key information in the text before you move on to more challenging questions.

Identify two pieces of information about saving water or energy and three pieces of advice about being green.

Examiner's tip

Practise analysing the ways language is used in different information texts.

Task

Using the annotations as a starting point, answer the following question:

In the text 'Tips for staying green', what is the writer's attitude to recycling? How does she use language to get her message across?

Analysing presentational features

Key points

- There will be a question in the exam to test your understanding of how the **layout** and **presentational features** are used in media texts.
- You will be expected to write about **why** these particular presentational features have been used and how they affect the reader.

Examiner's tip

Make sure you use the correct terms for any presentational features. Even more importantly, always explain the intended effect of the feature on the reader. Keep asking yourself while reading; 'Why has this feature been used? What is the effect?'

REMEMBER

Our eyes draw meaning from everything on the page, not just the text. Good designers use this to their advantage. So in your exam answer, analyse all the presentational features they use.

Identifying the features

- You need to be clear that **layout** means the way the text has been designed, or organised on the page whereas **presentational features** are individual elements, used to create the layout, such as pictures, headlines, choice of font and use of colour.
- When you comment on presentational features, try to explain how they work with each other to create an overall effect, not just what effect they have individually.

Here are some key presentational features used in media texts:

Headline	the main heading in a newspaper story is called a headline, designed to draw the reader's attention
Strapline	a second, introductory headline, below the main one, adds more information to the headline
Standfirst	the introductory paragraph in an article or report, which could be in bold print or with the first word capitalised
Subheadings	often used to summarise sections of the text or break it up into smaller sections, allowing the reader to skim over the whole text and see the overall point
Capitals	capitals used elsewhere than standard are often used to stress and reinforce particular words or phrases
Captions	the text under a photograph or diagram which explains it

The following texts show a range of presentational features.

Logo: an image that represents a product or company

Slogan: a word or phrase, linked to a product to make it memorable

Bold, italics, underline: different ways of making certain words stand out

Pull-quote: a quotation from a reviewer (or an article) and set apart, in larger or bold type

Photographs and graphics: used to add depth to the story or more information.

Font: style and colour of the typeface can vary throughout a text.

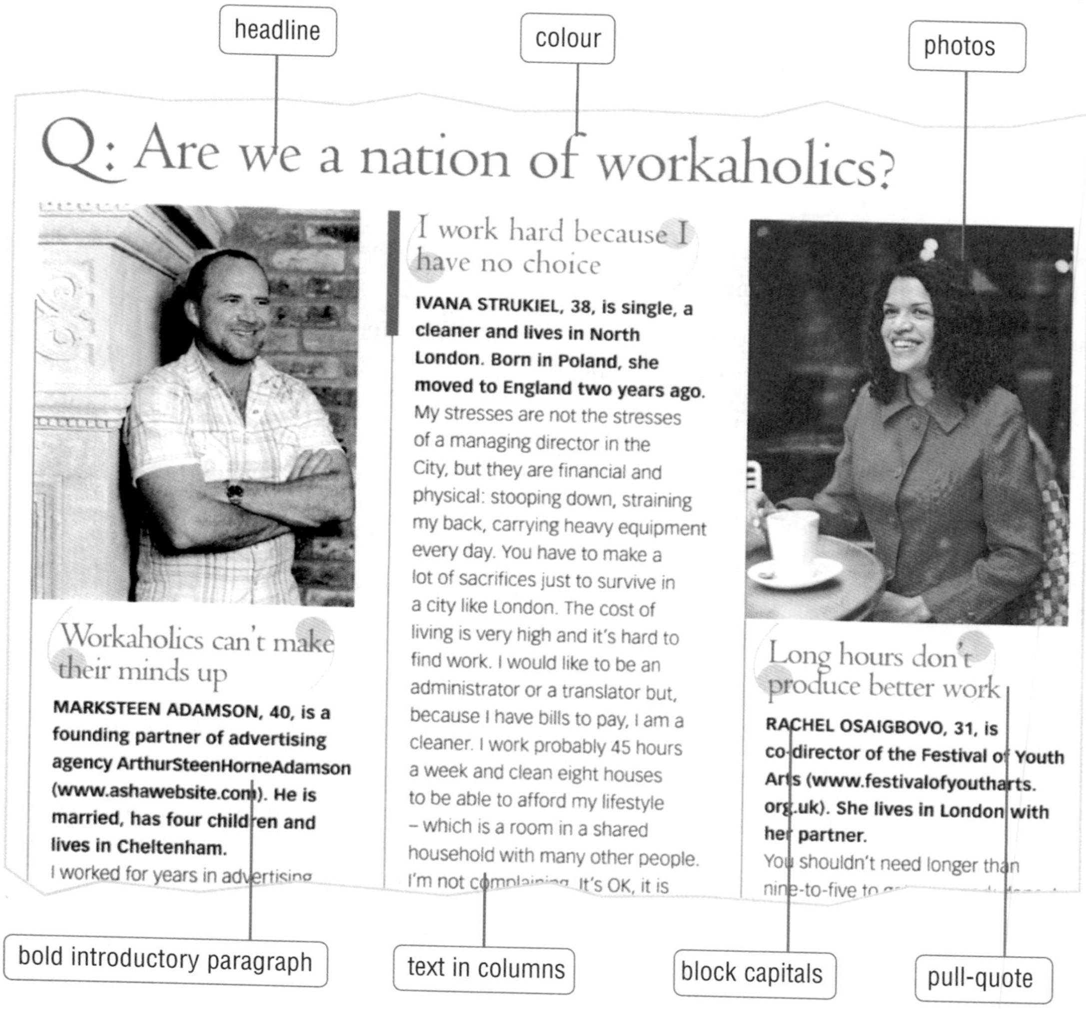
Q: Are we a nation of workaholics?

Workaholics can't make their minds up

MARKSTEEN ADAMSON, 40, is a founding partner of advertising agency ArthurSteenHorneAdamson (www.ashawebsite.com). He is married, has four children and lives in Cheltenham.

I worked for years in advertising

I work hard because I have no choice

IVANA STRUKIEL, 38, is single, a cleaner and lives in North London. Born in Poland, she moved to England two years ago.

My stresses are not the stresses of a managing director in the City, but they are financial and physical: stooping down, straining my back, carrying heavy equipment every day. You have to make a lot of sacrifices just to survive in a city like London. The cost of living is very high and it's hard to find work. I would like to be an administrator or a translator but, because I have bills to pay, I am a cleaner. I work probably 45 hours a week and clean eight houses to be able to afford my lifestyle – which is a room in a shared household with many other people. I'm not complaining. It's OK, it is

Long hours don't produce better work

RACHEL OSAIGBOVO, 31, is co-director of the Festival of Youth Arts (www.festivalofyoutharts.org.uk). She lives in London with her partner.

You shouldn't need longer than nine-to-five to

Writing about presentational features

Instead of just describing what is on the page, talk about **why** the text has been designed in a particular way. What effect does each feature have and what is the overall effect?

Here is how one student commented on the way layout and presentational devices are used in the article above:

> The article is designed in three columns to split up the three interviews clearly for the reader. The pictures give the impression that the people are happy, because both are smiling, so maybe there is an immediate thought that if we are a nation of workaholics, which is what the headline is asking, at least we are happy about it all. There is a lot of orangey red in the layout, which makes it seem upbeat and positive. Even the speech marks look like fun. The opening paragraphs are in bold each time, making them stand out and offer some variety, so the text is more varied and readable...

C

Good points

- There is clear understanding of the effects of the different features.
- Both layout and presentational features are included.
- Detail is apparent throughout.

Examiner's tip

If you can explain how effective the layout or presentational features are, you will gain a higher mark. Don't be afraid to give your opinion but always support it with examples from the text!

Task

Choose an article from your favourite magazine.

- List all the presentational feature used and explain their effect.
- Sum up the overall effect of the design.

Dealing with inference

Key points

- Two of the questions in the exam will ask you to show you can **read between the lines** or **infer** meaning from a text. This means looking beyond what is actually stated to discover deeper or different meanings.
- You can **infer** meaning in a variety of ways: from the **language** chosen, the structure and organisation of the text, the pictures and from other presentational features.

Inferring meaning from language

- There are a variety of ways in which **language** can be used to infer another whole meaning to the **actual words** themselves.
- One of the techniques to look for is irony, or subtle mockery – when what is being literally said is different to what is actually *meant*. Irony can be created by:
  - **Rhetorical techniques** – rhetorical questions, the repetition of words and phrases: *'We all agree that Wayne Rooney is fit, don't we girls? We think he is really, really fit? Mr McFittery of Fitland?'* (The the over-use of rhetorical questions here suggests that the writer does not, in fact, think Wayne Rooney is 'fit'!!)
  - **Exaggeration** – making a point seem silly or ridiculous by using larger than life detail. *'Yes, your hair looks gorgeous! It's absolutely the best example of a hair colour that I have ever seen in the whole world! It ought to be the colour the Queen uses to dye her hair!'*
  - **Understatement** – underplaying a point can make it seem as ridiculous as exaggerating it: *'I wouldn't say it tasted great'* (of a terrible meal) or *'You could say some size zero models are rather on the slim side'.*
  - **Quotations** – for example, quoting someone it is clear that we disagree with them or question whether they are telling the truth: *The Minister said that 'he had done nothing at all wrong' by claiming £175,000 on his expenses for a new lawnmower.*

Using humour

- Often we infer meaning as much by what is **not** said as by what **is** said.

Read the following text, which is an extract from journalist Bill Bryson's *Notes from a Big Country*. Use the annotations to help you identify what is not said!

People sometimes ask me. 'What is the difference between baseball and cricket?'

The answer is simple. Both are games of great skill involving balls and bats, but with this crucial difference: baseball is exciting and when you go home at the end of the day you know who won.

I'm joking, of course. Cricket is a wonderful game, full of deliciously scattered micro-moments of real action. If a doctor ever instructs me to take a complete rest and not get over-excited, I shall become a fan at once. In the meantime, however, I hope you will understand when I tell you that my heart belongs to baseball.

Implies that cricket is boring

Implying that cricket is hard to understand

Uses understatement to imply there is very little action

Implying that cricket is not exciting to watch

REMEMBER

The reader **infers** meaning from the text but the writer **implies** it. Use both terms correctly, when writing about inference.

Analysing inference

The next article, from *The Times*, is by the journalist Libby Purves. She is writing about the rate of changes to the education system.

Pupils Will Never Learn Unless We Make It Fun.

In their seven cheerful years of primary school – mostly in a small village – my children got through three Secretaries of State for Education. If they had been born 20 years later they could have scored four in even fewer years. And seen the Education Ministry itself bisected*. In UK education policy, everything accelerates except improvement.

Report follows review, white papers flutter weightlessly down as if from some celestial pillow fight, government initiatives sprout like mushrooms round a cow-pat. Infants who once footled around happily with Play-Doh, songs and stories are now formally assessed against 69 government targets, to the loud dismay of experts in child development

Suggests that children were happier when their education was not being interfered with

Use of the word 'scored' links with the idea of 'assessment' later on

Suggests that a great deal of reports are produced

Description suggests that the Government papers have no importance or meaning

Simile used to suggest humour and mockery of the work of the politicians

* **bisected** = split in two

Here is how a student has responded to the question:

How does the writer of this article use inference to make her meaning clear to the reader?

Libby Purves is saying that there have been too many education secretaries and that there has been too much change. She thinks that all this change is bad for children and that their learning might end up suffering – 'everything accelerates except improvement.'

She implies there are too many reports and describes them as fluttering 'weightlessly' which makes it sound as if she thinks they are not important at all and that all that work doesn't make any difference to the children's education. She says they are like 'mushrooms round a cow pat' which sounds a bit insulting but gets the message across that she thinks the work of the Education Ministers is a waste of time.

C

Good points

- The response shows a clear understanding of the content and point of view of the article.
- The student comments on the techniques used.
- Understanding of what the writer is implying is shown, and is supported by relevant quotations from the text.

Inferring meaning from presentational features

- Images and the layout of text items can carry deeper meanings in the same way that language does.

Take a careful look at this picture, which is part of an advertising campaign for PETA, an American organisation which campaigns for cruelty-free fashion.

- Notice how the dog is looking straight at the reader in a friendly way – as if it is a pet.
- Notice also how the dog is wearing one of PETA's shirts with the slogan 'fur is dead', even though the dog has its own fur itself and is obviously not dead.

Examiner's tip

In a text with images, 'read between the lines' and look for the messages implied by both these and the text. Explaining how these messages link will gain you higher marks.

Task

How does this photograph help the campaign organisers get their message across to their readers? Think about:

- What the slogan 'fur is dead' might mean (it could have two possible meanings)
- Why the word 'dead' might be in red
- How the slogan links to the picture of a friendly-looking dog.

Analysing language

Key points

- One question in the exam will always focus on **writing about language** in one of the three texts.
- Having a clear understanding of the kinds of things to cover when analysing language will help you tackle this type of question with confidence.
- Once you have scanned the text and identified its form, audience and purpose, concentrate on its key **language features**.

Key language features

- You will be asked to comment on the language features of a text and their effects. These might include:
  - Sentence and paragraph types
  - Significant vocabulary
  - Punctuation
  - Imagery (similes, metaphors and personification) and other linguistic devices
  - The style of the language.

Sentences and paragraphs

- Look out for the **length of sentences** and how they are **constructed**. Writers achieve a huge range of effects by varying use of the following:
  - **Short sentences** can suggest speed or excitement, e.g.

    He ran forward. The ball fell at his feet. He shot.

    They can also indicate surprise or despair, e.g.

    Her inspiration stopped. Her career ended.
  - **Long sentences** can indicate calm, e.g.

    The sergeant reported that right along the river, teams of men and women were resting at last and preparing to return to their headquarters for a much-needed break.

    Or they can build to a climax, e.g.

    The crowds gasped as the top of the mountain blew away, clouds of ash shot hundreds of feet into the sky and rivers of lava, terrifying in the early daw, shot upwards, then cascaded down into the valley.
- **Paragraphs**, too, can create different effects:
  - Very **short paragraphs** can be used to attract the reader's attention, or to pick out the main details in an article or to offer a 'punchy' idea. Popular newspaper articles often have short paragraphs so that they can be read more easily.
  - **Longer paragraphs** can provide more detail and analysis. Articles in more serious newspapers often have longer paragraphs

Examiner's tip

Look out for paragraphs of very different lengths. A one-sentence paragraph after a long paragraph, for example, aims to grab the reader's attention.

Significant vocabulary

- The kinds of words used in a text can also tell you a lot about the **purpose** of the text:
  - Powerful adjectives, such as 'fantastic,', and 'appalling', are often used to **persuade** the reader.
  - **Commands**, such as 'follow' and 'begin', suggest that the writing is giving **instructions** or **advice**.
  - **Connectives** like 'since' and 'because' suggest that the writing is **explaining** something.
  - **Connectives** like 'however', 'nevertheless', and 'indeed' may come from writing that is **arguing** a case.
- The words or **vocabulary** chosen can also tell you about the **audience** for a text:
  - **More complex vocabulary** indicates that the text is aimed at a more intelligent readership

REMEMBER

- There is no need write about absolutely everything in the text – you simply won't have time.
- It is always, always better to write 'a lot about a little' rather than 'a little about a lot'.

- A text containing **specialist vocabulary**, for instance ICT-based or scientific vocabulary, will be aimed at those with a special interest in that area.
- A text including **slang** and **colloquialisms** could indicate a teenage target audience.

Punctuation

Look out for exclamation marks and question marks. They have a purpose, e.g.

HOLLY HITS OUT!! – The double exclamation mark is to attract attention and suggest excitement, humour or even surprise.

WHY AREN'T WE BEING TOLD THE TRUTH?

The question also attracts attention by addressing the reader directly.

Examiner's tip

Be aware that writers of non-fiction texts use imagery for effect just as writers of novels and poetry do. Commenting on how imagery is used in your exam responses will help your grade.

Imagery

Imagery means using words to paint a picture. If a writer describes her son's room as a 'dustbin', she is using the image or mental picture of a dustbin to make you imagine how messy the room is. Clearly, he does not literally live in a dustbin!

Similes and **metaphors** are examples of imagery. Similies make a comparison using 'like' or 'as', and metaphors say things that are not literally true.

This short extract from an autobiography has three examples of imagery:

metaphor – being imprisoned is described as 'torture'

They held us in a small room. We felt like condemned men and smelt like battery hens. We had no idea of the day or the time and dreaded the dull echoes of sharp boots and the crank of the lock on the door. It was an eternity of torture...

similes – the word 'like' shows something is being compared to something else (an image)

REMEMBER

When you comment on language, it's important to use the correct technical term (e.g. simile), but the main thing is to describe what effect it has, and why the writer has used it.

Look at how this student has commented on the use of language in the extract above:

The writer uses imagery to show what their life was like. The simile 'like condemned men' stresses their desperate situation. Another simile ('smelt like battery hens') shows the terrible conditions they were kept in. They were like animals.

Finally, the metaphor 'eternity of torture' is used to express how long and painful it must have seemed to them at the time.

C

Good points

- Precise examples are given, backed up by quotations from the text.
- The effects of language features are discussed, not just identified.
- Some technical terms are used, e.g. simile, metaphor.

Style

- A text may be **formal** – with a more serious tone, e.g. serious newspaper articles or job applications. Here are some common features of a formal text:
  - close attention to all the rules of standard English
  - more difficult words
  - longer sentences.
- A text may be **informal** – with a warmer or chattier tone, e.g. emails, advertisements and light magazine articles. Common features include:
  - less attention to the rules of grammar and punctuation
  - the use of slang
  - simpler and more direct words and sentences.
- When commenting on style, always give examples to support your comments:
  - *The text is formal, using sentences like 'The government has taken a stance which…'.*
  - *The text is informal and targets drug users with phrases like 'get real…'.*

Stylistic techniques or linguistic features

Different techniques are standard features of specific text forms; for example writing to inform, persuade, advise, argue, explain, review or comment.

- **addressing the reader directly**, especially with **rhetorical questions**, used for added impact:
  Is it fair that they should have nothing to eat?
- **emotive language** to affect the reader's emotions:
  They are tiny and cold and they are starving.
- **irony** (subtle mockery):
  I have always thought it is a good idea to make the poor starve…
- **exaggeration**:
  The Royal Family eats nothing but caviar for breakfast.
- **contrast**:
  The seabirds sing, while the fishermen starve.
- **colloquial language**, as if people are chatting:
  If you want to pull, you have to impress the lads.
- **ambiguity**, where there can be more than one interpretation:
  Bird watching is a really exciting hobby.
- **inference**, where things are suggested rather than clearly stated:
  He met the girl of his dreams. He didn't come home that night.
- **examples, quotations or anecdotes**, giving credibility to what is written:
  Only yesterday, a shop assistant said to me…
- **humour**, to get the audience on the side of the writer:
  There was more life in my popcorn than in this film.
- **lists**, for emphasis:
  She packed the potatoes on top of the bananas, the bananas on top of the tomatoes and the tomatoes on top of the eggs.

This extract from a newspaper article is short, but uses several of the techniques above.

> So, the Prime minister claims that he has an excellent track record, does he? An excellent track record of what – destroying all areas of British life?
>
> People are paying taxes they can't afford, waiting in traffic that never moves, facing ever-mounting debt and an impoverished old age…

Here is what one student wrote about the style of the extract:

The writer begins by addressing us directly, which gets our attention. When she says 'claims' it makes us think it's not true. The next sentence is another rhetorical question, which contrasts the 'excellent' track record with the actual destruction of British life. Exaggeration is used here ('all areas') for added effect.

The list of three examples helps to build up the evidence against the Prime Minister. Exaggeration is used again ('never moves') and some emotive language when the writer refers to poor old people. This aims to get us on her side.

C

Good points

- The effects of the language features are described.
- The writer's purpose is clearly understood.
- Quotations are used to prove the points being made.
- Some technical terms are used, e.g. rhetorical, emotive.

Take a break where the sun always shines

All eyes turn to the sea on this 30-mile stretch of Italy's western shore, considered one of the most beautiful coastlines in the world, where Campania gazes out into the Tyrrhenian reaches of the Mediterranean.

It takes in Sorrento, Positano, Salerno and Amalfi – which gives it the local name *Costiera Amalfitana* – and even extends into the sea.

Sitting off the coast like a satellite at the end of the peninsula, the island of Capri is just a 20-minute cruise away from Sorrento. Fram the port of Marina Grande it's a short ride by funicular railway to the labyrinth of narrow alleyways that make up Capri town.

But it is at Anacapri, the island's second town, that you'll find Capri's very own Garden of Eden, where mythological statues sit like sentinels surveying the deep blue waters. Or where classically draped figures from Italy's past appear to hold command over clouds fleeing across the contrasting blue of the sky.

Task

This extract comes from *Take a Break* magazine. Its purpose is to attract people to visit Capri.

- See if you can find an example of:
  - – exaggeration
  - – a simile
  - – direct address to the reader
  - – a list
  - – a metaphor
  - – another simile
- Explain the intended effect of each example on the reader.

Comparing presentational features

Key points

- One question in Section A of your exam will ask you to **compare** the presentational features of two of the three texts you have been given.
- You are allowed to **choose which two of the three texts** you want to compare.
- This question will be worth **more marks** than three of the other questions so you will need to be prepared to give more time to this question.

Comparing presentation

The following question is typical of the sort of question you might face in the exam:

> **Compare the way presentational features are used in two of the Sources. Write about:**
> - **the title and subheadings**
> - **pictures and captions.**

- Remember your key approach to any non-fiction text:
  Decide how the writer has used layout and presentational features to match the text's form, purpose and audience. You might write about:
  - Colour and choice of fonts
  - Pictures
  - Headings and subheadings
  - Other presentational features

Organising your answer

- Your question is likely to come in two parts, which you will write in different sections. For example:

> **Comment on:**
> - **the pictures**
> - **other presentational features**

- To complete each section, you might find it easiest to write about one text, then write about the second one, making comparisons as you go, i.e.
  - Write about the use of pictures in Text 1.
  - Write about the use of pictures in Text 2, saying in what ways it is the same as, or different from, Text 1.
  - Then go on to do the same for other presentational features.
- When you refer to the texts, you need to link them together. This means using **connectives**. The words and phrases in this grid are really useful when you are linking ideas **within** or **between** paragraphs.

Similarities	Differences
Similarly	In contrast
Just as	Whereas
Likewise	On the other hand
Also	But/however

- As you compare, have a list of key questions in your head:
  - Do these texts have different target audiences?
  - Which presentational features will appeal to each audience?
  - What are the similarities and differences in the presentational features and why?

REMEMBER

Showing your ability to analyse and compare how **both** texts use presentational features – *what* has been chosen and *why* – will get you the marks.

Practising comparison

Here are two texts about healthy eating. As you read them, think about this question:

Compare the way the two texts are set out in order to appeal to different readers. Write about:
- **headings and organisation**
- **colours and images.**

Examiner's tip

The best marks are achieved by making detailed comparisons, using examples from both texts to support your points.

Item 1

This is a leaflet aimed at children.

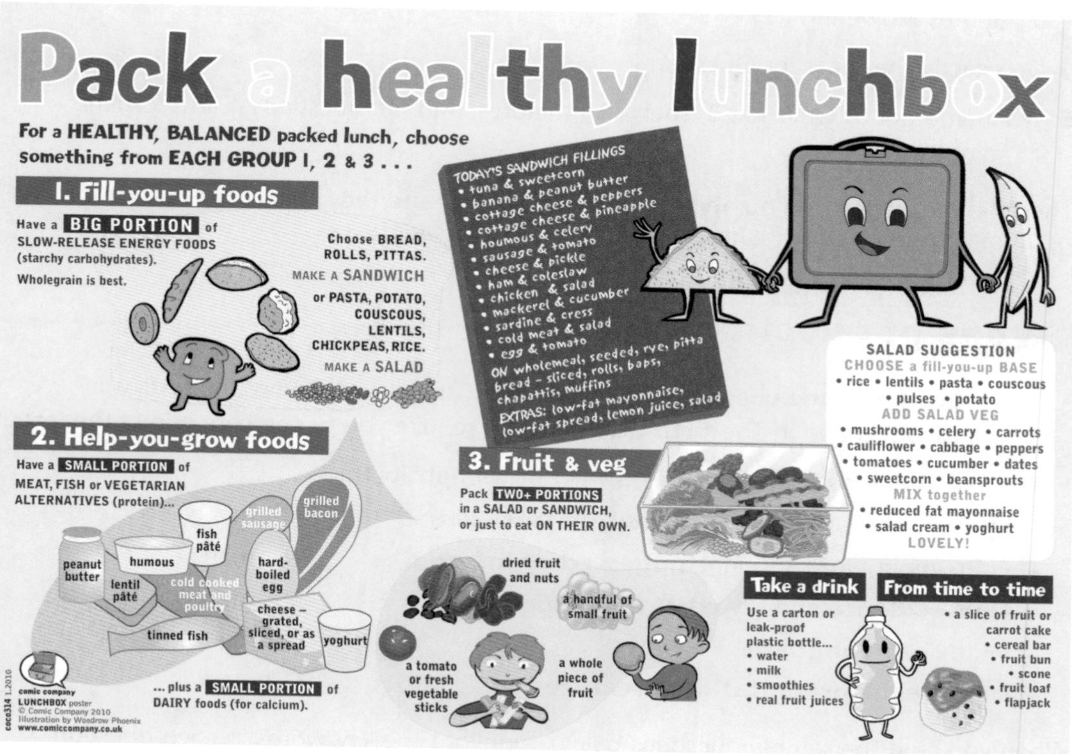
Pack a healthy lunchbox
For a HEALTHY, BALANCED packed lunch, choose something from EACH GROUP 1, 2 & 3 . . .
1. Fill-you-up foods
Have a BIG PORTION of SLOW-RELEASE ENERGY FOODS (starchy carbohydrates).
Wholegrain is best.
Choose BREAD, ROLLS, PITTAS.
MAKE A SANDWICH
or PASTA, POTATO, COUSCOUS, LENTILS, CHICKPEAS, RICE.
MAKE A SALAD
TODAY'S SANDWICH FILLINGS
• tuna & sweetcorn
• banana & peanut butter
• cottage cheese & peppers
• cottage cheese & pineapple
• houmous & celery
• sausage & tomato
• cheese & pickle
• ham & coleslaw
• chicken & salad
• mackerel & cucumber
• sardine & cress
• cold meat & salad
• egg & tomato
ON wholemeal, seeded, rye, pitta bread – sliced, rolls, baps, chapattis, muffins
EXTRAS: low-fat mayonnaise, low-fat spread, lemon juice, salad
SALAD SUGGESTION
CHOOSE a fill-you-up BASE
• rice • lentils • pasta • couscous • pulses • potato
ADD SALAD VEG
• mushrooms • celery • carrots • cauliflower • cabbage • peppers • tomatoes • cucumber • dates • sweetcorn • beansprouts
MIX together
• reduced fat mayonnaise • salad cream • yoghurt
LOVELY!
2. Help-you-grow foods
Have a SMALL PORTION of MEAT, FISH or VEGETARIAN ALTERNATIVES (protein)...
peanut butter
humous
fish pâté
grilled sausage
grilled bacon
lentil pâté
cold cooked meat and poultry
hard-boiled egg
tinned fish
cheese – grated, sliced, or as a spread
yoghurt
... plus a SMALL PORTION of DAIRY foods (for calcium).
3. Fruit & veg
Pack TWO+ PORTIONS in a SALAD or SANDWICH, or just to eat ON THEIR OWN.
dried fruit and nuts
a handful of small fruit
a tomato or fresh vegetable sticks
a whole piece of fruit
Take a drink
Use a carton or leak-proof plastic bottle...
• water
• milk
• smoothies
• real fruit juices
From time to time
• a slice of fruit or carrot cake
• cereal bar
• fruit bun
• scone
• fruit loaf
• flapjack
comic company
LUNCHBOX poster
© Comic Company 2010
Illustration by Woodrow Phoenix
www.comiccompany.co.uk
coco314 1.2010

Item 2

This is an online leaflet aimed at parents or adults.

Basic principles of a healthy diet

Eat plenty of starchy foods (complex carbohydrates)

The main part of most meals should be starchy foods such as bread, cereals, potatoes, rice, and pasta, together with fruit and vegetables. Some people wrongly think that starchy foods are 'fattening'. In fact, they contain about half the calories than the same weight of fat.

Eat at least five portions of a variety of fruit and vegetables each day

One portion is: one large fruit such as an apple, pear, banana, orange, or a large slice of melon or pineapple, OR; two smaller fruits such as plums, satsumas, etc, OR; one cup of small fruits such as grapes, strawberries, raspberries, cherries, etc, OR; two large tablespoons of fruit salad, stewed or canned fruit, OR; one tablespoon of dried fruit, OR; one glass of fresh fruit juice (150ml), OR; a normal portion of any vegetable (about two tablespoons), OR; one dessert bowl of salad.

Eat protein foods in moderation

Meat, fish, nuts, pulses, chicken, and similar foods are high in protein. You need some protein to keep healthy. However, most people eat more protein than is needed. Choose poultry such as chicken, or lean meat. Oily fish is thought to help protect against heart disease. For example, herring, sardines, mackerel, salmon, kippers, pilchards, and fresh tuna (not tinned tuna). Aim to eat at least two portions of fish per week, at least one of which should be oily.

Task

Using Item 1 and Item 2, answer the question at the top of the page in as much detail as you can. Remember to:
- Focus on how the named presentational features in both texts have been used
- Use detailed evidence from both texts.

How to tackle the exam

Key points

- You have one hour to complete Section A: Understanding non-fiction texts. You have **three texts** to read and **five questions** to answer in this time.
- Make sure you know what you need to do, and how to do it.

What to do with the exam paper

1 Spend 5 minutes skim reading the three texts. Decide what they are about.

2 Read through the questions.

3 Focus on Question 1: underline the important words in the question, then spend 5 minutes answering it.

4 Do exactly the same for Question 2.

5 When you get to Question 3, spend 10 minutes; and for Questions 4 and 5 spend 15 minutes.

These timings reflect the number of marks available – and they will leave you enough spare time at the end to check through and improve your work.

Examiner's tip

If you read the questions before you read the texts, this can save you time because you are reading *purposefully* – you already know what you should be looking for as you read.

Types of questions

- You will be asked **one** question on **each of the three** texts. One of the texts will have two questions set on it. The **fifth question** will require you to compare two of the texts.
- The five questions you will be asked will test your ability to:
  - find information (this is **information retrieval**) (4 marks)
  - write about what is being **suggested or inferred** (4 marks)
  - **find evidence** and say **what it is suggesting** (8 marks)
  - write about **language** (12 marks)
  - compare the **presentational features** used in texts (12 marks)

When you read the sample questions below, highlight the key words in each question. This will help you focus on exactly what you have to do.

Read **Source 1**, the magazine article called *The Last Polar Bear* by Paul Parry, and answer the question below.

1 Give <u>four</u> reasons from the article why polar bears are in danger. (4 marks)

> This question requires you to show that you have understood the text by picking out four specific pieces of information from it.

2 What are some of the ways Paul Parry suggests we can all help to stop global warming? (4 marks)

> This question wants you to show that you have understood what the text is suggesting by inferring meaning.

Now read **Source 2**, *The Journey Home*, which is an extract from a travel book by Martina Fellows, and answer the question below.

3 What reasons does the writer give for saying that her journey was:
- **'terrifying'**
- **'emotional'?** (8 marks)

> This question is asking you to infer from the text or read between the lines and give evidence for what is being suggested.

Now read **Source 3**, the leaflet called *Our Shrinking Planet* by the conservation society Save the Earth, and answer the question below.

4 How does the writer use language to make this article informative and shocking to the reader? Answer in two sections:
- **informative**
- **shocking**

(12 marks)

This question wants you to focus on the language feature used by the writer to meet the purpose and audience of the text.

Now you are going to compare the presentation of two of the texts.

5 Choose two of the Sources and compare them. Write about:
- **the title and subheadings**
- **pictures and captions.**

(12 marks)

This question asks you to write about the similarities and differences between the ways the two texts have been set out on the page and the effects created.

REMEMBER

Questions 4 and 5 are worth more marks because you are being asked either to **analyse language** in some detail or to **compare and evaluate the presentational features** of two texts. These both involve high-level skills.

See pages 46–49 for more on the technique of comparing texts.

Task

Below are five questions which are typical of the ones you will see in Section A of your exam.

Read the magazine article *The Flight of the Eagles* by Helen Dunham.

1 List four things this article tells you about eagles. *(4 marks)*

2 Why has there been so much interest in rare birds of prey? *(4 marks)*

Now read the text *One Boy's Journey,* which is an extract from an autobiography.

3 What are some of the thoughts and feelings that Aran has on his excursion into the forest? *(8 marks)*

Now read the text *Death of the birds*, a report about bird migration.

4 How does the writer use language to show the reader the birds' problems? Write about:
- imagery
- how the birds are described

(12 marks)

Now you are going to compare the presentation of two of the texts.

5 How are presentational features used in these texts? Write about:
- titles and subheadings
- pictures and colour

(12 marks)

Using a grid like the below, tick which Assessment objectives you think are being covered in each of the five questions.

Assessment objective	Question 1	Question 2	Question 3	Question 4	Question 5
Read and understand texts					
Select material appropriate to purpose					
Collate material from different sources					
Make comparisons and cross references as appropriate					
Explain and evaluate how writers use linguistic and grammatical features to achieve effects and engage and influence the reader					
Explain and evaluate how writers use structural and presentational features to achieve effects and engage and influence the reader					
Support comments with detailed textual references					

Raising your grade

If you want to boost your grade to C or above, you need to demonstrate these skills.

Answer all parts of the question

- Read the question carefully and answer it exactly.
- If the question asks you to comment on only part of a text then don't comment on all of it.
- If it asks you to comment on the language then don't comment on the presentational features.
- If bullet point 'prompts' are provided, use them to structure your answer.

Show that you understand the text

- If you show evidence of the following in your answer it will enrich your response:
  - Thinking about the **type** of text that it is (biography? Newspaper article? etc) and refer to this in your answer.
  - Thinking about **why** the text has been written (its **purpose**) and **who** it is written for (the **audience**).
- Make sure you support your ideas and develop your thoughts wherever possible.

Show that you can analyse and comment not just describe it

- **Analyse** *how* effects are created in the text and how it has been written. The examiner doesn't want to know just what is in the text.
- This means thinking about the writer's techniques, not just the content.
- **Offer your opinion** about how effective you think certain features are.

  After lots of long sentences there is suddenly a short sentence, 'No good'. ✗

  After lots of long sentences there is suddenly a short sentence: 'No good'. <u>This shows how the runaway has come to the end of the road and has nowhere to turn. The reader stops, just like he does.</u> ✓

Refer to the texts in your answer

- **Give evidence** for your ideas by quoting from the text.
- **Choose brief quotations** and make sure they are relevant to the point you are making.
- **Quote the words exactly**, and put them into inverted commas ('…'). Or, refer closely to the text by summarising.

REMEMBER

- Bear in mind **form, purpose, audience** when producing your response.
- Always **be aware** of the **question type** you are answering.
- Use **direct evidence** from the texts to support your comments.
- **Analyse** and evaluate the **effects of presentational and layout features**, as well as the **effects of language**, where appropriate.

- **Provide a comment** which explains why you are quoting from the text.

  The writer presents himself as a pathetic figure: he 'waves feebly at the taxi then steps away quickly as it races past him, covering him with muddy water'. ✗

  The writer presents himself as a pathetic figure who 'waves feebly' at the taxi then gets splashed as it races past him. This makes us laugh at him, but also feel a bit sorry for him. ✓

How to develop your skills

- Good quality texts are all around you. A great way to prepare for this exam is to read as much as you can. Remember that this exam is assessing your skills with reading a range of non-fiction texts, so your preparation can involve reading magazines, newspapers and web pages. We're not talking about revising by reading a whole novel every week!
- Remember that 'reading' means 'de-coding' in terms of this exam paper. Get yourself into good reading habits by being aware of the purpose, audience and form of every text you read.
- Junk mail can be annoying – however for your exam preparation it's a gift of free resources! Get your hands on every leaflet and free magazine that comes through the letterbox. You could keep a bag by the door just for this purpose; your family will think you've gone re-cycling crazy! Notice how leaflets are organised – look back at the section on Presentational Features and see how images, colour, layout and organisational features have been designed specifically to appeal to a range of target audiences.
- Analyse *and* evaluate when writing about language and presentational features.

Producing non-fiction texts

Examiner's tip

In Section B, one third of the marks are awarded for your use of sentence structure, punctuation and spelling. Be aware of this and leave some time to check your work for accurate spelling and punctuation, as well as choices of vocabulary and paragraphing.

REMEMBER

The analytical skills you have developed in your preparation for Section A: Understanding Non-Fiction Texts will come in handy when you need to write some non-fiction texts for yourself!

Section B: Producing non-fiction texts

- **Section B** of your English exam will assess your **Writing skills**.
- You will be asked to complete **two non-fiction writing tasks**. The first task is shorter and is worth 16 marks; the second task is longer and is worth 24 marks.
- You will have an hour to complete this section, and must answer **both** questions.
- You should aim to spend around 25 minutes on the shorter writing task and 35 minutes on the longer writing task. This should include 5 minutes to check your work once you have completed each task.

The tasks

- The **first writing task** will ask you to produce a relatively short non-fiction text, for example, a letter or e-mail. It is likely to be a functional task, such as writing to inform or explain.
- The **second writing task** will ask you to produce a longer non-fiction text in which you have a chance to develop your ideas in more detail, for example, an article for a magazine or newspaper. This might involve writing to argue or persuade.
- You will be given a clear **form**, **purpose** and **audience** for each task. Usually the audience of the text will be mentioned in the task, for example, 'Write an e-mail to a friend to let them know about...' If an audience is not given, you will be writing for the examiner.
- There may be a link between the tasks you are asked to complete in Section B and the texts you read in Section A.

The exam paper – Section B

Foundation Tier
Section B: Writing

Answer **both** questions in this section.
You are advised to spend about one hour on this section.
You are advised to spend about 25 minutes on question 6.
You are advised to spend about 35 minutes on question 7.

---

6 Imagine that you are applying for a part-time job in a local business.

Write a letter to the manager saying why you are interested in the job and explaining why you would be a good choice for the job. *(16 marks)*

7 Write an article for your local newspaper in which you persuade the readers to help in a project to improve the appearance of your area.

You might wish to write about

- when and where the work will begin
- the improvements which need to be made
- the benefits which will come from the improvements. *(24 marks)*

The skills you will be assessed on in Section B

The questions that you will be asked in Section B will also be based on Assessment Objectives. All the Assessment Objectives will be tested in both answers.

Assessment Objective	What this means in detail
Communicate clearly, effectively and imaginatively, using and adapting forms appropriate to task and purpose in ways which engage the reader	Can you write in the correct form, for the purpose and audience? Is your writing interesting – will people want to read it? Are your ideas clear and organised?
pages 74–91	
Select vocabulary appropriate to task and purpose in ways which engage the reader	Are you choosing interesting words? Do the words you have chosen interest your audience?
pages 66–67	
Organise information and ideas into structured and sequenced sentences, paragraphs and whole texts	Are you writing in clear sentences and paragraphs? Is there a clear beginning, middle and end to your writing? Are you linking your ideas together?
pages 58–59 and pages 72–73	
Use a variety of linguistic and structural features to support cohesion and overall coherence	Have you planned what you are going to write? Does it make sense? Are your ideas linked appropriately?
pages 54–57	
Use a range of sentence structures for clarity, purpose and effect, with accurate punctuation and spelling	Are there clear sentences in your writing? Have you tried to use more than commas and full stops to make your punctuation interesting? Have you checked your spelling?
pages 60–63	

Planning for purpose and audience

Key points

- You have two writing tasks to complete for Section B – Writing. The shorter task is worth 16 marks. The longer task is worth 24 marks.
- You will be given a **form**, a **purpose** and an **audience** for each task. If a task does not mention a specific audience, it will be for the examiner.
- Planning your response will be useful as it will help you to decide on what ideas to include and the order to arrange them in.
- There are three main stages to planning: **thinking of ideas**, **structuring** and **developing** your ideas.

Examiner's tip

Don't think that you have to write masses for these tasks. As a rough guide, the shorter writing response might be 1–1½ sides of A4 and the longer writing response might be 1½–2 sides of A4 in length. Don't worry about not writing enough – quality is more important than quantity.

Making good use of your time

How you use your time during the exam can make all the difference to your final grade. You should be busy and productive throughout the exam – either planning, producing answers or checking your work. Every minute counts on this paper and it is really important to use your time effectively.

Shorter writing task

- Ideally, you want to spend around 25 minutes on the shorter writing task, including around five minutes planning and checking.
- The examiner will expect your writing to be around 3–4 paragraphs in length.
- It is a good idea to make a short plan for this task because you want to make every paragraph count.

Longer writing task

- Spend around 35 minutes on the longer writing task, again including at least five minutes to check your work.
- Your response will be longer than the shorter writing task – possibly about 5–6 paragraphs in length. You might write up to two pages if you have average-sized handwriting.

Purpose and audience

The **task** is the question or problem you have been set. It might be, for example, to write part of a travel brochure or to write an article for a newspaper about animal cruelty.

- The **audience** is the reader (or readers) – the people who will read your brochure or article. A specific audience is often called a **target audience**, e.g. people who are looking for a package holiday.
- The **purpose** is the reason why you are writing your brochure or article. You might be trying to persuade your audience to travel to a place you have described or to donate money for a particular cause, or to campaign against animal cruelty. You might just simply want to inform your audience about cruelty to a certain species of animal or inform your audience about global warming.
- The **form** is the type of writing – for example, a brochure, a newspaper article or a letter.
- When you read the task you need to **identify** the audience (reader) the purpose (why am I writing this?) and the form (what am I writing?) in any writing task you are set.
- Think about the kind of **language**, **structure** and **tone** that will fit the form you are writing in.

Here is how one student made notes around a task to identify form, purpose and audience.

Form – a letter

Audience – a friend, so tone is informal

Write a letter to a friend explaining why you would like him or her to join you in a campaign to stop bull fights in Spain.

Purpose – persuading friend to my view on an issue of animal cruelty

REMEMBER

Both questions in Section B will identify the form, the purpose and often the audience for you. It is your job to choose and use the right structure, language features and tone to suit these.

The student went on to develop their notes likes this:

Notes

Form – letter (needs to have an address and greeting)

24 marks – longer writing task – needs to be about one-two sides of A4, so I need to make at least three clear points and develop them

Audience – can be quite informal as it's a letter to someone I know, but will need to be quite serious in tone because of the topic

Purpose – to persuade – I need to give good reasons to persuade my friend to my point of view so that she supports the campaign. Use persuasive techniques such as list of three, direct address and rhetorical questions.

Identify the form, purpose and audience from these writing tasks:

Write a letter to your local council which argues for more facilities for families to be made available in your area.

Write a review for a magazine about a film or TV programme you have seen recently.

Write a report for your local newspaper which offers advice on how to improve your town centre.

Write an article for a magazine persuading more people to adopt a healthy lifestyle.

Task

Look at the longer writing task question below and see if you can work out the form, audience and purpose – as in the examples above.

Some people believe there should be a curfew from 10pm–8am for young people to help to stop vandalism. Write a letter to a newspaper arguing either for or against this idea. *(24 marks)*

Then, use the example above to help you make some notes for your answer.

Producing and organising ideas

- Once you understand what you have to write about, the next thing to do is to get your ideas into some kind of order, or plan.
- The plan will not be marked but the examiner will be able to see that you have thought about the question.
- Your plan needs to:
  - answer the **main purpose** of the task
  - cover the **main things you want to say**
  - put your ideas into **order**.

  You can include **key words**, **phrases** or **sentences** you intend to use.

Look again at the idea of a curfew for young people. You can come up with ideas by using a spider diagram like the one below.

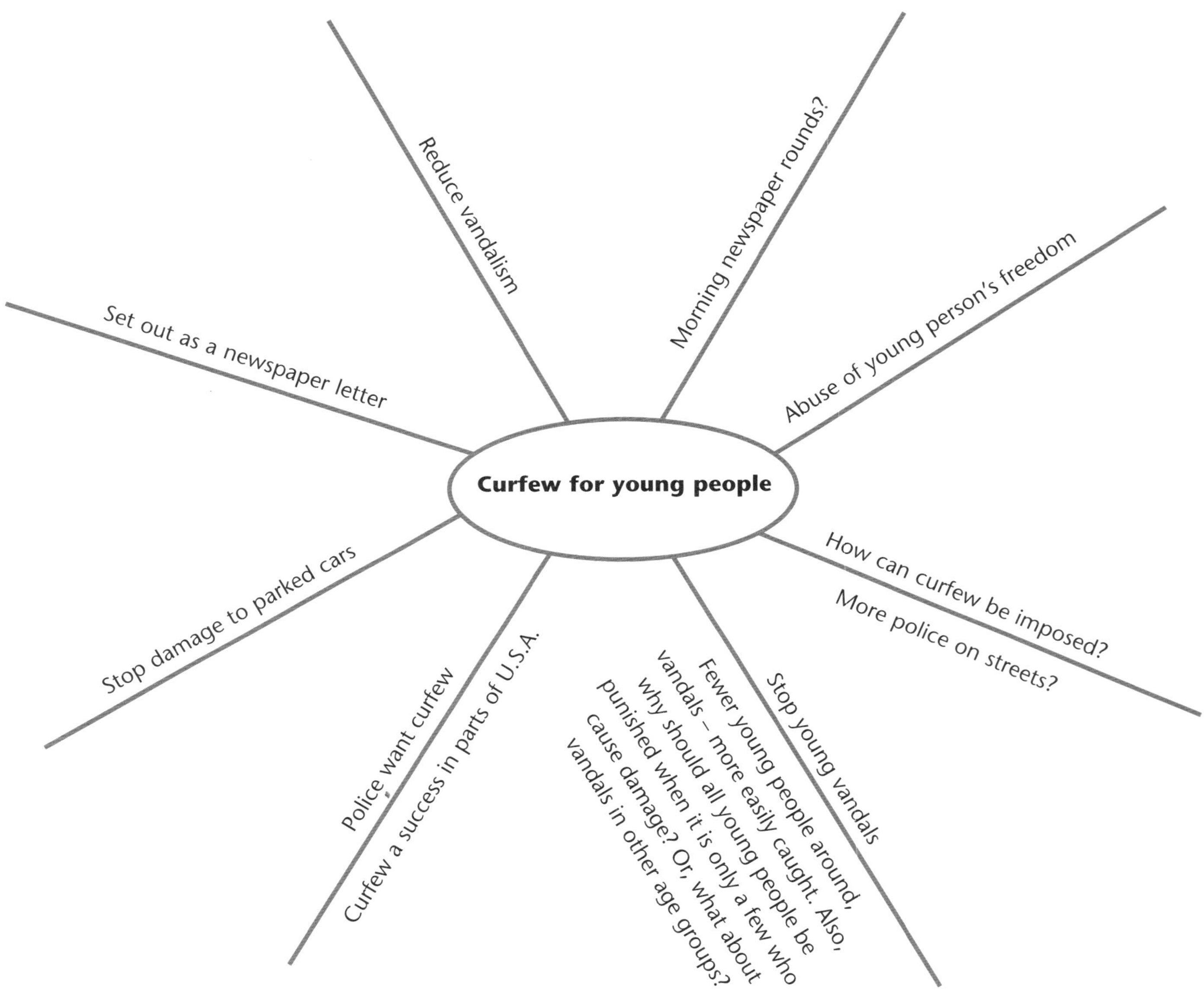

Of course, you do not need to use a spider diagram like this example. A list or a flow chart would be fine!

Developing your ideas

- The next step is to develop your first ideas by adding a little more detail to your plan.

Here is one student's first attempt at a plan.

1 Why I think a curfew should not happen
2 More reasons why a curfew should not be brought in
3 Some examples of things you'd have to do instead if there was a curfew

Examiner's advice for improvement

- This plan is rather thin and needs to be revised.
- The plan is not balanced – it is easier to argue if both viewpoints are represented.
- The points are all rather personal and vague.

The improved example below is based on the spider diagram:

1 Introduction – set out as a newspaper letter 'Dear Editor,'
2 Good points about a curfew;
 – Reduce vandalism in residential areas.
 – Those on streets easily dealt with (less of them.)
 – Police want curfew.
3 Bad points about a curfew
 – What happens to early morning workers? Newspaper boys/girls?
 – Abuse of young person's freedom – denied their personal choice.
 – Unworkable, not enough police to enforce it – cost of recruiting more.
 – Unfair to the young people who do not vandalise.
4 Clear conclusion – summing up my main argument

Good points

- The notes are broken down into sections which could be the basis of paragraphs.
- There is a 'core idea' for each section, with more detailed ideas in note form.
- The ideas have been ordered logically – this is vital.
- Less important ideas from first notes have been discarded.

Task

- Identify the key elements in this question – form, purpose, audience and important ideas.

Write the text of a speech for your year group, in which you attempt to persuade them to show more interest in what school offers out of lesson time. You might want to think about:
- **advantages to them from joining activities**
- **the kinds of activity in which they might become involved.**

- Make a plan of your ideas – a spider diagram or a list – that you could use to answer the question. Choose the type of plan that best helps you to organise, develop and add detail to your ideas and then to write them up in the time available.

Examiner's tip

You do not need full sentences in your plan or to explain the points fully. The plan is a tool to help **you** to write your response.

REMEMBER

The way you organise your writing will be assessed – so it is important to think of the order of your points to make sure your response is clearly structured.

Structure and paragraphs

Key points

- You will be awarded marks for how well you structure your writing. So organising your work clearly is important.
- A well-structured piece of writing has a clear **introduction**, developed ideas in the **main section**, and a strong **conclusion**.

Examiner's tip

You will have around 25 minutes to respond to the shorter writing task. Your writing might be only three or four paragraphs long, although you may write more if you need to.

Overall structure

- As you plan your response, think carefully about its **overall organisation**, e.g. how will you begin, how many main paragraphs will you need, will your conclusion refer back to the introduction?
- Create a clear structure, using paragraphs accurately and effectively to put across your main points or ideas. Making sure each paragraph has a **topic sentence** will help this.
- Use **connectives** to link paragraphs together, making the shift from one idea to the next smoother.

Organising and linking paragraphs

- Start each new paragraph with a topic sentence. Topic sentences act like sub-headings, signposting the main point or idea of each paragraph.
- The remaining sentences in the paragraph develop the idea in more detail, for example:
  The government has its priorities wrong… – you then say what the priorities should be
  There are three steps to perfect happiness… – which you then name and discuss
  Please attend to these safety requirements… – you then list the safety requirements.
- Link your paragraphs using **connectives** – words or phrases that show your reader how your ideas link and work together. Here are some different types of connective:
  time order (chronological), e,g, *At first, Then, Later*
  logical order, e,g, *Therefore, Consequently, As a result*
  contrast, e,g, *On the other hand, In contrast*
  simple ordering of ideas, e,g, *Firstly, Secondly, Finally*
  development of ideas, e,g, *Because of this, Also, What is more, In addition*

Look at how this student varies the length of paragraphs in response to this writing task:

Explain in a letter to a friend why a holiday was memorable.

Examiner's tip

Varying the length of your paragraphs for effect will gain you marks. A short paragraph, for example, will really stand out from the rest to emphasise an important point.

Longer paragraph – starts with topic sentence that sets the scene for the detail given in rest of paragraph

Sun, sea and sand. That is what everyone seems to want from their holiday, but I think that's boring. When people talk about ideal holidays, they all seem to have the same things in mind, like beaches, sun tans and night-life - but after that trip to Wales I told you about, all that changed for me. I really think adventure holidays are so much more fun and exciting.

Direct address – fits the audience

My holiday in Wales was the most fantastic experience of my life.

Short paragraph, making the most important point stand out

Powerful linking word to introduce next paragraph, changing the focus

Suddenly, I wasn't afraid of adventure activities any more, and felt more fit and healthy than I had ever felt in my life. We went canoeing, abseiling and climbing, and it was absolutely brilliant.

C

Task

Look through a magazine to find an article at least three paragraphs long. Identify:

- the topic sentences
- the linking words and phrases.

Notice how they help you to follow the stages of the article.

Examiner's tip

Reading high-quality writing by other people can help improve your own writing.

Structuring your writing

- Start by introducing what your writing is going to be about.
- Develop your ideas in the next two, three or four paragraphs.
- Keep to one main idea for each paragraph.
- Make sure you restate your point of view clearly at the end of your writing. You could also save a new idea for your conclusion.

Examiner's tip

Linking the ideas in your last paragraph to what you said in your first paragraph always impresses the examiner.

Here is how one student has planned their paragraphs for the following shorter writing task:

Write a letter [form] **to the local council** [audience] **explaining why your area needs a new youth club.** [purpose]

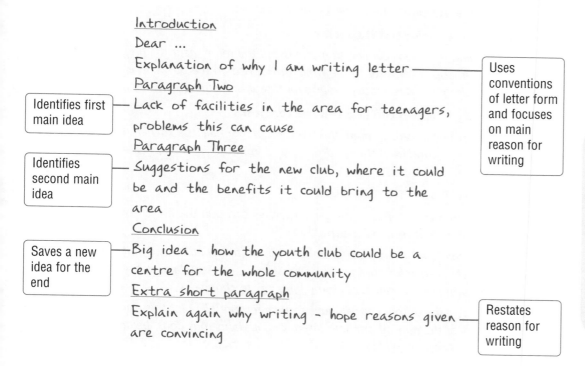

Introduction
Dear ...
Explanation of why I am writing letter — [Uses conventions of letter form and focuses on main reason for writing]
Paragraph Two
[Identifies first main idea] — Lack of facilities in the area for teenagers, problems this can cause
Paragraph Three
[Identifies second main idea] — Suggestions for the new club, where it could be and the benefits it could bring to the area
Conclusion
[Saves a new idea for the end] — Big idea - how the youth club could be a centre for the whole community
Extra short paragraph
Explain again why writing - hope reasons given are convincing — [Restates reason for writing]

Good points

- The writing is going to be controlled and purposeful, because there is a clear introduction and conclusion.
- The paragraphs follow on from each other very clearly and cover a range of relevant ideas.

Task

Using the example plan above, write the letter to the local council.

Sentences

Key points

- The way you use sentences in your writing is one of the things that the examiner will be assessing.
- Make sure the range and style of your sentences suit the **form**, the **purpose** and the **audience** of your writing.
- Include a mixture of sentence types: statements, questions, commands and exclamations, as appropriate.

Examiner's tip

Sentences are one of the ways you organise your ideas. If your sentences are clear, your ideas will flow easily.

Using a range of sentences

- It's important to use a mixture of long and short sentences: including simple, compound and complex sentences.
- Injecting this variety into your writing will help make it varied and interesting for the reader.

Short sentences

- A **simple sentence** contains **one main idea**, with one **subject** and a **verb**. It is a sentence which is complete in itself:

  subject (dog) | verb (trotted)

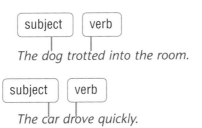

  The dog trotted into the room.

  subject (car) | verb (drove)

  The car drove quickly.

- Short sentences can be used one after another to **add excitement** to your writing:

  He began to run. The man followed. His heart was racing. The man was catching him. He had no choice. He plunged into the icy water.

- Short sentences can also **build tension**:

  The scratching noise was coming from the left of the room, near the fireplace. Sarah moved closer. She put her ear to the wall. She tapped on the bricks. The fireplace was hollow. Sarah looked desperately around for a tool, something to make a hole in the wall.

  However, short sentences can also **relieve tension**:

  Back and forth he paced, through the living room, the hall, the kitchen, back through the hall again, to and from the window, to and from the letterbox, waiting, pacing, endlessly...

  And then the knock at the door. At last.

- A short sentence after a series of longer sentences can pull the reader up short and **make a quick but powerful point**.

  Time after time, the Government promises to listen to the public sector, to provide funding so desperately needed for our hospitals, our schools, our social services – and time after time those promises are not kept. Something has to change.

  Sooner or later the authorities will have to take responsibility for this rising tide of attacks on members of the public from unlicensed, illegal, dangerous dogs, before we see another tragic death. Another child lost.

- A **single word sentence** can be used effectively to create a particular effect, but don't use this technique too much. In this case the single word at the end emphasises the silence.

  The fog stretched ahead of her, enclosing and wrapping itself around the house, the car, the world. Silence.

Longer sentences

- You can join two short sentences together to form a **compound sentence**. This type of sentence must be 'balanced' – each part of the compound could stand on its own as a simple sentence. For example:

  It is now or never. We need to do something today.

  becomes

  It is now or never and we need to do something today.

  It is now or never so we need to do something today.

  It is now or never; we need to do something today.

  Each half of the compound sentence is balanced by 'and', 'but or 'so' or by a semi-colon.

- A **complex sentence** has one **main clause**, which contains the main point of the sentence, and at least one subordinate clause. A **subordinate clause** links to the main clause but cannot stand on its own as a sentence. This means it does not have a main verb. Its job is to add extra information to the main clause. For example:

  The boy walked across the field. — Simple sentence

  The boy, who was alone at last, walked across the field as if nobody knew him. — Complex sentence containing two subordinate clauses

- You can 'expand' a sentence by adding extra detail to make the writing come alive for the reader and enable them to picture what you are writing about. Take care, because too much expanding can sound ridiculous!

  Look at that first simple sentence again:

  The boy walked across the field.

  Subject noun (boy) — Verb (walked) — Object noun (field)

  At the moment, it is rather dull and flat. To make it more interesting, it could be 'expanded' with some more descriptive vocabulary. The rule is:

  – Adjectives link to nouns

  – Adverbs link to verbs

  One student expanded the original sentence like this:

  The thin, pale boy walked slowly and cautiously across the muddy field.

  Adjectives (thin, pale) — Adverbs (slowly, cautiously) — Adjective (muddy)

  Notice how this expansion adds much more detail and interest to the sentence.

  Advertisers use this technique all the time. Here is an example from a travel brochure:

  Come to Portugal, where you will happily spend long, warm, lazy days wandering through glorious, green, picturesque countryside.

  Adverb (happily) — String of three adjectives (long, warm, lazy) — String of three adjectives (glorious, green, picturesque)

REMEMBER

Showing range and variety in your writing gets you marks. This applies as much to the sentences you use as to vocabulary, punctuation and ideas.

Examiner's tip

Beware of adding an adjective before every noun. Do it for effect and be selective.

Task

Look for a leaflet or a magazine article. Choose one paragraph and count how many sentences it has. Then identify the complex and simple sentences. How much variety is there?

Sentencing for effect

- Compound and complex sentences can create a range of effects, for example grouping ideas together:

  If the Government doesn't act quickly to do something about the crisis in public funding, there will be disastrous consequences for the whole of the public sector, including schools, hospitals and social care.

  The use of long clauses adds weight to the feeling that there is a long list of services that will be affected badly.

- You can also **add detail** to an idea with a complex sentence:

  Alone at last, the boy walked across the field; he was solitary but he did not seem lonely.

Look at this example of a good student response. Notice how a variety of sentences have been used deliberately for effect:

Good points

- The first three sentences are long, complex sentences, used to make the journey seem like it is taking a long time.
- The final sentence is short, suggesting that the writer is trying to ignore what is going on.

I was stuck in a car with my family on that last car journey to the ferry, feeling imprisoned by the slow traffic on the motorway. There were loads of hold-ups, loads of road-works, loads of my dad's really bad temper - not a great start to our annual family holiday.

My brother jiggled and rattled the seat next to me, kicking me with his little trainers and getting chocolate all over my jeans. My mum wanted her 'Coldplay' CD on over and over again, and even my headphones wouldn't drown out the sound of that on repeat.

I stared out of the window. I wanted a holiday from my family.

C

Questions, commands and exclamations

- Questions and exclamations should be used sparingly, so that they have an impact.
- They can be used very effectively in writing to argue, persuade or advise.

REMEMBER

Clear, accurate sentencing is possible when you know the rules of punctuation. The two skills go hand in hand.

Examiner's tip

Different effects suit different audiences and purposes. For example, rhetorical questions are useful in writing to argue or persuade.

- **Rhetorical questions** don't require an answer. Their job is to gain the reader's attention or to make a powerful statement.

  Can you imagine the effect of this lack of public funding on our society?

  This really means: 'the effects are going to be terrible'.

  Try beginning or ending a piece of writing to argue, persuade or advise with a rhetorical question:

  Is it ever acceptable to value animals more than humans?

  This really means: 'it is never acceptable to value animals more than humans'.

- **Commands** are a way of addressing the reader directly:

  Buy this book and your life will change overnight!

- **Exclamations** show strong emotional reactions, for example humour or anger:

  This is a disgrace!

  The results were stunning!

Take a look at this response to a persuasive task. The student is persuading other students to use charity bags to recycle their unwanted items.

> If you think about it, your stuff is just going to sit in cupboards and drawers anyway. It will take up space and make your house look untidy. If you use those charity bags when they come through the door you are helping other people as well as yourself. You are giving other people good stuff that they can use and you are tidying your house up at the same time. Everyone needs to use these charity bags.

D

Examiner's advice for improvement

This response is appropriate for the purpose and audience, however, it could be improved by:

- Including more variety in sentence lengths and types
- Using techniques such as rhetorical questions
- Including an exclamation mark or other different type of punctuation for variety
- Varying the vocabulary.

Here is the student's improved response, having taken this advice:

> Think about it, please. When you don't need your stuff any more, what do you do with it? It sits in cupboards, drawers, or even under your bed, taking up space and gathering dust. Wouldn't it be better for everyone to spend a few minutes filling a bag? That way, you get a tidier home, someone else gets the benefit of your unwanted items, and you get to feel that you've done something to help another human being. Everyone's a winner!

Imperative softened with 'please'

Rhetorical question – relates topic to reader's own experience

Rhetorical question – for persuasive effect

Short sentence to end – rounds off the piece with exclamation mark

C

REMEMBER

Sentence range and variety improves your work when it is done **deliberately** to create an **effect**.

Examiner's tip

An examiner would usually advise you to use exclamation marks sparingly – no more than one or two per response.

Task

Look at the following extract which describes an important event and uses only simple sentences.

Rewrite it so that the sentences are more varied and interesting. You can alter the order and add extra words if you need to.

> The day finally came. It was time to put the plans into action.
> We had been waiting for a long time. Everyone was very excited.
> We had one final meeting. The plans were looked through again.
> We wanted to make sure we had made all our preparations. We wanted to be certain that we hadn't missed anything.

Punctuation

Key points

- You need to use basic punctuation, such as full stops and capital letters in your writing responses.
- To obtain better marks, you will need to use a range of punctuation.
- You should aim to use: commas, apostrophes, question marks, exclamation marks, speech marks, brackets and dashes. If you can use colons and semi-colons, that is even better.

Commas

- Use commas to:
  1. separate the **items in a list**:
     When I was only a young boy I was battered, bruised, scalded and totally neglected.
  2. separate **clauses** from the main part of the sentence:
     I escaped from my family as soon as I was able, setting out for a new life in Australia.
     Relying on my own abilities, I was planning, step by careful step, during my childhood, to work my way out of that situation.
  3. separate a phrase that adds **extra information or detail** to a sentence:
     Ralph O'Hara was a very rich man, as far as I could tell.
  4. **introduce direct speech**:
     She told him, 'No way will I marry you!'
     or, when there is no question mark or exclamation mark **at the end of a sentence in direct speech**, a comma is used in place of a full stop.
     'The tide has turned against us,' he said.

Apostrophes

- Use apostrophes to:
  1. show **possession**.
     If the 'owner' is singular the apostrophe goes before the 's':
     Terry's watch
     the snail's trail
     If the 'owner' is **plural** and **does not** end in an 's', you add an apostrophe and an 's':
     the men's hats
     the children's toys
     If the 'owner' is **plural** but ends in an 's', you just add the apostrophe after the 's'.
     the parents' views
     the boys' bikes
  2. show where a letter or letters have been removed (an **omission**):
     'Do not talk!' ➜ *'Don't talk!'*
     'I am going to the shop' ➜ *'I'm goin'...'*

Speech marks

- Follow these guidelines for punctuating direct speech.
  – Speech marks go around the actual words spoken. They show the beginning and end of direct speech.
  – Punctuation at the end of speech is placed before the final speech mark.
  – There should be only one speaker for each paragraph.

'Is that your wallet?' asked the policeman.

If details of the speaker follow the speech, punctuate, close speech marks, use a lower case letter to continue.

'Yes, it's mine,' answered Jake.

If the speaker comes first, put a comma, then open speech marks and start the speech with a capital letter.

The policeman replied, 'That's very strange because the name on the wallet is Christine.'

'Easily explained,' said Jake, 'that's my surname.'

When the speaker comes in the middle of a sentence of speech, add a comma and open speech marks and use lower case to continue the speech.

'I think you'd better accompany me to the station,' said the policeman. 'A lady by the name of Christine Withers has just reported her wallet was taken by a boy of your description.'

If the speaker is placed between two complete sentences of speech, add a full stop, open speech marks and start the next speech with a capital letter.

Examiner's tip

Although you are unlikely to be writing a story in your exam, you might want to include some direct speech in a piece or writing, so you need to be aware of the rules about its punctuation.

REMEMBER

If you know how to use a wide range of punctuation, you are more likely to use a range of sentence lengths and types. All this adds interest to your writing.

Adding information

- A **colon** (:) can introduce a list, following a general statement:
  This country has been involved in many wars: the Civil War, the Napoleonic War, the Boer War, World War One and World War Two.
- A **colon** can also introduce a clause that explains the first phrase:
  'I'm sorry I didn't show up: I had a heavy cold and my head hurt.
- A **semi-colon** links two clauses or simple sentences that are equally important:
  I was uncertain what to do next; I couldn't let them down.
- A **semi-colon** can also separate phrases in a complicated list:
  I love my aunts for different reasons: Auntie Rachel because she's so kind; Auntie Kate because she's so funny; and Auntie Zulema because of the cash she doles out for birthdays!
- **Brackets** can mark off extra information in a sentence:
  The gloomy teachers (including Mr Morse, Miss Wignell and Mrs Tutty) trooped on to the stage.
  The BAFTA (British Academy of Film and Television Arts) awards were worth watching the other evening.
- **Dashes** can be used in the same way:
  Billionaire Chelsea owner Roman Abramovich has bought himself a new toy – a £72 million yacht – for his birthday.

Examiner's tip

Using an ellipsis (...) means you leave things to the reader's imagination: 'He opened the door and was horrified by what he saw...'

REMEMBER

Use dashes and brackets occasionally for effect, otherwise it can look like you are adding extra information needlessly.

Task

Add correct punctuation to these two sentences:

My mums boss rang shes got to go into work after all

Hes finally agreed to let us go we havent been to a home game for years

Language to engage the reader

Key points

- Choosing language that is appropriate to the **form**, the **purpose** and **audience** of the writing task set is very important in Section B of the exam.
- Using words in **imaginative** and **interesting** ways will be rewarded by your examiner.

Using appropriate words

- Choosing vocabulary appropriate to the **form**, the **purpose** and the **audience** of your writing is vital if you want to gain a good mark. It is one of the things your examiner will be looking for.
- Write in a **style** that suits the form, purpose and audience for your writing. For example, a letter to a Government Minister would be **formal**:

  'I sincerely hope that you think carefully about the points that I have offered for your consideration.'

  However, a letter to a close friend giving them advice about how to deal with moving home would be informal:

  'Don't you worry – you'll soon be you'll chatting and laughing with everyone. They won't be strangers for long!'

REMEMBER

Don't ever use text language in your responses! Text language does not follow normal spelling or grammar rules of standard English. So, if you use it, your work will be inaccurate and you will lose marks.

Using more interesting words

- If you want to achieve really high marks, you need to show that you can use a wide **vocabulary**. This means aiming for **variety** and **interest** with the words you choose.
- Regular use of a **thesaurus**, which offers alternatives for word choices, gives you more practice at using wider vocabulary.

  Your letter to a Government Minister might substitute 'think about' for:

  consider/contemplate/deliberate over/take into account

  Your letter to your close friend might substitute 'worry' for:

  lose sleep/agonise/fret/be anxious
- Using subject-specific or **technical vocabulary** that are linked to the topic you are writing about shows that you have clearly understood the **purpose**. For example, if you were writing about the elderly, you might use terms like 'social services' and 'primary carers'. If you were dealing with a subject like football, you might use 'offside', 'in the box', 'goalie', 'defensive move', etc.

Examiner's tip

When you come across unusual words in your reading, look them up and find out what they mean. This is another way of increasing your word power.

Connectives

Connectives are used to link paragraphs and ideas together. These might be to:

- order ideas, e,g, *Firstly, Secondly, Finally, To begin with , then*
- give logical reasons, e,g, *Therefore, Consequently, As a result, Accordingly*
- contrast/offer alternatives, e,g, *On the other hand, In contrast, Nevertheless, Whereas*
- develop an idea, e,g, *Because of this, Also, What is more, In addition, Taking this further*

Connectives make your writing flow and demonstrate that your ideas are well thought out. Examiners call this type of language 'markers' and will look to see that you know how to use them.

REMEMBER

Variety in your choice of words gets you marks. So avoid using the same word. Repetition should only ever be used deliberately for effect.

Look at how this student uses wide vocabulary and connectives to ensure that their writing is appropriate to the form, purpose and audience:

> One of the main reasons that the Government should listen to what people are saying about educational funding is that school exam results are being affected. If they invest in education now, it is going to help future generations as well as current students. Firstly, if teenagers are having to compete with each other for fewer and fewer places in further and higher education, they need the best possible exam results to help them. Secondly, the country is struggling to find talented doctors and scientists and so has to employ people from abroad.
> As a result, ...

- Use of linking phrase to introduce first point ("One of the main reasons")
- Connective to order ideas ("Firstly, if teenagers are having to")
- Connective to develop an idea ("Secondly,")
- Connective to summarise ideas ("As a result,")

C

Good points

- This response uses a range of connectives to organise ideas and clearly mark them out for the reader.
- It avoids repetition, for example using 'students' and 'teenagers'.
- It includes varied vocabulary.

Using more precise words

- Try to avoid nouns and verbs that sound very general, for example:

  She ran to the shops.

  improves when the words become more precise:

  She jogged all the way to the newsagent's on the corner.

- Be aware that the specific noun or verb you choose creates a particular effect. Compare:

  Ali leaned against the wall.

  with

  Ali lounged against the conservatory wall.

Try inserting some more precise verbs or nouns into the following sentences:

- Michael walked towards the bus stop.
- Hannah picked up her homework from the table.

Task

Look up the meaning of the following words in a dictionary. Practise stretching your vocabulary by choosing a few at a time and writing a sentence using each of the words:

furious	heavenly	whimpered
clashing	influential	dubious
scrupulous	unacceptable	morose
drastic	naïve	habitual
eventually	deliberated	assertive

Using language creatively

Key points

- **Engaging** the reader's interest is really important in your responses to the writing tasks – it is something the examiner will assess!
- Using language for effect, for example by using **imagery**, **stylistic techniques**, **irony** and **rhetorical devices**, is an effective way of improving your written work.

Creative language in non-fiction

- Creative and engaging language has a place in non-fiction texts just as it does stories and poems or other types of fiction. In terms of the exam, if you use imaginative and interesting language you are likely to achieve better marks.

Using imagery

- Using imagery, such as similes and metaphors, will bring your writing to life and make the examiner take note. You don't have to be a poet to use imagery –writers of non-fiction texts often use it in their work.
- **Similes** make a comparison using 'like' or 'as': e.g.

  The chance of working for that company might seem like a ticket to paradise right now, but…

  Her lessons do sometimes seem as dull as ditchwater, but you can still learn something.
- **Metaphors** state things that are not literally true, but the comparison has a strong effect: e.g.

  Even though your teachers come from the time of the dinosaurs, they can teach you important lessons….

  You exploded when I last suggested this, but, at the risk of causing another full-frontal attack…
- **Personification** is a particular type of metaphor, giving inanimate objects 'live', often human, characteristics: e.g.

  Greedy, hungry flames licked the sides of the building ferociously.

In this extract from an autobiography, the writer uses imagery and stylistic techniques to communicate their feelings to the reader:

Filled with disgust and remorse, I threw the bottle onto the hard concrete floor. It shattered, and shards of glass scattered; they formed a pattern in a circle like some mystic fortune teller's handiwork.

I lurched towards the window and glanced downwards. Below, cars crawled along the busy road like ants. Dizziness overcame me – whether from vertigo or the booze ... I wasn't sure.

I was on the top floor of a deserted tenement block and somehow I made my way to the wrong doorway. I opened the door and there was a yawning gap – a nothingness. I knew something profound and knew it in an instance. That was my life! My life!!

Only I could do something about it, step back – take back my life. Be in control!

It was that moment, when I teetered on the edge, that I decided to do away with the demon drink. I haven't touched alcohol since that day. Never!

Engages reader – makes them want to read on.

Overused simile – a cliché?

Personification – 'yawning'

Metaphor – again over used?

Uses semi-colon to link two vivid images together

Effective simile

Ellipsis used to indicate uncertainty

Short sentences, pulls reader up, keeps their interest

Continues metaphor of the 'yawning gap

Single-word sentence to reinforce writer's feelings'

Avoiding clichés

- A **cliché** is an over-used phrase that has become so common that most people have heard of it. Clichés tend to be similes and metaphors that have been so repeated that they have almost lost their meaning. Try to avoid using these in your own writing!

Take a look at how this student has over-used clichés in the start of their account of a family trip to a theme park.

> By the time we got to the theme park my little sister was as white as a sheet. She had been as sick as a parrot on the car and still wasn't feeling well. She looked the spitting image of a patient in a hospital bed, to be honest! Anyway, I was climbing the walls by then because we'd had to stop the car three times for her. Even though she was as pale as a ghost, we'd got rides to go on and I was sick to the back teeth of waiting.

REMEMBER

Alliteration can create different effects. In the sentence 'the sensuously slippery snake slithered silently over the silvered rock' the alliteration echoes the movement and the hissing of the animal itself.

Stylistic techniques

- **Onomatopoeia** is a way of capturing sounds in words. It is the term we use when a word sounds like the sound it is describing: e.g.

  Imagine the dull thud as the head teacher's door closes behind you.

  The leaves crunched and crackled deliciously underfoot.

- **Alliteration** is when words begin with the same sound: e.g.

  What a weary way you will have to tread without further qualifications.

  The quiet queue crept forward.

Task

Describe the effect of the alliteration in each of these examples. How does it affect the way you read the sentence?

Emotive language

- Writers use **emotive language** to make the reader respond with a particular feeling: for example, sympathy, anger, passion, guilt…
- Emotive language is often a feature of writing to argue or persuade.

Read this short extract which includes several examples of emotive language:

> If we don't try harder to encourage more people think carefully before buying a puppy from these unscrupulous breeders, the animal shelters are going to be even further crammed to the rafters with unwanted, abandoned, helpless dogs – dogs that could be given happy homes with loving families instead of being discarded, forgotten and abused.

Task

Write a paragraph that uses emotive language to make a point strongly.

Irony

- **Irony** can be when a writer means something rather different from what they are saying. It is a good technique to use – but don't overuse it. Include, at most, two or three examples in a piece of writing: e.g.

  'Oh, great, I really wanted a bruise on my arm.'

  It can be used in a humorous way:

  'That lump on my neck will really improve my looks.'

  It can also be used for serious effect:

  The robbers were really brave people – beating up a defenceless 98-year-old pensioner.

Task

Re-write the three ironic sentences above, making them literal – in other words, saying exactly what the writer meant.

Look at the following diary extract to see how the writer has used irony to make a clear point in a humorous way:

> Dear Diary,
>
> I'm feeling great today. I'm meeting friends I haven't seen for almost six years and I've woken up with a sore throat, a headache and I feel sick! Perfect timing, as usual.

REMEMBER

There may be some relevant evidence, facts or statistics in the reading extracts from Section A. It is fine to include some of this material in your writing responses as long as it is appropriate and you put it into your own words.

Evidence, statistics and quotations

- Your examiner does not expect you to be an expert on all the topics you are asked to write about. It is fine to make up 'evidence' but it must make your writing sound more believable.

Read this extract from a student's article about the RSPCA:

> Lots of animals come get sent to the shelter in January. It is nearly half of all the animals they get in a whole year. They get loads sent in January. This probably means that people are buying pets for Christmas and then they are abandoned.
>
> People who work at the shelter say that they need money from the public so they can stay open. They only get to provide their service because of public donations.

D

Now look at how the same student has used evidence in order to make his article about the RSPCA more powerful:

Over 42% of the animals that come into this shelter arrive in January, which means that nearly half of their intake arrive straight after Christmas. That's lots of animals abandoned within two weeks of them being given as presents.

We spoke to someone who works at the shelter. 'We are dependent on members of the public for funds to keep us going. It is donations from the public that mean we can stay open. Unfortunately we get lots of sadder donations as well and this is why we are needed. I would prefer it if people gave less to charity and thought a bit more instead before buying a dog as a present in the first place.'

C

Good points

- The use of two numerical statistics makes the article sound believable and accurate, as if the material has been researched.
- Using a quotation from a 'representative' is a common technique in articles. In this case it makes the student's work seem authentic.

Rhetoric and humour

Look at this student response to the writing to argue task:

Write a comment piece for a magazine on the topic – 'Should we receive organs from animals?'

I'd rather die than receive an organ from an animal donor. Some scientists see animal donations as solving the problem shortage of donor organs. Other people see it as their right to receive organs from animals. Do the animals have any rights? Do they deserve to die so that we might have a few more years of life? Surely not!

Compare it with using organs from humans. I'd rather die than rob other people of vital organs. It isn't morally right, it isn't just and it isn't fair to take organs from third world peoples who'd take the money for their starving families without knowing the full facts and consequences of what they are doing. So I feel almost as strongly that it isn't feasible and it isn't right to rob animals of life, just to survive a few more years on this earth and see what's going to happen in 'Home and Away'.

C

Strong, emotive opening statement – clear sense of writer's voice

Rhetorical question – includes direct address 'we'

Strong personal voice reinforced by rhetorical list of three

Humour added

Emotive language to pull at reader's heartstrings

Short exclamation to reinforce argument

More emotive language to create guilt /sympathy in reader

Good points

- The response has a strong personal voice – remember the examiner does not have to agree with the message of the essay.
- Rhetorical questions appeal directly to the reader.
- This is a successful response because it engages the interest of the reader, uses a range of sentences for effect, focuses on the question very well and uses accurate punctuation and spelling.

Task

Re-write the response above, adding some evidence and statistics to give weight to the writer's argument.
You can invent these details if you wish.

Openings and endings

Key points

- Your examiner is looking for clear structure and organisation in your writing.
- The **opening** and **closing** paragraphs of your writing are very important – they are the first and last things your examiner will read. Your opening will create a good impression and your closing paragraph might give a last boost to your work.

The opening

- The first paragraph in your writing has an important job – to grab the reader's attention.
- Don't 'play safe' with your opening. Try to avoid:

  In this essay I am going to… ✗

  I am writing to you because… ✗

  I think that… ✗
- Try a more effective start. What about:

  A short piece of conversation ✓

  An anecdote (a story about someone or something) ✓

  A description ✓

Here are two examples of how students have begun their response to the task:

Write a speech for your teachers arguing for the school's homework policy to be changed.

Hello everyone. I have come here today to talk to you about our school homework policy. I have been asked to talk about how the students feel about homework, the kinds of homework we get at our school and to give some suggestions for how we could change our homework policy.

D

Examiner's advice for improvement

- This is a clear, polite start – but simply lists the things they will cover in their speech.
- This opening could do more to grab the attention of the audience.
- It could also adapt its tone better to the audience.

The second response is instantly much more engaging as the annotations show:

'I'm not accepting that Jo, it's copied from Melissa.'

'So, Michael, mum 'helped' again, did she? Good old mum, she's on her way to a good GCSE in Chemistry at this rate!'

Sound familiar? I'm sure it does. We all know there's a problem with homework – and we all accept that something needs to be done about it. I am going to give some suggestions that might mean that Jo and Michael – and the rest of us – spend time on homework of real value, rather than the homework we do at the moment.

When I was asked to speak about the value of homework, what did I do? No, Mrs Hussain, I didn't 'google' homework' – well, not at first, anyway!

C

Annotations:

- Uses humour to gain the audience's interest
- Starts with two short anecdotes
- Question engages the audience
- Identifies topic of the speech
- Introduces form, purpose and audience
- Makes direct mention of member of the audience to maintain interest
- Use of humour to engage the audience

Task

Look at these different openings to a formal letter of complaint. Which is more effective?

Dear Sir/Madam
I am writing this letter to you because...

To the Customer Services Manager
I recently purchased a phone from your Salford store and was initially delighted with the service I received. However...

REMEMBER
Your examiner is a real person! They want to read responses that interest them.

Different openings

Look at these two different introductions in response to the question:

Write an article for a school magazine which argues either *for* or *against* banning mobile phones in school.

A Banning mobile phones? That should never happen. Some teachers think they are a nuisance and can disrupt a good lesson. In my view, mobile phones do have their benefits. They allow students to communicate effectively – an essential skill in the world of work.

Rhetorical questions engage reader in the topic.

Responds directly to the question, communicating a clear point of view

B Last month, a boy was sitting in a science lesson when his mobile phone rang. The teacher was fuming and cursed the use of 'these modern toys.' The phone was confiscated. If only the teacher had waited a few valuable seconds. The boy was me and the text message was; 'meet me outside the school gate now. Your dad has had an accident. We are going to the hospital. Love mum.' So no, I don't think mobile phones should be banned!

Uses an anecdote to engage the reader's interest

Then finally reveals the main point of the argument

Look at both answers and consider their different approaches:

A Uses rhetorical questions to engage the reader and then offers a good reason to support the opinion.

B Opens with an anecdote to engage the reader's interest and offers an inventive approach.

Examiner's tip
Adapt your tone and style to suit your audience. For example, using an anecdote could suit a persuasive piece but will not suit all non-fiction writing tasks.

The ending

- Your final paragraph should always leave your reader with a clear impression of your ideas and your point of view. It should also link back to the opening to round off your writing.

Here is the concluding paragraph of the piece of writing about homework.

The most important message I want you to take from everything I've said is that a major review of the effectiveness of homework policy is absolutely necessary. In its current format it is outdated, ineffective and, quite frankly, a waste of time. Please consider the points I have outlined today, and, in conclusion, I hope I have managed to convince Mrs Hussain (and the rest of you) that, this time at least, I definitely didn't 'google' my homework!

Clear summing up of the views expressed

Uses the rhetorical list of three

Summarising connective

Links to the humour in the opening paragraph

Task

Read some magazine articles. See if you can identify the different techniques the writers use to engage the interest of the reader in their first and final paragraphs.

Writing letters

Key points

- A letter is one of the forms you may be asked to write for either the **shorter** or **longer writing tasks** in Section B.
- You will need to be aware of the **purpose** and **audience** for the letter and adapt your style accordingly to suit these.

REMEMBER

- This part of the exam is assessing your writing skills. So focus carefully on the text of your letter but also make sure that you get the opening and signing off conventions of the letter right.
- The same applies if you are asked to produce a web page or a leaflet; it is still the text that you should focus on. You are not expected to design a web page or a leaflet.

Adapting your style

- If you are asked to write in the **form** of a letter, your **purpose** could be to inform, to explain, to argue or to persuade, to describe or review. Look carefully at the question to identify what your purpose is.
- The **audience** is a very important part of letter writing. If your audience is someone you don't know, or to someone in authority, such as your head teacher, a Government Minister or local council representative, your writing will need to be **formal**: e.g.

Form — Audience

Write a letter to the Minister for Education explaining your views about the current education offered to Key Stage 4 students and suggesting ways in which it could be improved.

Purpose

If your audience is someone you know, such as a friend, a family member or to a group of people your own age or younger, your letter will need to be informal: e.g.

Form — Audience

Write a letter to a friend who has recently moved back to your area, informing them about the things to do where you live.

Purpose

Setting out letters

- Your letter needs to **look like** a letter. Look at the following response to this shorter writing task:

Write a letter to a mobile phone company complaining about the contract they asked you to sign. Your letter should include:
- **Where and when you bought the phone**
- **What the problem is with the contract**
- **What you would like the company to do**

596 Main Road
Basingstoke
Hampshire
BS3 4R

29th January 2011

Customer Services Department
Anyphone Ltd
Long Road
Basingstoke
Hampshire
BS1 9K

Dear Sir/Madam

I recently purchased a new mobile phone from your Basingstoke branch after being attracted by the advertising on your website. One of the reasons for my purchase was the offer on the website for a package deal including free evening and weekend calls to all other networks, as well as 200 free texts per month.

When I came into your store to buy the phone, I was pleased with the customer service. The advice was clear and helpful and the store assistant quick to deal with my purchase. I got the model of phone I wanted and the paperwork did not take much time. It was only when I got home that I realised that the contract I had signed was not the same as the online offer. The offer on your website made it clear that the free tariff applied to all other networks, whereas the paperwork I was given said it was only the current network and calls to other networks did not apply to this free offer.

When I rang to ask about this difference, I was told that the offer only applied to online purchases. However, this was not made clear to me when I bought the phone; in fact when I checked with the assistant who served me she assured me that the offer was the same as the one advertised on the website.

Therefore, I would like you to either change my contract to the free tariff offer or cancel it immediately. I feel that I have been misled by your sales assistant and would appreciate it if you could contact me in writing to let me know what you intend to do.

Yours faithfully,

Moniza Hussain

C

Good points

- The purpose of this letter is very clear.
- The letter follows bullet points suggested in the task and includes relevant detail.
- The letter is well structured with each paragraph having a clear purpose and the addresses and date set out correctly.
- The writer uses the right greeting (Dear Sir/Madam) and signing off phrase (Yours faithfully).

Signing off

- There are clear rules to signing off at the end of a formal letter.
  If you are writing to someone you don't know, your letter would use the greeting:
  Dear Sir or Dear Madam

  Then, you always end with:
  Yours faithfully
- If you are writing to a named person or someone you know formally, for example:
  Dear Mrs Jones or Dear Customer Services Manager

  Then, you always end with:
  Yours sincerely

Remember: **never have** double 's' – 'Sir' and 'sincerely'!

- If you are writing to a friend or someone you know well, you can sign off with:
  Yours, Best wishes or even *Love*

Examiner's tip

- A letter is to a **specific person** unless it is a 'general audience' letter, for example to a magazine letter page
- A letter needs to **look like** a letter – address, greeting, signing off phrase
- Think of a letter as an essay in a different package – it's the content that matters most but basic **layout** must be right too.

Task

Write a letter to a friend who lives abroad, informing them about a recent school or family day trip. You might include:

- Where you went on the trip and why
- The kinds of things you did there.

Remember to use the right style and to sign off correctly.

Writing reports and articles

Key points

- **Reports** usually have a **functional purpose**: to inform, explain and sometimes to argue a point of view.
- **Articles** tend to be more **'open' in purpose**: to discuss ideas and issues.
- You may be asked to write for a *specific* **audience**: for example a report to your Year Group. However, you may be asked to write for a more *general* **audience**: for example an article for a magazine.
- This type of writing task will be based on **facts** but you might be expected to offer your own **opinions**.

Writing reports

- A report is usually a mainly **factual account** of a recent event or set of circumstances, for example:

  Write a report for the school magazine on a recent sporting event.

- The information you supply will usually be a mixture of facts and opinions:
  - **facts** provide the basic content on the event or issue
  - **opinions** provide more of an assessment of the material, making it more lively to read as well as more personal.

Here is one way you might plan the response to this task:

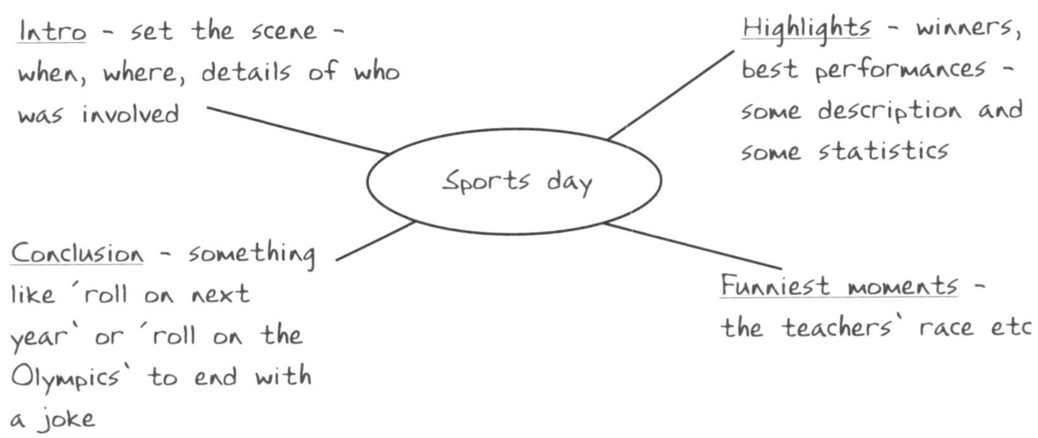

The same student has used no opinions at all in the start of their response to this task:

> Sports Day was held last Friday on the school field, as usual. They had planned to use the massive new sports centre with the proper running track, but something went wrong at the last minute. Mr Scott and the PE department did another great job with the organisation. The weather was fine all day. This meant that no part of the day was cancelled which was unlike last year when some of the Year 7 races had to be put off until the following week. This year all year groups were able to take part in the whole day and all the awards could be given out afterwards, with Mr Scott providing his usual jokes.

D

REMEMBER

You can invent details – your examiner will not be checking to make sure the account of Sports Day happened exactly as you say it did!

Examiner's advice for improvement

- The student responds to the form and purpose, but could offer extra detail to engage the interest of the reader.
- The style is dry and although technically accurate, this response could benefit from the addition of more opinions.
- The paragraph contains ideas that are not all well linked.

Here is the same student's rewritten version which now includes a mixture of facts and opinions:

Sports Day was held on Friday, rather than the awful mid-week event last year, meaning this year the athletes got the weekend to recover. The weather was lovely all day, so there were no events cancelled unlike last year when some of the Year 7 races had to be postponed until the following week, which was a shame. This year all year groups were able to participate in the whole day and all the awards could be given out at the ceremony afterwards, with Mr Scott providing his usual hilarious jokey commentary.

Of course, it was a shame that the planned trip to the new all-singing-all-dancing sports arena had to be cancelled at the last minute. We were really looking forward to having a Sports Day which felt slightly more professional and less like an infant school sack race event, but never mind – there's always next year!

Star turns this year included the now usual sight of Jordan Brown winning the 100m, the 400m and heading up the relay team. What would Year 10 do without him? And of course the staff race was as thrilling as usual (as a comedy event rather than a sporting event though).

C

Good points

- This is an engaging response with a good mixture of facts and opinions.
- The inclusion of opinions and lively detail creates a tone which communicates well to the reader and provides engaging detail.

Examples of the good points have been underlined in the first paragraph. Underline some more in the rest of the response.

Sports Day can be competitive – and fun.

REMEMBER

Detail is just as important in non-fiction as in creative writing. Setting the scene for your reader is a very important, effective part of good non-fiction writing.

Task

Write a report of a recent school event that you have taken part in. You are writing for your school news bulletin. Try to include:

- Facts and details about the event
- Your own opinions.

Writing articles

- Articles are normally written for magazines or newspapers.
- An article has a clear **purpose**: to discuss or express ideas usually from a particular **point of view**.

Here is the plan produced for the following longer writing task:

Write an article for your school magazine explaining your ideas for ways schools can address the issue of bullying.

REMEMBER

Making a plan first, perhaps including topic sentences, will help you to organise your ideas

Plan

Paragraph 1: Intro - exploring different types of bullying

Paragraph 2: Different types of bullying - violence, verbal, written, cyber, etc

Paragraph 3: How schools can make a difference and what they can do - anti-bullying charter

Paragraph 4: What I believe - 'I strongly believe' etc

Paragraph 5: Conclusion - Finally... what schools have to do

Look at the following extract from the student's response to the same writing task:

Surely we can get rid of bullies in school? I would like to explore different types of bullying and discuss ways in which schools can make a difference... by signing up to an anti-bullying charter.

Rhetorical device to begin

Clear explanation of main purpose

All types of bullying are harmful. The most obvious is physical bullying and it's when a victim receives physical violence. Verbal and written threats are also types of bullying and nowadays bullies use text messaging and the internet to bully as well, which makes it even easier.

Main point of discussion emerges – topic sentence to begin

Range of bullying identified

Schools can make a difference by signing up to an anti-bullying charter. This would show that a school is against all forms of bullying. Schools should look at their own anti-bullying policies and check if the policies are actually working. They need to realise that some students see their school as a violent, lonely and miserable place and this needs to be changed.

Restates student's opinion using emotive language – before going give more reasons why bullying needs to be addressed

Rhetorical rule of three to enforce point

I strongly believe ....

Finally, schools must ....

Final paragraph starts with connective, going on to state own solutions and sum up reasons why

C

Good points

- The response is clearly organised, using topic sentences effectively.
- Rhetorical techniques and emotive language emphasise point of view.
- Paragraph structure makes the arguments clear and powerful.

Layout and presentational features

Read the student response below to this longer writing task.

> **Some people think schools should be closed and all subjects should be taught via computers.**
> **Write an article for a school newspaper, arguing either for or against this idea.**

HOME ALONE?

It's been suggested that students learn better at home

SCHOOL DAYS OVER FOR EVER?

Some educational advisers are suggesting that students can learn better at home, via computers. They claim students learn more from a computer than they do from a teacher. Apparently, school could soon be a thing of the past!

However, think of the benefits school gives us. We get to see our friends every day, we get our equipment provided, and most of us are lucky enough to have some very good teachers who are very good at their job. Most of them are really good at their jobs and we learn better by listening to them than we would on our own.

It's obvious, isn't it? Nobody wants to learn on their own. Why would anyone bother to switch on their computer to watch someone talk about a Shakespeare play or show us a scientific experiment, at long distance? And what about being supervised? I don't know about you, but I'd be much more likely to flick a button or click a mouse and go on some entertaining games, check my Facebook page or see what Amazon is offering....

If these advisers want to change the education system, a better way to do it would be to spend money improving our schools rather than completely doing away with the system. What is wrong with schools at the moment is that they are under-funded. We could easily sort that out..

C

Headline – grabs reader's attention

Strapline – a second level heading giving more information than the headline

Subheading – summarises first part of the text

REMEMBER

Magazine articles use a range of layout and presentational features. You don't have to design these in the exam, but, as this example shows, you can include a **headline** and a **strapline** to prove your understanding of these features to the examiner.

Good points

- The tone is appropriate to the audience.
- Presentational devices show it is an article.
- The headline and strapline encourages the audience to read on.
- The purpose is clearly identified and is sustanined to the end.

Task

Using the plan below:
Write a report for a travel magazine about places to visit near you, explaining why the area is interesting for everyone.

<u>Intro:</u> set the scene - explain where we are, where we are near, the type of area

<u>Main points of interest (2 paragraphs):</u> good things about the area - things to do, the shops, where to go

<u>Conclusion:</u> give recommendation - why it's a good area

Writing to argue

Key points

- One of the questions in Section B may ask you to argue *either* for *or* against something.
- When you write to argue, you need to **present and develop a point of view**. Your aim is to convince the reader of this view.
- Your answer should refer to the **other point of view**, be **well structured** and use a range of **techniques** to convince the reader.

REMEMBER

Writing to argue doesn't mean getting annoyed or angry! It means presenting a clear point of view and supporting it.

Including both points of view

- Your main aim when you write to argue is to present your point of view. For example, it could be that students should be not have to wear school uniform, or that people should not eat meat.
- Make your point of view clear from the start of your answer.
- When you plan, list the 'arguments for' and the 'arguments against' your point of view. That will help you think about what to include when you are writing.
- Mention the opposite point of view in your writing. Try to counter it and as you do to develop your own point of view. This should help your argument.

Structuring your argument

- It is vital to structure your argument carefully – remember, this is assessed as part of your overall mark in Section B of the exam.

  You will be expected to include:
  - An introduction – a paragraph which presents the subject and probably suggests your attitude, or point of view
  - Your argument, which uses paragraphs to present your main ideas in a structured and systematic way
  - A conclusion – a paragraph which sums up your overall point of view.

Introductions

- Take a look at these two introductions, which have been given different grades. The students are writing an article for an employer's magazine, arguing either for or against work experience.

When I was told about work experience I wondered whether I would like it, and it was quite a difficult thing to do but in the end I quite liked it. Some people say work experience is a waste of time, and I know what they mean because I felt that too. Though I suppose it helps students to know what real life is like.

D

Examiner's advice for improvement

- The student introduces the topic, but isn't clear about what their point of view is. Are they arguing for or against work experience?
- The response moves from work experience being difficult, to being enjoyable, to being useful – this is confusing for the reader.
- There is rather a lot of repetition of 'I' in this response. It is better not to over-use personal pronouns.

Good points

- The Grade C response expresses a clear point of view from the start.
- It makes reference to another point of view.
- It signposts how they are going to develop the argument (by discussing the things in its favour).

In my opinion, work experience is a good thing. Some people argue that it is a waste of time, but I am going to show that it helps students get to know what real life is like. There are many things in its favour...

C

Conclusions

- The most important job of a good conclusion is to remind the reader of the main point of view. It should link back to the way you started, if that is appropriate.
- Try and write an ending which will stick in the memory.

Here is the way the Grade C response ended:

So, when I looked back on the two weeks, I realised that the problems didn't mean I hadn't learnt a lot or enjoyed myself. It was great to be covered in oil and I feel that I am now even better prepared for a working life. I would recommend work experience to everyone!

Good points

- This conclusion provides a clear summing up.
- The main point of view is repeated.
- The student gives a personal response about how they feel.
- It is a positive and enthusiastic ending – supporting the point of view.

Techniques of argument

- You might want to include some of the following to engage the reader in your argument and to emphasise your key points:
  - reasons for your argument
  - evidence (if possible)
  - short anecdotes (where appropriate)
  - facts and figures
  - rhetorical questions
  - direct address to the reader
  - lists and sentences varying in type and length.

REMEMBER

Of course, it would be tricky to include all of these techniques in a 30 minute response. Instead, use a range of techniques relevant to the task. Examiners will reward an appropriate selection of techniques.

Have a look at the following extract, which uses some of these techniques. It is the start of a student response to the question:

Write an article for a magazine arguing for or against this idea:

The government should give grants to ensure that every home in the UK has high-speed broadband access by 2016.

The government have promised to make sure that everyone in the country will have access to high-speed broadband by 2016. Will they achieve it? It's a very impressive promise. However, good quality internet access is one of the rights of modern society, proven to improve quality of life. And looking after the quality of our lives - yours and mine - is one of the government's responsibilities.

At the last count, 77% of homes in the UK had broadband access. Of these, over 60% have high-speed connections. However, the majority of these are still in densely-populated areas such as towns and cities. In more rural areas over a third of the country without access to high-speed broadband in the home...

Rhetorical question – engages reader

Inclusive pronoun – addresses the reader directly

Use of figures and statistics

Task

Write a letter to a newspaper arguing either for or against this idea:

The internet is a great resource and does more good than harm.

Writing to persuade

Key points

- One of the questions in Section B may ask you to **write to persuade**.
- When you write to persuade, you are trying to get the **reader** to **do something** or **believe something**.

Good points

- The response uses some persuasive language techniques effectively.
- It is clearly structured with a strong introduction and uses topic sentences in the following paragraphs.
- There is a clear sense of purpose and audience.

Persuasive techniques

- There are certain techniques that you can use to make your persuasive writing stand out:
  - effective **structuring of ideas**
  - **emotive language**
  - **examples** and **anecdotes**
  - **rhetorical techniques**.
- Make sure you use these for particular effect in your work, selecting the techniques that best suit the purpose and audience of your task.

Structuring ideas

- There are different ways of persuading people, and different ways of organising what you are going to say.
- The main difference between writing to **argue** and writing to **persuade** is: a piece of **argument** involves the presentation of two **different points of view.** **Persuasive writing** does not usually present the alternative point of view. More often it presents **one view** on a topic or issue.

Look at the following extract from a response to a persuasive task. A student was asked to write a letter to their headteacher suggesting how the school could be improved.

Dear Headteacher,

[Use of introductory paragraph to outline main suggestions] You asked for some suggestions for how we could spend the school buildings budget. There are a number of points I would like to raise. In general, the outside of buildings need to be improved. There are also no facilities outside for students. The state of individual classrooms is awful and there are a number of health and safety issues for each year group.

[Strong persuasive tone] I feel that each of these concerns is serious and requires immediate attention.

[Organised persuasion] First of all, the outside of buildings are tatty and paintwork is peeling. Isn't it reasonable to expect that a school should be nice to look at? Parents of new students visit the school, and what do they see? They see buildings that appear to be run down, damaged and uncared for. [Rhetorical questions to persuade the reader and emphasise key points] I suggest the painters are brought in to give the buildings a new coat of paint. [Example for improvement]

The area around the school is a wasteland at present. [Emotive language] There are areas here that some students would love to work on, growing plants and flowers. Then, the school could supply benches for students at lunchtime. Wastepaper bins could be provided to clean up all the litter that is all over the playing fields. The whole place would look better. [Persuasive ending to paragraph]

As for our classrooms: these are gloomy and dull. There has been no attempt to...

C

Emotive language

- **Emotive language** is language which makes the reader feel something strongly, such as guilt or anger. It can be a very effective technique in persuasive writing.

Look at how the student continues their letter about the state of their school:

As for our classrooms, these are gloomy and dull. There has been no attempt to provide a positive environment for learning for many years, so that now the classrooms are dark, dreary and dull places to be. They are often freezing in winter and boiling hot in summer, and this makes concentrating very hard. The younger students are really affected by this, coming from their bright, sunny and colourful primary schools. It must be a huge shock for them.

C

List of three drives home this point

Use of emotive language creates feelings of guilt and encourages changes to be made

Second list of three provides contrasting description with 'dark, dreary and dull'

Examples and anecdotes

- Using **examples** and real-life stories can make a point you are making more persuasive, if used occasionally and appropriately.
- An **anecdote** is just a short story which supports what you are trying to say. The reader is more likely to be persuaded if you can write about something that actually happened.

Consider how this student has used examples and anecdotes to illustrate her points:

As we know, there was a lot of concern after the last Open Evening – several parents said they were worried about the state of the temporary classrooms. One parent in particular asked you some very challenging questions about the last plan to replace them, in front of the new students. We need to make sure that this doesn't happen again.

Example given, as if from real life

Short anecdote used to support the point

REMEMBER

You are allowed to invent your own examples and anecdotes in the exam – they don't have to be true!

Rhetorical techniques

- **Rhetoric** is 'language used for effect' originally in 'the art of public speaking'.
- You have already seen some examples of rhetorical techniques in the response above, including rhetorical questions, the list of three and using anecdotes.

Now read the final paragraph of the student's response. Notice how she finishes her piece:

Pronoun 'we' – makes reader feel involved

List of three adjectives

Powerful vocabulary for emphasis

We all know the school is a mess, Mrs Smith. We all know the budget is limited. We share your concerns about finances. But if we don't attract new, enthusiastic, eager students to our school because of the disastrous state of our buildings, soon we won't have a school at all.

Repetitive phrasing emphasises points and builds to main conclusion

Use of exaggeration to persuade reader to act

Examiner's tip

Rhetorical touches like these can improve your grade.

Task

Write a persuasive letter to your Head of Year about part of your school that needs updating or improving. Use the persuasive techniques you have learnt about on these pages.

Writing to inform

Key points

- One of the questions in Section B of your examination may ask you to write to inform.
- The question is likely to focus you on a particular form and audience as well as purpose.

Effective information writing

- When writing to inform, you should concentrate on:
  - **choosing information** to suit your purpose
  - organising your ideas into **clear paragraphs**
  - writing an effective **opening** and **ending**
  - including **facts** and **opinions**
  - creating the right **tone** for your audience and purpose.

Examiner's tip

An information text does not need to be dry or dull; it can be more than a list of facts and figures. Try including some personal response (for example, a well-chosen anecdote, example or comment). This will raise your grade as your writing will immediately be more interesting.

Choosing the information

- Focusing on the main purpose, think first about the types of information you will provide to your reader. Come up with 5-6 main ideas and produce a clear plan. Spider diagrams work well for this but it could also be a simple list.
- Better answers will develop some of these main ideas in detail rather than include lots of undeveloped material.

Look at this spider diagram that one student produced for the following task:

Write a report for a teen magazine about a topic you are interested in.

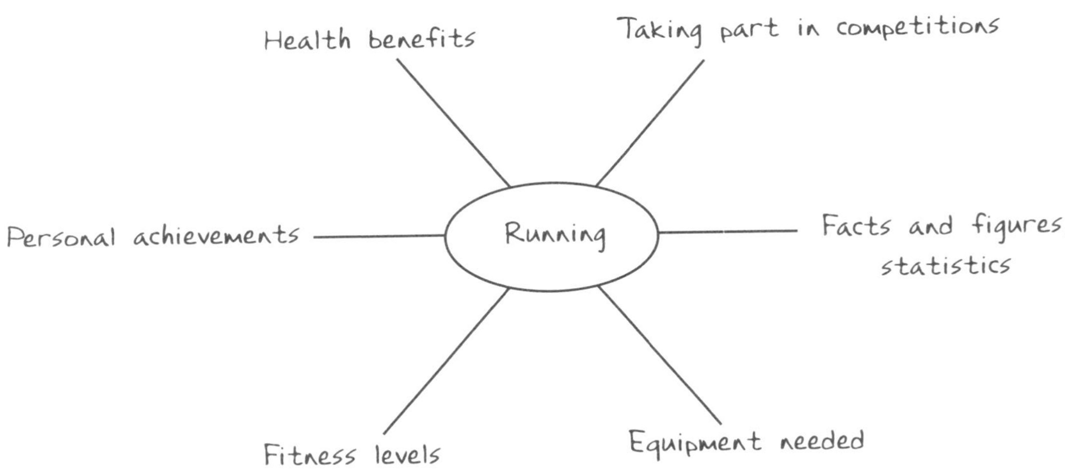

REMEMBER

You don't need to be an expert in your chosen subject, but it helps if you *sound like* one! Make up some survey results, include some figures and numbers – this gives your writing more credibility.

Developing the structure

- **Group** your ideas together and **link** them effectively. Unless you plan carefully, you run the risk of writing disjointed pieces of information which lack direction.

On page 85 is the same student's **detailed plan** for a response to the question above. Notice how each main idea is given a new paragraph and how then a few points of information are covered within each paragraph.

Plan

Intro: why I have chosen this topic

- background information – why I like it, when I started

Para 2: what running involves

- time commitment, equipment needed, how to start

Para 3: making progress

- health benefits, how to make progress, how running improves fitness (stats/ figures)

Para 4: taking it further

- getting into club running, training for races, competitions

Conclusion: passing the baton

- why starting running changed my life, why I recommend it to others

Good points

- The plan is clearly divided into separate paragraphs.
- The ideas within each paragraph are connected which should give a strong sense of purpose to the article.
- The information from the spider diagram has been developed well in the detailed plan.

Making the information clear

- When you are writing to inform, you must make the information clear for your audience. You can assume the reader knows nothing about what you are describing.
- The more details you can give, the clearer your information should be.

Decide how well these two different extracts from a 'How to start running' article offer clear, relevant information to an audience who have no knowledge of the subject.

REMEMBER

The longer writing task should only take you 35 minutes. So aim to complete between 5 and 6 developed paragraphs in this amount of time. Any more might lead to undeveloped ideas.

It is important to take it easy when you first start running. Don't go for a run too often and don't go out every day. You need to make your training suit your body.

D

Examiner's advice for improvement

- This is a clear response to the question, which provides some basic information.
- The information doesn't really go into detail about why it is important to do what is being suggested, and is in danger of sounding more like writing to advise than writing to inform.

It is really important to take it easy when you first start running, so you don't get injured. Don't go for a run too often and don't go out every day. Depending on your fitness level and your previous sporting history, you need to adapt your training to suit your body. Most new runners want to run every day, but this is a really bad idea because you are not allowing your muscles chance to recover and get even stronger between runs. Most top runners got a bit too enthusiastic at the start, and paid the price for it with pulled muscles!

C

Uses detail and gives reason for advice

Gives facts that might affect a new runner's ability to run every day at first

Shows knowledge of subject to reader with this fact

Provides example of other's experience – which will encourage new runners

Good points

- This is a clear response which provides some basic information.
- The direct address to the reader ('you' and 'your') makes the information personal.
- The occasional use of exclamation marks helps create an appropriately friendly tone.

Task

Write an article for the Year 7 student brochure informing new students about their first term at your school, from the perspective of an older student.

Writing to explain

Key points

- One of the questions in Section B of your examination may ask you to produce an explanation text.
- Explaining does not just involve supplying information. You need to explain **how** or **why** something happens, not just **what** happens.
- The question is likely to focus you on a particular form and audience as well as purpose.

REMEMBER

Functional writing is any writing that could exist in the real world and has a clear transactional purpose – for example to provide information. Types of functional writing could include letters, reports, articles and reviews.

Examiner's tip

Students often confuse writing to explain with writing to inform. Remember that writing to explain requires more than just information. Think about feelings, background and reasons as well as the facts.

Types of explanation task

- When you write to explain, it is vital to give reasons for what happened, or how you feel, or why something is important.
- You are likely to be asked to respond in one of these ways.
  You may be asked to **write an account from personal experience**. For example:

Most of us have a mixture of good and bad memories from our past. Choose a memory of an event in your past and explain why it was so significant for you.

> The examiner doesn't want a long detailed story – your focus should be an explanation of why it was significant.

or

Write about a time in your life that you felt particularly proud of yourself. Explain why you felt so proud of yourself during this time.

> Here, the examiner is interested in why that time was significant, not just what it was that made you proud.

- You will be asked to **write a functional non-fiction text**. For example:

Write a letter to a relative explaining why they should visit a place you think is very special.

> This task is asking you to explain why this place is special to you, rather than just information about the place.

or

Write an article for a school magazine explaining why it is important to take regular exercise.

> This task asks you to explain why and how exercise is important not just supply information about exercise.

Presenting the explanation

- Explanation texts often present a situation, then explain **the cause(s)** of it (why it came about) and **the effect(s)** it had.
- All the way through, an explanation text gives **reasons**. This is the key part of writing to explain.

Look at this example introduction from a response to this writing to explain task:

Form | Audience | Purpose

Write a letter to a friend explaining why a recent holiday was so memorable.

As you know, we went on holiday to Greece last year. It was very memorable. We stayed in a place called Milos. There were not many British people there. It was memorable because we had quite a bad time there, not because we had a good time.

D

Examiner's advice for improvement

- Sentences are clear but they are all short and simple. More variety in sentence length would add interest.
- The student does explain why the holiday was memorable but too simply; 'we had a bad time.' The main reason could be mentioned even in the Introduction.
- The language is basic – adding more detail would help.

Here is the student's improved response:

About six years ago, I went on holiday with my family to Greece. We stayed on the island of Milos, and there were not many British people there. I am sure we could have had a good time and then it would have been 'just another holiday'. However, there were also some seriously bad moments which made the holiday particularly memorable.

C

Task

Using the same question, make a plan of between five and ten things about a recent holiday that you feel made it memorable.
Now, choose three of the things you have chosen. For each one, write a short paragraph explaining why that particular aspect was memorable. You might choose things like:

- A person I met
- Something which made me laugh
- Something that went wrong
- A new food I had not tried before
- Something embarrassing that happened
- Something I learned

Using the language of explanation

- There are certain phrases that are really helpful with writing to explain. Here are some examples:

Phrases to explain the reasons and causes of something:
As a result of this
This meant that
This is because
As a consequence
Therefore

Phrases to show when something is uncertain:
It might be
The reason could have been
It may be that
Perhaps
Possibly

Task

Modern technology is advancing rapidly in the world.
Choose a piece of modern technology, for example a mobile phone or an mp3 player, and write an article for a gadgets magazine to explain how it has affected your life.

Good points

- Background information is clear, offering some detail.
- Examples to come are introduced: 'some seriously bad moments'
- Punctuation is used to suggest this holiday was not 'just another holiday'.
- Introduction ends well by referring directly to the key word in the question – 'memorable'.
- The tone is chatty and friendly to suit the audience.

REMEMBER

- The writing tasks in Section B may be linked in some way to the reading texts in Section A. Don't worry – the tasks will only ever ask you to write about things that you will be able to do. (You don't have to be an expert on every topic!)

Examiner's tip

It is absolutely fine to 'create' material – your examiner is not expecting every word you write to be 'true'. For example, you could invent details or statistics about a new mp3 player!

Writing reviews

Key points

- One of the questions in Section B of your examination may ask you to produce a review.
- A review is normally **an account and an evaluation** of an event or experience, giving a clear point of view. Reviews are designed to be read by a **wide audience** rather than one person.
- The **purpose** of a review can be to inform and/or explain, but it can also be to persuade as well, as it normally expresses a point of view.

Review structure

- The first part of a review explains what the review is about. It usually gives a short description of the concert, holiday, film, book or the TV programme.
- The second part goes into more detail, with some examples that give more information about your topic and why you liked or didn't like it.
- The final part is where you can give your overall opinion of what you are reviewing.

Planning

Here is an outline plan for a review of a film:

Plan

Title: catchy, might show whether I liked or disliked the film

Paragraph 1: summarise the film, early indication of my opinion

Paragraph 2: what was good (story, settings – don't give too much away)

Paragraph 3: what else was good (characters, actors)

Paragraph 4: what was bad – what I didn't like and why

Conclusion: final comments, what I'd say to make others go and see it (or not)

Give a rating (between 1 and 5 stars)

REMEMBER

Don't give away too much of the story in your review! This means not ruining the story for the reader by retelling crucial parts – especially the ending.

Tone and point of view

- When you write a review adopt a definite **point of view**. Give an opinion and explain that opinion. Do not be afraid of stating your opinion clearly.
- You want people to read all of your review, so choose your words and your tone carefully to match your audience.

Look at how this student has responded to the task below. They have used an imaginary film for their review.

Write a review of a film you have seen recently for a teenage magazine, persuading your audience either to go or not to go and see it.

Examiner's tip

It is fine to invent an imaginary film or band to review if you cannot think of a real one. The examiner is interested in how you write, not in whether to go and see the film you are recommending!

Three Little Pigs Leave Home

The film version of this well-known children's tale works well. It's not for tiny tots as it has a fifteen rating. The use of language is 'modern' to say the least – I don't think I ever expected to hear so much 'effing and blinding' from the mouth of Mr Wolf – thought it was supposed to be 'huffing and puffing'!! 'The three pigs...' is certainly for a teenage audience that like to laugh and know the original story-line. Well, who doesn't know

> Clear opening opinion in first sentence

> Language appeals audience – comparing 'effing and blinding' with 'huffing and puffing' – with humorous effect too

the story-line? The special effects are good, too. Seeing Mr Wolf blown off a chimney top in 3D was hilarious.

What a pity, then, that the director, Claude Sinclair, chose such a clumsy mumbling actor as the eldest pig! Ronald Ross was out of his depth playing such a vital role and, for some reason, spoke his lines in a boring tone that was difficult to hear. It reminded me of Lincoln Burrows in 'Prison Break'. The newcomer, Andrew Coles, was brilliant as Little Pig and he produced a performance that made the film so entertaining and watchable.

The film's settings were excellent, with lovely exotic locations. The camera angles were great, too - focusing on the wolf's lips and tongue and the dribbles of his saliva when he thought about eating a pig.

I'll definitely be getting hold of the DVD which includes extras, such as extended scenes and outtakes. Overall, you should go and see this film - but don't take your gran or your little sister, it might be a bit much for them!!

Star rating: 4

Specific example of special effects.

Clear structure - example of a negative feature of the film starts new paragraph

Reference out to another film

Comments on range of technical aspects with example

Finishes with an evaluation and rating of film

C

REMEMBER

Structure and organisation are really important in review writing. Make sure that you use each paragraph for a separate purpose. Imagine you have got sub-headings!

Good points

- The tone and style of this review is appropriate to its audience.
- The response presents both good and bad points giving a sense of balance.
- It comments on a range of aspects such as setting, camera angles.
- It gives an overall evaluation and a rating.

Vocabulary

- Use well-chosen descriptive words in reviews to match your opinion. These will engage your reader.

Here are some examples of descriptive words you might include in a review.

Positive	General	Negative
irresistible	plot	bewildering
hilarious	type	disappointing
classic	form	confusing
superb	hype	unbelievable
entertaining	effects	imitation
suspense	mood	typical
thrilling	typical	
impressive	scenes	

- Try using alliteration in your descriptive phrases to make them more memorable, for example:

lovely locations *sizzling scenes* *classic comedy*

Task

Adapting the plan on page 88 and using some of the vocabulary above, respond to this task:

Write a review of either a film or TV programme of your choice to persuade a general audience that it is not worth watching.

Writing to advise

Key points

- One of the questions in Section B of your examination may ask you to produce a piece of advice writing.
- Advice writing aims to encourage the **reader** to do **something** or to **behave in a particular way**.
- You should **organise** your **ideas**, offer **logical solutions** using **examples** and adopt the right **tone**.

Types of advice task

- An advice task will give you a specific **audience**, as well as a specific **form** for your writing and these may vary. For example:

  Write an article for your school magazine in which you advise its readers how they could welcome newcomers to the school.

  Write a letter to parents advising them of ways in which they could help improve their child's exam results.

  Write an article for a young person's magazine advising readers about how they could lead healthier lives.

Presenting your ideas logically

- Your advice will not be convincing unless you are logical. Writing to advise involves clear thinking, good organisation and presenting fair and balanced ideas. You could:
  - begin by presenting the subject clearly
  - offer advice that is logical and convincing
  - demonstrate the benefits of following your advice.

Getting the language features and tone right

- Your tone needs to fit your purpose and audience. When writing to advise you are **addressing your reader** directly, so tone is very important.
- You may be asked to write a **formal** response – a letter or an article for a magazine – or you may be asked to write an **informal** response – a letter to a friend.
- Here are some different language features you can use in your writing to vary your tone:
  - **Commands** which tell the reader directly what to do: e.g.

    Make sure you add...

    Don't forget to visit...
  - **Verbs** like **must** and **should** which encourage the reader to act: e.g.

    You must wash...

    You should exercise...
  - **Softer verbs** like **can** and **may** or **could** and **might** which give suggestions: e.g.

    You may want to put your planner...

    You could ask your parents...
  - **'If...(then)...** sentences... shows what would happen if you follow the advice: e.g.

    If you make sure you are well prepared, then you are less likely to worry that you won't perform well...

Look at the extract on page 91 from one student's advice writing, which uses some of these techniques.

Command

Softened command

If… clause shows result of following the advice

Don't worry when you come to our school. You need to get to grips with a whole new situation, including the crowds, the size of the school and all the new people. But take a deep breath and try not to panic. If you keep your cool, you will soon get used to it all.

Command

C

Good points

- This response uses commands to offer clear advice.
- The other approaches have a softer tone and will give the new student more confidence.
- The mixture of two approaches makes the writing varied and creates the right tone.

Offering solutions

- Offering possible solutions to the problem is a key part of writing to advise.

This student has offered a solution to a problem, using an appropriate tone:

Our school corridors can get very busy at changeover times and this can mean it is confusing and hard to get to lessons on time, especially when you're new. One solution to this problem might be to check your map of the school at the start of each day, so you know exactly where you will be going.

Using examples

- Giving **examples** is a good way of making your writing more convincing and reassuring.

When Tejinder joined the school last year, she soon got used to the place. She said that using her map of the school and always following the signs around the building made everything easier. Her brother, Majid, did the same and had no problems at all. In fact, he'd only been here a week before he told me, 'It feels just like home'...

Examples

A direct quotation adds weight to the advice – a reassuring ending

C

Examiner's tip

A great way of ending your writing is to sum up what the benefits would be if the advice is followed.

Task

An older person (perhaps a grandparent) has asked you to give them some advice before they buy their first laptop.

Write a letter, advising them on how they should choose their laptop and about the sorts of things they need to be aware of.

Remember to:

- make your advice points clear and logical
- use the language features of advice text to help you get your tone right for an older person.

REMEMBER

Getting tone right is vital to the success of advice writing. In this case, although you know the older person you are advising and so can be quite informal, you will still need to be reassuring as they are new to this type of shopping.

Checking your work

Key points

It is important to check your writing for errors as it is being assessed for several things at the same time:

- Your **ideas** and whether you can write in the right form for the audience and purpose you have been set, using interesting vocabulary
- Your skills in **organising** and **structuring** – openings, endings, paragraphing
- Your use of **sentences**, **punctuation** and **spelling**.

Spelling and accuracy

- To gain a Grade C, you need to show you can spell a wide range of words accurately, so be sure to check your spelling as you read through your work at the end of the exam.
- There are some spelling rules and strategies that can help to make sure that your spelling is as accurate as it can be.
- You also need to make sure that your handwriting is easy enough for the examiner to read. They will not know your handwriting as your teacher does.

Common spelling patterns

- Where words **follow a set pattern**, learn that pattern so that you can spell other related words, or words affected by the same rule. For example:

  – Words ending with **a single vowel and single consonant – double the consonant** if you **add an ending beginning with a vowel**:

  sit ➔ sitter/sitting *ban ➔ banned/banner*

  – **Add 's' to make a plural**:

  house ➔ houses *pool ➔ pools*

  but be aware of these **exceptions**:

words ending in *–ss, –sh, – ch, -x*: add *–es*	*glasses, bushes, matches, foxes*
words ending in consonant + *y*: change *–y* to *–ies*	*lady ➔ ladies, try ➔ tries*
words ending in *–f*: usually change to *-ves*	*wolf ➔ wolves, leaf ➔ leaves*
some words ending in *–o*: add *–es*	*tomatoes, potatoes*
some plural words don't follow these rules	*children, women, mice, sheep*

  – **Remove the final 'e'** from a verb **before adding 'ing'**:

  love ➔ loving *have ➔ having*

REMEMBER

You need to make sure your handwriting can be followed by the examiner, but it does not need to be perfect!

Knowing the difference

Some words sound the same or very similar but are spelt differently and have different meanings Learn these common examples and look out for others when checking your work:

your *(belonging to you) and* ***you're*** *(you are).*

their *(belonging to them),* ***they're*** *(they are) and* ***there*** *(any other use.)*

where *(place),* ***were*** *(verb) and* ***we're*** *(we are).*

too *(as well or very),* ***two*** *(the number) and* ***to*** *(any other use)*

whose *(belonging to someone) and* ***who's*** *(who is)*

quiet *(calm),* ***quite*** *(a bit)*

accept *(take),* ***except*** *(apart from)*

effect *(noun),* ***affect*** *(verb)*

Examiner's tip

Don't be afraid to make alterations. As long as your writing is legible, you won't lose marks. However, if the examiner can't make sense of what you have produced, that will let you down.

Spelling strategies

- Make sure you can spell these words which are frequently used and frequently misspelt in students' writing responses:

all right	*business*	*environment*	*occasionally*
argument	*coming*	*favourite*	*persuade*
beautiful	*definitely*	*friend*	*receive*
beginning	*develop*	*immediately*	*sense*
believe	*disappear*	*necessary*	*separate*

- When you are working, either in class or at home, get into the habit of underlining and then checking with a dictionary if you are not sure how to spell a word. (You are not allowed a dictionary in the exam.)
- Try to avoid relying on spell check on the computer. It is often wrong and it can make you a lazy speller.

Spelling tips

- Group words into families, where part of the word is the same, e.g.
  success, successful, succeed, unsuccessful
- Use memory jogging phrases (or mnemonics), e.g.
  'There is *iron* in the *environment* or *a rat* in *separate*.
- Say the word in your mind as it is spelt, e.g.
  Feb*ru*ary, Wed*nes*day, fr*i*end
- Chunk or break words down into smaller parts, e.g.
  ex-treme-ly, dis-appear-ed, def-in-ite

Checking and correcting

- Spend five minutes at the end of Section B of the exam **checking** and **improving** your writing.
- Failure to do this can affect your mark considerably, because vocabulary, punctuation and spelling can **all be improved**.
- Ideally, read through your response very slowly, as if reading aloud, and be prepared to **alter** your work whenever necessary.
- With regard to spelling, check for:
  - Words **spelt differently** in different parts of your answer – decide which version is correct.
  - Words which are clearly **spelt incorrectly** – try to apply spelling rules.

REMEMBER

Although you should never copy text from Section A, the text extracts can contain vocabulary that is useful for Section B.

Editing your writing

- If you realise that you have missed out a paragraph break, simply mark it in – either using two diagonal slash marks (//) or with a note in the margin with an asterisk (*) in the appropriate place.
- If you have used evidence, make sure you have put quotation marks around the words you are 'quoting'.
- If you need to move any text around or add a sentence or further information, do so. Your examiner will not mind and it is never too late to pick up a few more marks.

Examiner's tip

There are no marks for neatness. As long as the examiner can read your work, alterations are likely to improve your marks.

Answers to Tasks

Answers

Understanding non-fiction texts

page 11

Grade C

The audience for this report seems to be for adults. It is from a national newspaper so is aimed at a general adult reader. It uses words like 'sabotaging' and 'appropriateness' which are quite high-level vocabulary choices, so is designed to be read by someone with a reasonable level of education.

The tone of the article appears to be balanced and unbiased. The writer doesn't express any personal opinions but does give two points of view to make the article seem that it is not taking any sides. The critics are not named: it refers to 'critics' rather than saying who it is that is making these claims. However we are told who is giving the other point of view. This makes it seem as if lots of people are the 'critics' rather than just one or two people.

The headline makes the point of view more biased. It is rather emotive and uses two exclamation marks as if the idea is very silly and shocking. Even though the article itself sounds unbiased, the point of view is made clear by this headline and the pull-quote 'studying wigging', where the quotation that has been chosen and the exclamation mark both indicate the idea is being mocked.

page 15

Grade C

This is a news report from a local paper. The purpose of the report is likely to be to tell the reader what has happened, without giving any particular point of view. News reports are often unbiased.

This news report doesn't sound like it has any particular point of view at first. It reports the events that have happened without giving any opinion on why the bus company had to take down their decorations.

The bus company wants the driver to take the decorations down because of health and safety. The word 'claimed' in the second paragraph makes it sound as if this is only the bus company's view, however, and possibly that the writer of the article doesn't agree. Perhaps the writer thinks the bus company is being over-careful.

However, the quotations that are reported are only from one side of the argument. The lady quoted says that the passengers were 'delighted' with the decorations. There is no real explanation about why they had to take them down, apart from a mention of 'health and safety' which sounds dry and boring and a bit of a silly reason to take them down. It is clear that the writer is on the side of the passengers.

So, overall, the report is more biased than it first appears, mainly because it only presents one side of the argument and makes the bus company seem mean and unfestive – nobody likes 'bureaucracy'.

page 17

Grade C

The report breaks into several clear and logical sections. To begin with, it sets out what it is looking into: uniform, the school day and lunchtime arrangements. These are bulleted so that they stand out clearly.

Next, the report explains how the research was conducted – using questionnaires in pastoral time – and how long it all took.

When it moves on to the results, these are given in separate paragraphs. The first one deals with school uniform, offering percentages to make the results obvious and to show how strongly people feel. The second section is about school timings, giving a percentage again and the students' opinions. Then there are the findings about the lunchtime, again with relevant details.

We imagine it might have gone on to summarise the findings in its conclusion.

page 18

Grade C

From the start, this report is biased. The headline is critical of Simon Cowell, saying he has a 'smug grin', and this is repeated in the first paragraph. We learn that Rage Against The Machine are opposing the X Factor winner, who is supported by Simon Cowell, and Tom Morello is quoted at some length, which means the writer wants to put across his point of view.

He describes Joe McElderry's single as an 'abyss of blind mediocrity', which does not sound good. To make us be on his side, he also says the band are giving their royalties to charity. However, McElderry sounds angry and says Rage Against The Machine's music is 'dreadful'. He does not sound very nice. In fact, he was throwing darts at Zack de la Rocha's picture.

To show whose side the writer is on, he ends by quoting Morello, who is being kind about McElderry, which makes the man supported by Cowell seem even worse in contrast.

page 19

Completed Grade C response

This article says that homeless people are treated very badly. It uses some strong emotional words to make the readers feel sorry for the homeless, such as 'attacked, abused and robbed'. The writer makes use of the persuasive technique 'list of three' in order to make the point about the dangers faced more powerful. Also, these words make the homeless sound like victims and are used to make the reader sympathetic and want to help.

It uses words like 'we' and 'us' in order to include the reader in the article. Using this technique is effective because it speaks directly to the reader, which is part of the purpose as the article wants the reader to get involved and help to change the way the homeless are treated. Also, using a technique like this stops the article sounding like it is accusing people.

Saying the people should be 'eliminated' makes the homeless sound worthless and they are like refuse and should be 'swept from our streets'. This is emotive language which makes us feel sorry for them again.

The final sentence is very powerful because it is a simple statement but very effective: 'how much better would it be…'. It makes the point sound definite as if nobody could argue with it, which is effective because if the reader can't argue with that point, maybe they can't argue with any of the others.

page 21

Completed Grade C response

Layout

The first thing we notice in the picture is the couple wandering off into a rich sunset. The whole advertisement is in late evening shades, which are romantic and warm. The footsteps lead us to the couple, and the way they curve into the distance suggests the lazy, relaxed mood they are in. The body of the text follows that same curve, showing everything is in harmony. The idea of footprints is reflected in the red heading, which is like the red of the sun and it connects with 'Devon' at the bottom, as if Devon is the place for a romantic walk.

Other presentational features

The use of 'Devon' in the bottom right is clever, because it seems to be the only solid thing in the advert, so you notice it more – which is useful because the advert is about Devon. Also, it's on its side, so it sort of makes you look up to the title at the top. When you do look at the top, the third line is effective, because it has the words 'escape' and 'Devon', and these are the last part of the heading – the picture shows people who have escaped and Devon looks lovely so it all ties together.

Right at the bottom there appears to be a logo in the left-hand corner, and that will be there to show someone responsible has produced the advert. Also, all on its own, there is a line asking us to ring or look at the Devon website, and that is the final thing on the page, so it might be the thing we remember at the end.

page 23

Grade C

The leaflet shows someone with swine flu, so it immediately grabs our attention. As well as giving information, the leaflet is also persuading people to act responsibly about swine flu in order to stop the virus from spreading. The use of a very large picture with an image of the virus spreading into the air makes you realise how quickly the virus could spread and how important it is to do something about it. This is, of course, the purpose of the leaflet.

The photo takes up most of the space which suggests that it is the most important message. There is hardly any text on the page. The text is in capitals and large print which is designed to be read quickly. Using capitals also makes it stand out and seem vitally important – which it is, because people's lives are at stake. There are only two colours, blue and white, so that the writing is not confusing but simple and straightforward. The writer wants to give the reader a straightforward message.

The words 'keep it safe' are in capitals which draws your eye. It looks very definite so it might imply that if you don't do as they say you will not be 'safe' but 'in danger'. The black background makes it seem as though there is darkness all around the man and this creates a sense of danger as well. The hand is very large on the page but the germs are all around it and this suggests that the hand is useless in preventing swine flu from spreading.

The leaflet has been presented to highlight the dangers of not following the government advice and taking precautions against the spread of swine flu.

page 25

Grade C

Clear

The blog reads like a typical diary so we know exactly what is happening ('We've reached a fish camp…) and when ('Last night…'). There are the sorts of language people will easily understand: 'it was pitch black'. It is just like he is speaking to us. This is especially true of the way the entries begin: 'Hi it's Glenn. It's very late up in the Arctic'. Here, he seems to be telling us things in short sentences, to make it all clear. There is nothing in the second entry that is out of the ordinary, because phrases like 'we got on fine' are all easy to understand.

Interesting

In the first entry especially, there is also language to try to excite the reader: 'absolutely astounding' makes the view seem amazing, and 'stunning' is the same. There is also a simile ('like green inverted curtains'), so the sights are linked with something we can visualise. When 'stunning' is repeated, that just makes it seem even better. He also describes the scene as 'this great black expanse of the Arctic winter' and the words make us think it is all huge and somehow empty. However, it is also a bit like being at the pictures, because it is all 'entertaining'.

page 28

Completed Grade C response

To begin with, the expression is just matter-of-fact, with the long quote from John Wilson as he describes the experiment. It is quite 'everyday': 'There was a rubber tube…'. Then, the account begins to sounds more interesting as Wilson's childishness is stressed. He was sitting on a 'high stool', as if he was not big enough to stand, and was 'playing with the blue flame'. The word 'playing' makes it all sound like a game.

Of course, it all changed in an instant when it 'suddenly exploded'. This phrase is to shock the reader and bring a longer sentence to a sudden halt. After 'exploded', there is 'explosive', for emphasis, then 'explosion', almost as if there is an echo.

Wilson's description that 'it was quite an explosion' and that 'it wrecked part of the room' almost seem like understatements, considering the way the accident changed his life forever. The biographer uses another first-hand account from an eye-witness: 'There was a huge bang' and 'I got some glass in my face.' This gives authenticity to John's account of events and backs up what he has said about the event.

The extract ends with a short sentence, confirming that John Wilson was blinded in both eyes. The short sentence is effective in that we are aware of the impact upon John's life as he 'was blinded in both' eyes. Things would never be the same for him again. John notices the colour of the 'blue flame' because he will never see colour again, and this adds to the impact of the accident. He also tells us 'they say' because he would never see the damage done to the room.

page 29

Grade C

The extract is about the different reactions people have had to Rossetti's work. He has produced paintings and poetry, both of which have sometimes been ignored and sometimes really admired.

People seem to have liked his poetry in the past. The writer uses the word 'acclaimed' to suggest that everyone thought his poetry was really wonderful and talked about all the time. His work apparently got 'strong reactions' from people in the past, which means that lots of people talked about it, either loving it or hating it but at least it was not ignored.

The writer also says that his paintings are seen everywhere: 'grace countless items of merchandise', as if his painting is so popular that it is used all the time. The paintings are described as 'iconic' as if they are so famous that everyone recognises them. The word 'iconic' also makes it seem as though his work is very influential and powerful.

Of course, there is another side to him. His poems are now 'unfashionable', and perhaps he should not be admired because he chased many women and even got his poems back from his dead lover's grave after seven years. His 'grandly romantic gesture' went all wrong.

page 31

Grade C

Orwell uses language to suggest a negative attitude towards his experience. In the first two sentences he uses 'exhausting', 'every quarter' and 'traversed'. He sounds rather unenthusiastic about his experience – 'traversed' makes it sound as if he has gone on a very difficult expedition, like across a desert.

He uses metaphors to describe the 'monstrous' chimneys, coupled with them 'pouring forth smoke'. This makes it seem like a dangerous place, as if it is being compared to being in hell, surrounded by monsters. Not only is there a suggestion of hell in the imagery and language used, but Orwell creates a sense of danger. He repeats the mention of 'smoke' and 'misty' several times as if it is hard to see in Sheffield and this also makes the place seem dangerous. He also describes the 'huge jets of flame' which randomly appear out of the chimneys, as if they shock and surprise because they are not regular but 'periodical'. This also increases the sense of danger. He ends his description with the powerful metaphor of 'fiery red serpents' which reinforces again the image of hell created in this description of Sheffield.

Orwell wants the reader to think that Sheffield is a dangerous, ugly place, full of factories and smoke.

page 33

Grade C

The Monkey Island review opens with a metaphor, using 'set sail', 'journey' and 'come into port' to suggest that playing the game is going to be like an exciting expedition. The first sentence explains about the review generally and then goes into more detail with a description of the characters and setting of the game.

The writer clearly likes this game because there is language like 'amusing twists' which suggests the game will be entertaining. The use of the word 'unconventional' is clearly meant as a compliment to the game also, as if the game offers something new and exciting and out of the ordinary. Other examples of positive language include 'engaging' and 'funny' to describe the tone, and 'wacky' to suggest that this will please gamers who are 'wacky' as well.

The final sentence sums up the reviewer's opinion of the game. 'Lengthy' is used as a positive thing about the game, as if it offers real value for money and won't be finished quickly. The last sentence mentions 'new gamers' and 'veteran gamers', stressing by the repetition that all gamers will like it.

page 35

Grade C

Pictures

The overall appeal in The Real Gap Experience is one of cheery colours, so the pictures fit that style. The main picture of the rhino is in orange and red surrounds, making it look almost pretty. The top boat is in a lovely blue-green sea and the lion cubs stand out and look cute. It is all about trying to make the experience seem attractive. The other pictures seem to be of people enjoying the experience – like the three in the bar – and of exciting things happening. The whole idea is to make the reader want to be involved.

The WWF webpage is much more serious. Here, the pictures are worrying, with the contrast from 1941 to 2004. The 2004 picture could actually be quite lovely, but the reader will be concerned and so want to find out what is happening and perhaps what they can do to help. The smaller pictures are attractive because they are different things you can click on to find out information, from Obama to furry animals.

Other presentational features

The other features have some similarities and some differences. There are lots of links to click on in both cases, which makes everything more interesting for a surfer. But the colours work differently, with the Gap Year site being bright and fun and the WWF colours being much more serious, somehow, and depressing, so people will read on because they are worried...

page 37

Grade C

It is clear from the beginning that the writer of this information text is very positive about the need to recycle all sorts of items. In fact, the whole piece is a series of ideas of ways to 'help save the planet'.

The writer uses language carefully, to persuade the reader to be more 'green'. Firstly, it starts with the word 'we' which gives the article a friendly tone and also includes the person reading the article. This has the effect of making it seem that the reader and the writer are both on the same side. The first sentence is a simple sentence which acts as a kind of summary of the article in the same way as a sub-heading. It introduces the topic and subject clearly and simply. This is ideal because the writer want to attract younger readers, since this is from the CBBC website.

The text uses persuasive language techniques like command sentences which are repeated right through the text. This gives instructions to the reader but makes it seem easy and clear. The friendly tone is also created by using informal language like 'mates'. This is effective because it seems like the writer is on the same level as the reader, rather than being an adult telling you what to do.

The text is clearly aimed at a young audience. As well as language like 'mates', there are lots of simple sentences like 'cycle to places!' and the language is easy to understand. The content also suggests that the readers are at school, with 'get a lift to school in the car'.

page 41

Grade C

The slogan 'fur is dead' might mean two different things. On the one hand it might mean 'dead' like 'not fashionable', which is a good technique as the advert is trying to encourage people who are fashionable to not buy fur. Therefore the slogan is likely to appeal to the people who are the audience for the advert.

However, on the other hand the slogan is also talking about the way that fur is made, using 'dead' to remind the audience that a real live animal would have to be killed in order to make a fur coat. 'Dead' is also in red which reminds the audience of blood and violence, which is very effective as it makes you remember again that an animal would have to die.

This links with the photo of the dog as it is an example of a live, friendly animal that nobody would want to die. Using a dog on the photo is very effective because most people like dogs, and even if they didn't they certainly wouldn't want to see one being killed for no reason at all, which is what the people who make fur coats do all the time.

page 45

Grade C

Note that there are alternative answers in the extract.

- **Exaggeration:** all eyes turn to the sea

  This is to try to make the reader think it's all so good that you can't stop looking at it.

- **Simile:** like a satellite

  This makes the island seem quite a way away, so it is more exciting perhaps – as if it was something dropped from the sky.

- **Direct address to reader:** you'll find

  This is involving you and telling you what here is to see.

- **List:** Sorrento, Positano, Salerno and Amalfi

  The list is of towns, as if there are lots of them, so it must be a big place and they are probably famous too so you might want to go there.

- **Metaphor:** fleeing across

  The metaphor makes it seem as if the clouds are escaping – or perhaps they are running away because the clouds do not stay around here for long.

- **Simile:** statues sit like sentinels surveying

  This simile also has alliteration so it all seems smooth and calm and the statues are sitting like that just watching, which might make the reader think they will all be very beautiful as if they have been there for a long time.

page 47

Extract from a Grade C response

The first text is designed to persuade young children to eat more healthily by taking healthy foods for their packed lunches.

The leaflet uses lots of bright colours which would appeal to young children. There are also characters used which look like cartoon 'foods' that again appeal to that audience. It is all jumbled together so it is attractive for young readers. This is designed to make the leaflet appeal straight away by looking friendly and fun to read. This is important because the writers would want to make sure that children are attracted to reading the leaflet, persuading them that healthy eating is 'fun' rather than boring.

The information is broken down using colour. All the sub-headings are in red, which helps the information to be organised and clear, making it easy to read. Also, this means that your eye is attracted to the colour red, making it easy to look over the leaflet quickly and understand the main points it is making.

The second text is also about healthy eating, but this is much more for an adult audience. There are lots of lists, with sub-headings to guide the reader through the information and the lists are quite long, meaning you would have to have quite an adult reading age to be able to find the information you needed. Importantly, though, there is also a 'five a day' symbol, which is attractive – perhaps more to women than to men, because of the colours – and will attract readers. In its way, it is just as attractive as all the 'busy' details in the leaflet for children…

page 55

Form: Letter – so needs to have the correct format

Audience: Readers of a newspaper – so quite formal, and quite serious in tone

Purpose: To argue for or against the introduction of a curfew – will need to be well organised and logical

page 57

A possible plan might offer:

Introduction:

Why it is important to have interests/hobbies

Part 1:

The kinds of things school offers – music, sport, extra lessons (Science)

Part 2:

- Why it is a good idea
- Free/cheaper cost
- Familiar surroundings
- On-hand expertise

Conclusion:

What you stand to gain and how the school would improve

page 59

Extract from a Grade C response

Dear Sir,

You have been asking residents for their suggestions about what we need in this area. As a teenager, I am writing in the hope that you will give us something we need very badly – a new youth club.

I imagine you are well aware of the fact that we need a youth club urgently. There is simply nothing for us to do at nights or at weekends and this causes a lot of problems. Many of them could be avoided if we had somewhere else to go. For a start, we would not be hanging around on street corners; local people would not be complaining about youngsters making noise; and there would certainly be less litter.

So much would be improved if we had a base for young people, so the rest of the community would not be troubled. Since there is waste ground behind the swimming baths that is owned by the council, it would be an obvious place to put the new facility...

page 63

Possible response:

Finally, the day came and – the time when the plans had to be put into action. We had waited a long time for this, so everyone was excited. In our one final meeting, the plans were looked through again, because we wanted to make sure we had made all our preparations. We had to make sure that nothing had been missed. Nothing.

page 65

My mum's boss rang. She's got to go into work after all.

He's finally agreed to let us go. We haven't been to a game at home for years.

page 67

furious: extremely angry
My Mum was furious because I'd stayed out really late again and hadn't done my homework.

clashing: colliding, or working against each other
I didn't like the new football strip because the colours were clashing.

scrupulous: very careful or precise
She was always scrupulous about getting her homework in on time.

drastic: extreme, severe
It got so serious that I knew it was time for drastic things to be done.

eventually: finally, at last
It took an awfully long time but we did finish eventually.

heavenly: wonderful
She looked heavenly in her new dress.

influential: having an effect on something or on other people
He was a very influential member of the local council and could often persuade other members to agree with him.

unacceptable: unsatisfactory, can't be tolerated

If students keep behaving in an unacceptable way, they risk being excluded.

naïve: innocent, not sophisticated

She was so naïve that she didn't even realise there was a problem.

deliberated: thought out something carefully

We deliberated for a long time before deciding where to go.

whimpered: sobbed

The young child whimpered quietly because she had fallen and hurt her leg.

dubious: doubtful, not certain

That's a very dubious excuse for not turning up to sports practice – can't you think of something better?

morose: miserable, gloomy

He always seems so morose, which makes everyone feel bad.

habitual: done regularly and often

She is a habitual liar so no-one believes anything she says now.

assertive: putting forward your own opinion strongly

When they worked in a group, Sam was always assertive and took the lead.

page 69

Extract from a Grade C response

It was terrible when you looked at the people. There were small babies with flies all over their small faces, and they had bellies all swollen, and their mothers were crying all the time. The villages looked like something from many years ago and there were hungry dogs with blood-shot eyes and their ribs showing…

page 70

That bruise really hurts and it's the last thing I want.

That lump on my neck looks awful.

The robbers were so cowardly picking on an old person to beat up.

page 71

Example answer:

I'd rather die than receive an organ from an animal donor. Some scientists – for example, Professor Steven Braithwaite – see animal donations as solving the problem shorting of organs. However, up to 70% of people see it as their right to receive organs from animals. Do the animals have any rights? Do hundreds of thousands each year deserve to die so that transplant patients have, on average, an extra five years of life? Surely not!

page 75

Extract from a Grade C response

Dear Samira,

How are things with you? We've been having an amazing time here recently – and not just because my dad got a new job and Kiran got a new boyfriend!

Last week the whole school all went on a trip to Alton Towers and it was just brilliant. There was a fleet of coaches in the car park and queuing up right round on to the main road and, of course, hundreds of us in all our best gear, waiting to get on and get started. Phones were ringing and it was like the start of a demonstration or something – except that we knew we wouldn't be complaining when we got there – we just wanted to get on all the best rides and scream till the end of the day…

page 77

Extract from a Grade C response

My mum said, 'You'll never do it!' My dad said, 'If you get round, I'll treat you to a slap-up meal in town.' They had no faith in me at all. I think that was why I had to finish the whole fun run and raise as much money as my sister Faith. She's an athlete and I'm not – but I wasn't going to let her beat me.

I did some training, then when we turned up on the day it was brilliant. Most of the kids in the school had turned out, even though it was a Sunday, and there were banners everywhere and the teachers were all in fancy dress. Miss Timmins was particularly outstanding. You would have thought the Queen was really with us..!

page 79

Extract from a Grade C response

I've never heard of people recommending West Yorkshire as the perfect place to visit, but believe me the Americans who come to Britain would have a much better experience if they came up north, rather than wasting their time in London. As an area, it has lots of history, especially of the industrial revolution, and there are villages, towns and cities which are all linked by rail and have motorways to get you there too.

There are not many places better than visiting Salt's Mill, at Saltaire in Bradford. Just think, it is a whole area designed by the man who owned the mill so that all his workers could live there, and it is just the same as it used to be…

page 81

Dear Editor

I am tired of people writing to your paper attacking the internet and saying it does no good. It is about time some members of the older generation accepted that the world changes and that new things are not necessarily bad. The internet offers a huge opportunity to all kinds of people and makes information available instantly, as well as letting people play games and play music.

With broadband, we can even watch television programmes and films; then there are even books on line for those who like reading. How would those who say it does no good answer that point.....?

page 83

Extract from a Grade C response

Dear Mr Wills,

In response to your request for ideas about how we should improve our school, I should like to offer you a range of ways in which you could make the buildings more in line with what might be expected in the 21st century.

The biggest need is for the maths block to be modernised. It is not just that the rooms are too small and the corridors too narrow, it is also the fact that the fire escape can't be used from the front of the building. What are we supposed to do if there is an alarm? Jump out of the windows? It is essential for the basics of the building to be made much better.

My cousin was in a school which actually did have a fire, and when some students had to struggle to get out, it was the senior teachers in the school who were blamed. That means that you would be one of those held responsible, Mr Wills…

page 85

Grade C

To our new students

Hello and welcome! It is very good to welcome you all to your new school. I still remember how excited and nervous I was when I was coming up to secondary school.

You should have had your Welcome Pack by now and visited the school once at least. It all feels very confusing but don't worry. Your form tutor will go through everything with you and make sure you have everything you need. Also, your form will have Peer Mentors who are Year 10 students who are attached to your form and are there to support you and answer any questions. In a couple of weeks you will feel like you've always been here!

You will probably be worried about the same things everyone always worries about, like bullies and equipment and getting lost. Don't worry, it isn't really that bad at all. The Peer Mentors will guide you around until you get the hang of the building. You also need to make sure you listen to your Form Tutor carefully as they will go through everything with you. Check the lists in your Welcome Pack as they have all the details of standard dress and equipment that you will need.

When I was just starting, I used my homework diary all the time at first for writing everything down. You'll get a lot of information in your first week or so, and it can seem a bit like a lot of information, so just make a note of everything you might forget. And remember the homework diary has got a map of the school in it as well, which is another reason to hang on to it!

I'm sure you'll be fine and will really enjoy coming up to secondary school. We're waiting to welcome you, and please remember – if you don't know something, just ask. The teachers are all great (well, most of them!) and the students are much more friendly than they look, generally!

We will all look forward to seeing you in September

page 87

Extract from a Grade C response

It might seem strange to a lot of people, but I never wanted a mobile phone and I was the last person I know to get one. I just thought they took up everyone's money and wasted their time and I had better things I could be doing. My friends thought I was crazy of course, but my grandma said I was wonderful. How sad is that? I was my grandma's hero.

Eventually, of course, I moved into the modern world, and it was when I got a girlfriend. Then, you do really need to talk and there was no way our relationship was going to continue, she said, if she had to train carrier pigeons to bring me messages round.

That was when I went out and bought my first Samsung phone and my life has never been the same since. I am now properly in touch with what everyone else in my gang is doing and I can even access the internet when I want. The apps are great…

page 89

Extract from a Grade C response

(Terrible) Tales of Terror

When I sat down last night to watch 'Tales of Terror' I was really looking forward to it. I had heard that it was genuinely scary, which is what you want on a cold Christmas night after all. But it was a huge disappointment.

The cast list is impressive. There is the new star Mary Fawcett who won an award recently, and the famous Mike from 'EastEenders'. The writer, Paul Morello, has had lots of success as well. However, the acting was truly awful – I have never seen people die so unconvincingly – and the writing didn't live up to normal standards. Even the scenery was the worst I've ever come across: are walls supposed to wobble when door slam shut.....?

page 91

Extract from a Grade C response

Dear Gran,

I am very impressed that you are moving into the modern day and getting a laptop. Congratulations – I bet you will never want to be without it, once you have got the hang of what it can do and how to use it properly.

The first thing you need to do, of course, is select the best model for you. I could advise you about memories and internet connection speeds and so on, but you really need to go into a shop first and look at some models. In the shop, there will be salespeople who will be more than happy to talk things through with you and they will even let you try out some of the functions. Be brave enough to ask them to help, and you will find they will change the way you see computers for ever…

Collins

Revision

New GCSE English

✔ For GCSE English from 2010

Foundation

Exam Practice Workbook

Written by Keith Brindle

How to use this workbook

How this workbook is organised

This exam practice workbook is designed to help you develop your exam skills and test how well you are doing. Hopefully, it will show you are working 'on the right lines' as well as allowing you to spot some areas in which you might be able to improve.

It deals with the exam only because your controlled assessments will be prepared with the help of your teacher.

Its coverage links closely to the AQA English and English Language exams which are assessed like this:

	English	English Language
Examination paper (Reading and Writing)	2 hours Section A: 1 hour Reading non-fiction texts 20% of final marks Section B: 1 hour Writing two responses – one shorter, one longer 20% of final marks	2 hours Section A: 1 hour Reading non-fiction texts 20% of final marks Section B: 1 hour Writing two responses – one shorter, one longer 20% of final marks
Speaking and listening	3 assessments • Presentation • Discussing and listening • Adopting a role 20% of final marks	3 assessments • Presentation • Discussing and listening • Adopting a role 20% of final marks
Controlled assessments (Reading and Writing)	2 assessments Literary Reading 20% of final marks Producing Creative Texts 20% of final marks	3 assessments Extended Reading 15% of final marks Creative Writing 15% of final marks Spoken Language Study 10% of final marks

There are two major sections in this exam practice workbook:

Examination reading:

Examination writing:

As you work through the book, you can check how well you have done by referring to the Answers section that follows.

How to use this workbook

Work through the tasks provided in these two sections and then mark your own work, to see how well you have done. This will test your ability to respond to the requirements of the exam.

You can also consider what else you might have done, which would have brought you higher marks.

Exam Section A: Understanding non-fiction texts

First, you will have the opportunity to examine different kinds of media and non-fiction texts and answer questions on them. These will be the kinds of questions which you will meet in the exam.

Then, you will work though sections focusing on the sorts of questions you will be asked, one sort at a time. The same skills are tested each year, so you will know exactly what to expect in the exam.

Finally, you will tackle a complete practice Section A.

Exam Section B: Producing non-fiction texts

First, you can work through practice sections which focus on the skills you will require for the writing section of the exam.

Next, you will be guided through fundamental requirements for the writing tasks, for example: planning, writing in varied sentences, using punctuation and paragraphs appropriately.

Then, there are opportunities for you to practise the different kinds of writing you might have to face: for example, persuasion and argument.

As you move through these important sections, there are extra writing tasks, so that you can practise writing at length.

Exam Section A: Understanding non-fiction texts

Responding to the questions

Section A of the exam should take you one hour to complete. It is important that you manage to finish in the time, because the tasks in Section B are still to come. The exam paper will contain three texts. On the Higher Tier paper, there will be four questions; on the Foundation Tier paper, there will be five questions.

The questions will be based on the following assessment objectives, which expect candidates to:

- Read and understand texts, selecting material appropriate to purpose, collating from different sources and making comparisons and cross-references as appropriate.
- Develop and sustain interpretations of writers' ideas and perspectives.
- Explain and evaluate how writers use linguistic, grammatical, structural and presentational features to achieve effects and engage and influence the reader.

These may seem difficult or confusing, but when you respond to texts in the exam, you will be asked to:

- find information
- explain what writers are saying and suggesting
- say how language has been used
- compare presentational features of texts, like pictures and heading

The way the marks are awarded is predictable, so you will know in advance how long to spend on each question according to how many marks are awarded for the answer.

The key to success is to:

- read the texts carefully, so you know exactly what they are saying and so that you can find the material necessary for the answers
- read the questions carefully, so that you include the detail and interpretation for which you can be rewarded. You will not gain marks for writing about the wrong things. Consider underlining the important words in any question, so that you focus on them when responding
- respond in appropriate detail and in the right amount of time, so that you answer all the questions but still have enough time to complete Section B without having to panic
- support what you say with evidence from the texts. Usually, the best technique is to offer point/evidence/explanation or analysis.

What the questions involve

The Reading section of the exam is slightly different for each tier.

For the **Higher Tier exam**, you will have to:

- read three quite detailed texts
- answer four questions, testing your ability to

– find information (this is information retrieval)	8 marks
– write about presentation	8 marks
– analyse what is being suggested or inferred	8 marks
– compare how language is used in texts.	16 marks
	Total 40 marks

For the **Foundation Tier exam**, you will have to:

- read three texts
- answer five questions, testing your ability to

– find information (this is information retrieval)	4 marks
– write about what is being suggested or inferred	4 marks
– find evidence and say what it is suggesting	8 marks
– write about language	12 marks
– compare the presentational features used in texts.	12 marks
	Total 40 marks

Section A questions will look like this:

Paper has two sections: only Section A is given here

Foundation Tier

Section A: Reading

Answer all questions.

You are advised to spend about one hour on this section.

You need to allow a few minutes to read through the texts before answering the questions

You will be given three 'unseen' texts in the exam

Read **Source 1**, *Mattie is a hero*, a newspaper report, and answer the question below.

This is a retrieval question, so you just need to find relevant information

1 Give four reasons from the article that show that Mattie is a hero.

(4 marks)

2 What did Lucy Downes think of him?

This question is asking you to look beyond what is being said to what is being suggested

(4 marks)

Now read **Source 2**, an article from a travel magazine entitled *How the Eskimos survive*, and answer the question below.

You will need to find the evidence in the text then explain what is being suggested

3 What reasons are we given to make us think that the Eskimos deserve enormous respect? Write about:
- the conditions in which they live
- how families work together.

(8 marks)

Now read **Source 3**, *Real Heroes*, an extract from a biography about a family who lived through an earthquake, and answer the following question.

4 How has the writer, John Hallett, used language to make us sympathise with:
- Oliver
- Melanie?

You are not just finding language, but saying how it contributes to the impression being created

(12 marks)

Now look again at all three **Sources**. They have each been presented to attract the interest of the reader.

This question demands a detailed comparison of how presentational features are used. You may choose which other text you would like to write about

5 You are going to compare the presentational features of two of the texts. Choose two of the **Sources** and compare them, using these headings:
- pictures and headings
- other presentational features.

(12 marks)

Remind yourself of the number of marks given to each question and allocate your time accordingly

Purpose and audience

Why are purpose and audience important?

The terms 'purpose and audience' are often a vital starting point when you are answering the exam questions, because everything in the text is likely to be targeted at a particular purpose and audience. For example, the purpose and audience are the reasons why the writer chooses particular language and presentational features.

Focus on the **purpose** of this text.

We'll be there in a minute – teenagers fly on school run

Some children moan about having to get a bus to school. A small group of teenagers on a remote Scottish island, however, have the rather more exciting prospect of going to school by plane on what is believed to be the world's shortest commercial flight.

The journey from Papa Westray to Westray in the Orkney Islands takes 96 seconds, covering a distance of just over a mile. With a tail wind, it can take as little as 47 seconds. Normally the teenagers go by ferry but when the vessel was taken out of service for refurbishment, Loganair stepped in and offered to fly them to Westray Junior High. It has changed its schedule to ensure the children get to school on time.

Willie McEwen, acting head teacher at Westray Junior High, said: "We're delighted that Loganair has come forward with this solution. Our children will enjoy the flying especially as, at this time of year, it can be quite rough on the boat."

Guinness World Records said that it did not recognise the world's shortest scheduled domestic flight. "The category is currently under research," a spokesman said.

The Times, 06.11.09

1 Why has the writer written this text? Try to support what you say with evidence from the text.

____

____

____

____

____

____

____

____

(4 marks)

2 For each extract in the grid opposite, say:

- who you think they were written for – the audience
- why you have come to that decision.

Extract	Audience	Reason for decision	Marks
My husband snores all night. Why not do something about it..?			2
Stop throwing things away. Householders need to be more environmentally aware.			4
After centuries, nurses are starting to get some credit for all they do.			2

(8 marks)

Focus on the **purpose** and **audience** of this text.

3 What is the purpose and audience for this text and how does it appeal to its audience?

Support everything you say with evidence from the text.

Continue on lined paper if necessary.

(8 marks)

Selecting relevant information

What information will I have to select?

In the exam, you are tested on your ability to find exactly the right details to answer questions correctly.

Read this newspaper item.

Get your votes in for heroes

THE nominations are in – and now the voting can begin for the Your Heroes Award for 2009.

The response we received was staggering, with more than 100 individuals and organisations being put forward.

As previously stated, the competition now separates into a voting and judged section.

This is because we felt some categories required further careful consideration before winners and runners-up were chosen.

In other categories, we felt it was fairest to let the community decide who should take the plaudits.

And in this week's *Express* there will be another chance for you, our readers, to cast your votes in the categories for Health Service hero, Teenage Hero Award, Top Teacher and Police Community Support Officer Award.

All the nominations are featured on our websites www.wakefieldexpress.co.uk, www.pontefractandcastlefordexpress.co.uk and www.hemsworthandsouthelmsallexpress.co.uk to help you make an informed choice before casting your vote.

In true X-Factor style you can vote as many times as you like but each vote must be on an original coupon. No photocopies will be accepted.

The coupon will be printed in this week's *Express*. The judges will be examining the nominations in the other categories during the next few weeks.

Once all the choices have been made, we will be left with a top three in each category and they will be invited to the final event, which takes place at Wakefield Town Hall on November 30.

Compere for the night will be Ian Clayton, and also represented will be the competition's sponsors, Wakefield Council and NHS Wakefield District.

Wakefield Express, 28.10.09

1 Find two details in the text which show that the competition is popular.

____

____

____

(2 marks)

2 How can the public be involved in selecting the winners? List four things they can do.

____

____

____

____

____

____

(4 marks)

Read these letters to a newspaper carefully.

Booking agents bleeding us dry...

Thanks for your article last week. It is disgraceful that we are faced with extortionate booking fees for concert and theatre tickets. If a ticket 'costs' £30 but you are forced to pay £4.50 on top, it should be advertised at £34.50. The booking agents are guilty of deception and the law should do something about it. Why doesn't someone use the Trades Descriptions Act to sort them out?
Steve Forbing, Hackney

I wanted to go to see my favourite band recently, but the booking agent had added a huge 40% booking fee to the price of the ticket. If something isn't done soon, the artists will suffer because fans will simply refuse to pay.
Janice Barrell, NW7

Last year, I went to see Leonard Cohen in concert at the Albert Hall. I paid £90 plus a booking fee of £3.50. I saw my hero 20 years ago in the same place and I paid £12.50 and no booking fee. Is it me, or is this appalling?
Danny Southern, Bromsgrove

3 Find four details in these letters which indicate that people have a right to complain about booking fees.

____

____

____

____

(4 marks)

4 Write down four words or phrases from the text which are critical of the current pricing policy.

____

____

____

____

(4 marks)

Reports

Will there be a report in the exam?

It is likely that there will be a newspaper report in the exam, which you will be expected to analyse. You might, for example, be asked to look at the language or the presentational features or at what the report says or is suggesting.

Read this newspaper report.

BOOTY & BEAST

Blonde bruiser kicks up storm

by RICHARD PEPPIATT

FOOTBALL babe Elizabeth Lambert is facing a life ban for sticking the boot in.

The blonde bruiser, 20, has been branded the dirtiest player in the women's game after a series of violent fouls in one match.

She yanked a player to the ground by her ponytail, punched another in the back and lunged into knee-high tackles. And it was all caught on camera.

Face

Midfielder Lambert was finally booked for booting the ball into the face of an attacker who was flat out on the ground. The vicious incidents came as her University of New Mexico team lost 1-0 to Brigham Young University in America. Her university has suspended her and she could now be banned from all football.

Coach Kit Vela said: "She clearly crossed the line of fair play."

But Lambert said: "I am deeply regretful. My actions were uncalled for. I let my emotions get the best of me in a heated situation."

HEAD CASE: Elizabeth pulls ponytail

TAKE THAT: She boots ball into girl's face

Star, 11.11.09

1 What are the purposes of this text? Explain your ideas.

(2 marks)

2 How does the report try to attract the attention of the reader?

(4 marks)

3 What is the effect of the headline, sub-heading and captions?

(6 marks)

4 What impression of Elizabeth Lambert is created in the main section of text? (Do not comment on headings, captions, etc. in this answer.)

(8 marks)

Next read this newspaper report.

Gales, floods and chaos on the roads... it's Friday 13th

By **John Ingham**

BRITAIN is on alert for a Friday 13th storm with violent gales of up to 70mph and half a month's rainfall in a few hours.

Forecasters yesterday issued an early severe weather warning ahead of the first major storm of the autumn tearing in from the Atlantic overnight into Saturday.

The West, North-west and Wales face the worst pummeling although no-one is expected to escape.

Much of the nation is on high alert for flooding and treacherous driving conditions. Motorists have been told to expect severe delays with power lines and trees likely to be brought down.

Intense downpours of more than two inches (60mm) – half the average for November – threaten towns such as Bocastle in Cornwall, devastated by flash floods in August 2004.

A Met Office spokesman said: "The West and North-west will be worst affected. In the South there'll be gale force winds gusting to 50mph and 60mph with the potential for storm force winds gusting to 70mph in the north of Scotland."

Daily Express, 11.11.09

5 What is the purpose and audience for this text, and how successful is it? Explain.

Continue on lined paper if necessary.

(8 marks)

Aren't articles the same as reports?

Articles take a more considered view of events, including opinions and sometimes referring to related issues. Reports are more immediate and are usually about what has just happened.

Read this article carefully.

Sporting value

Heroes leading on from the front

ON and off the cricket pitch, Sir Ian Botham has always been a larger than life character. His barnstorming performances inspired a nation, and his relentless charity walks, in aid of Leukaemia research, have added to the aura and invincibility of the former all-rounder who lives in North Yorkshire.

Typically, he was not going to allow the 25th anniversary of his first walk from John O'Groats to Land's End, to pass unmarked as he looks to build upon the incredible £10m that he has already raised for the charity. His latest marathon effort deserves the fullest possible support.

But, just as importantly, Sir Ian, and former Olympic champion Sebastian Coe, who was revisiting his Sheffield childhood roots yesterday, continue to show that the impact of sports stars is not consigned to the field of play. What they do, away from the sporting arena, counts just as much, if not more so.

Thirty years after they captured the public's imagination, Lord Coe hopes the 2012 Olympics will inspire a grassroots sporting revolution, while Sir Ian believes that his fundraising can save lives. Typically,

STRIDING OUT: Sir Ian Botham, with leukaemia sufferers, launches Beefy's Great Forget Me Not Walk in London

he has pledged to continue his charity walks until childhood Leukaemia is beaten. Without such determination, Britain would be a much poorer place.

Yorkshire Post, 11.11.09

1 What is the purpose and audience for this text? Explain.

(4 marks)

2 Find four words or phrases which are intended to show Ian Botham as a hero.

(4 marks)

Next read this article.

Facebook generation knits with the WI for a rest

Will Pavia

Sometimes it's hard to be a young woman. City life is relentless: there are work pressures, home pressures and the worry of constantly updating one's Facebook profile.

The answer, according to thousands of young people in cities across the country? Join the Women's Institute.

In the upstairs rooms of pubs in New Cross and Borough, South London, they gather to knit. In lofts in Shoreditch and Islington, London, they cross-stitch. In universities up and down the country, they learn crafts their grandmothers knew all drawn by a modern cry: modern life is stressful, let's make some chutney!

The phenomenon of the urban Women's Institute was first noted in 2005, when a group of young ladies in Fulham, West London, began meeting every month. The next year there was a group in Islington called N1WI. The Shoreditch sisters formed in 2007, sparking copycat WIs in Leeds and Manchester. A network of university WIs is now forming, with branches at Goldsmiths College and King's College London, and in Newcastle upon Tyne, Sheffield, Birmingham and Reading.

An investigation into what drives the new urban WIs suggests that it is the jam-making, crocheting and even darning that draws members. The very crafts that WIs have taught since 1897 are suddenly attractive.

At this week's meeting of the King's College WI, 20 women sat at tables learning how to make jewellery and spoke of the joys of meeting each other in actual physical locations.

Holly Thompson, 21, a theology student, said: "You're on your BlackBerry or iPhone the whole time. If there is an opportunity to talk to people in real life, that's appealing." Jenny Parker, 18, an English student from South London, said: "People don't go to youth clubs any more – there is nothing like this around."

A few said that their parents were worried. One feared that her daughter would become a Young Conservative.

At the end of the evening, Jade Landers, 19, a medical student from southeast London, put on her home-made bracelets and went to leave. "I'm going to the Black Eyed Peas after a party at the Ministry of Sound," she said. "It's a pretty random evening."

Just as it was: women learning crafts

The Times, 06.11.09

3 How does the writer use language to interest the reader?

(8 marks)

4 How does the writer want us to react to:

- the first three paragraphs
- the last three paragraphs?

Continue on lined paper if necessary.

(8 marks)

Advertisements

What am I most likely to be asked about advertisements?

You are most likely to be asked about how an advertisement uses language and presentational features, or what it is suggesting to the reader, and to relate these to its purpose and audience.

Read this advertisement.

1 What impression of fostering is presented by this picture? Use detail to support your ideas.

____

____

____

____

(4 marks)

2 How does the language used try to persuade the reader to become involved?

____

____

____

____

____

____

____

____

(8 marks)

Next look at this advertisement.

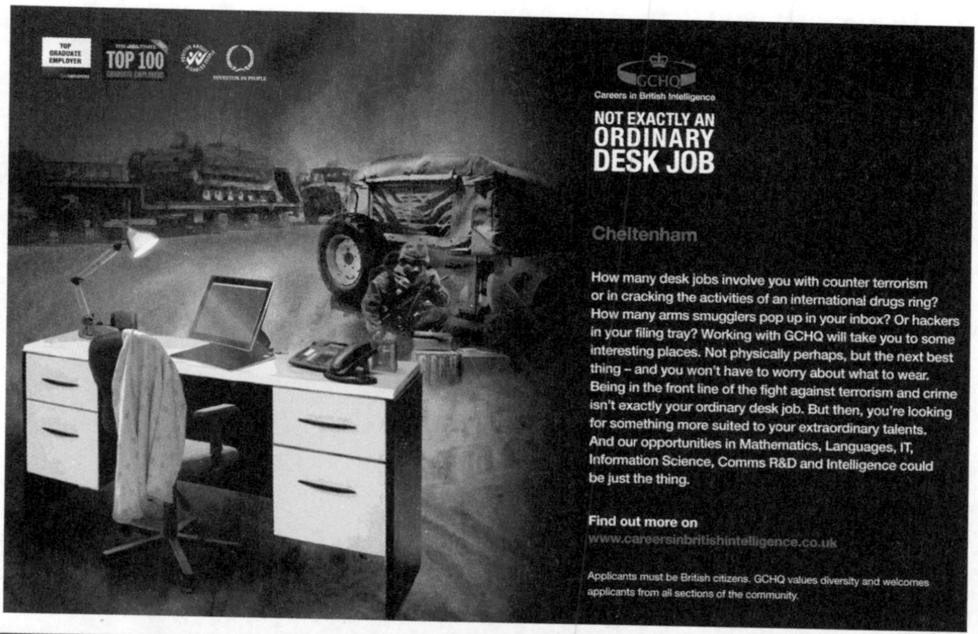

3 How does the advertisement try to capture the reader's imagination in the following extracts?

Extract	How is the imagination captured?
Not exactly an ordinary desk job	
How many arms smugglers pop up in your inbox?	
Being in the front line of the fight against terrorism...	
...you're looking for something more suited to your extraordinary talents	

(8 marks)

4 What effect is created by the picture and other presentational features?

Continue on lined paper if necessary

(8 marks)

Leaflets

Some leaflets can be very long. Won't writing about them be difficult?

Some leaflets can sometimes stretch to four or six pages, sometimes folded, but you are likely to be asked to focus on just the front of a leaflet and perhaps one other page.

Read the front of this leaflet.

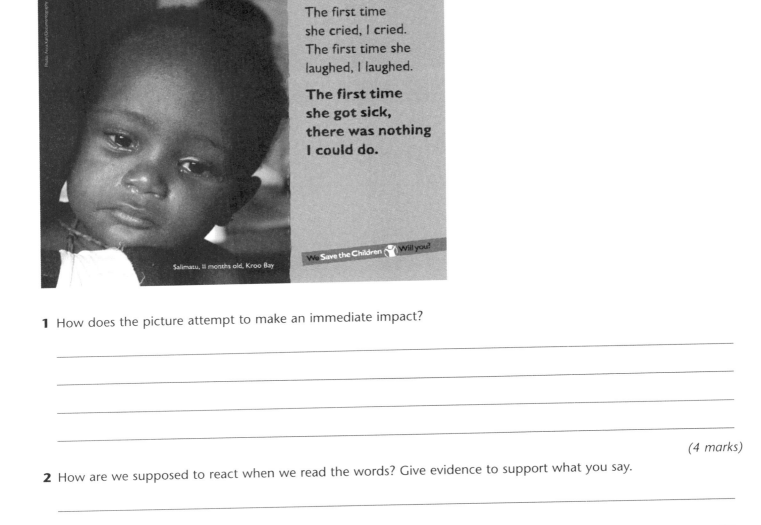

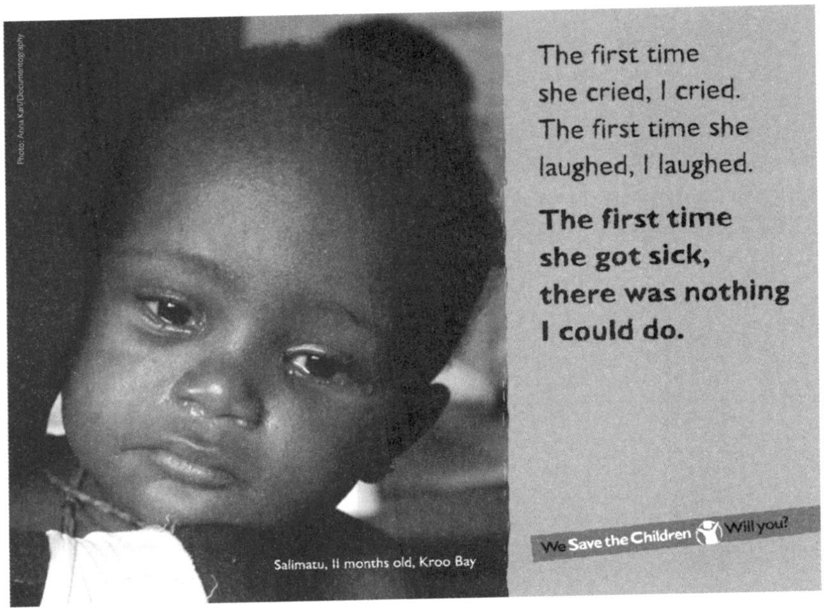

The first time she cried, I cried. The first time she laughed, I laughed.
The first time she got sick, there was nothing I could do.
Salimatu, 11 months old, Kroo Bay
We Save the Children Will you?

1 How does the picture attempt to make an immediate impact?

(4 marks)

2 How are we supposed to react when we read the words? Give evidence to support what you say.

(4 marks)

Now read the second part of the same leaflet.

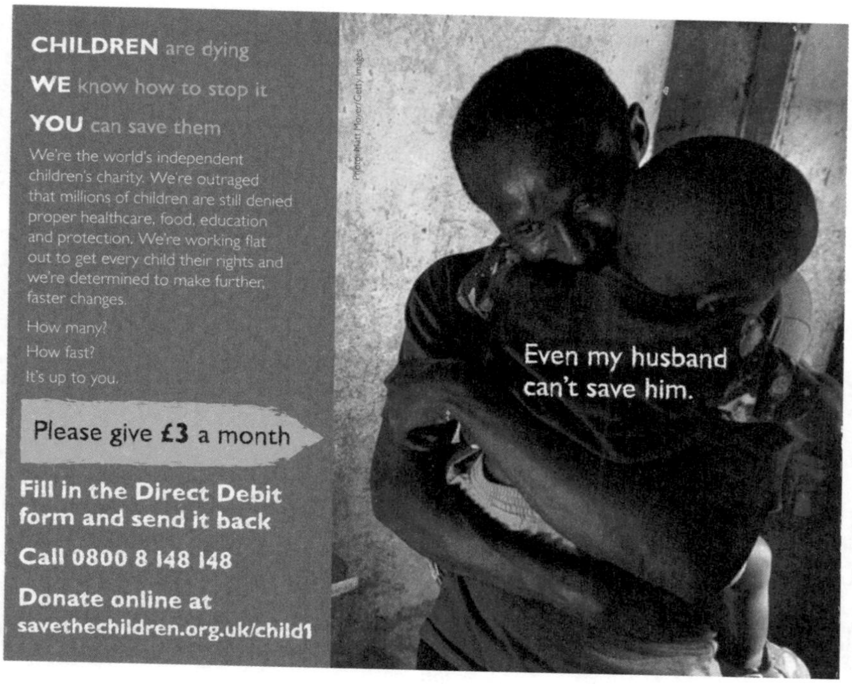
CHILDREN are dying
WE know how to stop it
YOU can save them
We're the world's independent children's charity. We're outraged that millions of children are still denied proper healthcare, food, education and protection. We're working flat out to get every child their rights and we're determined to make further, faster changes.
How many?
How fast?
It's up to you.
Please give £3 a month
Fill in the Direct Debit form and send it back
Call 0800 8 148 148
Donate online at savethechildren.org.uk/child1
Even my husband can't save him.

3 How does this second part of the leaflet link with the first?

(4 marks)

4 What is the effect of the short sentences?

(4 marks)

5 What is the purpose of this leaflet? Do you think it would be successful? Give reasons.

(4 marks)

Are we likely to be faced with a letter or diary entry?

You might be asked write about *any* form of media or non-fiction text. It is best to be prepared. Be aware that letters can be very formal and functional or they can offer more personal views.

Read this letter from a regional newspaper.

Colourful local language that is disappearing

From: W Michael Waite, Carr Lane, Sutton on the Forest, North Yorkshire

I FIND the letters regarding our dialect fascinating, as they evoke many happy memories for this old Leeds loiner.

Regarding the use of the word "whisht", my old landlord in Edinburgh, a Scot born and bred, used to say "hod your whisht" meaning stop talking.

There are many other words which I recall as a child but no longer hear, such as my mother telling me to stop moidering her when she was busy and I wanted attention.

In the midlands, the word mithering was used with the same meaning. We used to have our bins emptied by the midden men, and road gulleys were fever grates, harking back to the days when disease was thought to be caused by bad smells.

Mother used to use scouring stone to edge the doorstep while I sat on the causer edge watching her. When I was older, I went apple kipping, and occasionally took a bit of tusky (rhubarb).

When playing taws, a cardinal sin was gibbing, or jibbing, when the forearm was used to supplement the impulse given by the thumb. My father-in-law, who came from Sheffield, used terms such as broddling your lug, meaning a vigorous poking of the ear, and taldering meaning tuneless singing.

It is sad that our colourful dialect is being replaced by sloppy television-derived speech from American sit-coms and rap. I know language is continually evolving, but I'm like, no way man.

Yorkshire Post, 11.11.09

1 What is the writer's main point? How does he attempt to convince the reader?

(4 marks)

2 Find four examples to support his viewpoint.

(4 marks)

3 How does he use language in the final sentence? Compare it with the language used in the first sentence.

(4 marks)

Diaries usually give a personal angle on what has happened.

This extract is taken from a teacher's diary.

> *The whole day was dreadful again. I am sick and tired of standing in front of kids who don't want to learn anything and, worse still, seem determined to stop anyone else learning. First it was Year 7s: they look like little cherubs if you see them on their own, but put them together and they turn into a pack of deranged hounds. Uncontrollable at times. Then it was Year 9s, then 11s, then 10s but none of them were any better. They just get bigger and even more confident. It's shocking, it's demoralising and it's a daily occurrence. I can't help thinking that if an inspector walked in on any ordinary day, she would wonder where the senior members of staff are and why the ordinary teachers are just left to flounder. My previous school was so different...*

4 Comment on the following language. What does it make the reader think?

Language	What the reader thinks
they look like little cherubs	
they turn into a pack of deranged hounds	
Uncontrollable at times	
It's shocking, it's demoralising and it's a daily occurrence	

(4 marks)

5 Why does the fact that this is written in the first person make it more effective for the reader?

(2 marks)

6 Who does the teacher hold responsible for what is happening and how does she make this point?

(4 marks)

Biographical writing

What sorts of writing does 'biographical' include?

The term biography refers to the story of someone's life. In the exam, you could be presented with a biographical extract, an autobiographical extract (where someone tells their own story), or even a piece about someone's adventures when travelling.

This is an extract from a biography of Florence Nightingale, who, with her nurses, introduced cleanliness into the care of injured soldiers during the Crimean War (1853–56). She had not been allowed to help much, but then there was a rush of casualties.

> It was Miss Nightingales's opportunity – at last the doctors turned to her. In this urgent work she met no opposition. Just as it was no one's business to clean the lavatories, so it was no one's business to clean the wards. She ordered two hundred hard scrubbing brushes and sacking for washing the floors. Her next step was to try to wash the men's clothes. The men said they preferred their own lice to other people's and refused to part with their shirts, stuffing them, filthy and vermin-ridden, under their blankets. The total amount of washing satisfactorily accomplished for the vast hospital was seven shirts. Miss Nightingale made arrangements to rent a house outside the barracks and have the washing done by soldiers' wives. She said she wished to have boilers put in by the Engineers Corps. The boilers were installed and paid for.

1 Find two improvements Florence Nightingale made.

____

____

(2 marks)

2 Whose fault was it that the conditions were so dirty? Offer evidence for your ideas.

____

____

____

____

____

____

(4 marks)

3 What sort of woman does 'Miss Nightingale' appear to be in this extract? Explain.

____

____

____

____

____

____

(4 marks)

This extract is taken from the autobiography of a nurse in the First World War. She is writing about one of her patients who tried to commit suicide rather than fight.

> When he could stand it no longer, he fired a revolver up through the roof of his mouth, but he made a mess of it. The ball tore out his left eye, and then lodged somewhere under his skull, so they bundled him into an ambulance and carried him, cursing and screaming, to the nearest field hospital. The journey was made in double-quick time, over rough Belgian roads. To save his life, he must reach the hospital without delay, and if he was bounced to death jolting along at breakneck speed, it did not matter. That was understood. He was a deserter, and discipline must be maintained. Since he had failed in the job, his life must be saved, he must be nursed back to health, until he was well enough to be stood up against a wall and shot. This is War. Things like this also happen in peace time, but not so obviously.

4 How does the nurse want us to feel about this man? Support your ideas with close reference to the text.

(8 marks)

5 How is language used to make this incident particularly shocking?

(8 marks)

Will we be expected to write about internet texts?

You can regard the web page as just another form of text. Any question(s) about it will be of the same kind you might be asked about an article or an advertisement. (You will not be asked about the function of any buttons or navigational tools shown on a web page, for example.)

Look carefully at this web page.

the specialists in customised athletics clothing for clubs & teams
Leeds Road, Ilkley • Tel: 01943 601 581
www.fastraxrunning.co.uk

UK results

COMPLETE RUNNER
Ilkley: 01943 601581 • Nelson: 01282 690111
www.completerunner.co.uk

This page is sponsored by Fastrax and Complete Runner, Ilkley and Nelson - click the logos above to visit their sites

- Home
- New On Site
- Contact Me
- Race Calendars
- Results Index
- York RRL
- Entry Forms
- Search site
- Links
- Other Pages
- Login

Site Map
Register as an Organ Donor and save a life
UKResults supports the following organisations:
Lewa Wildlife Conservancy (Kenya)
Tusk Trust (UK)

Associate sites:
VLA Events
Sport Systems

In partnership: St John Ambulance
St John Ambulance for all your event's First Aid Cover

Welcome to UKResults - Skype *ukresults* or *ukresults.ontheroad*

For friendly advice and assistance relating to your event, please contact me. My associates **VLA Events (Ramsbottom, Bury)** and **Sport Systems** are also available to lend their expertise to your event. Contact me for availability.
If you're thinking about chip timing, please contact me to discuss availability and suitability for your event.

Are you a charity? Do you have places available in races which you want to advertise to runners? Use my NEW FREE service - **Click here to register your places.** If you are a runner looking for a charity place, maybe this would be a good place to start (once details start to come in of course!!).

Aches and pains due to a sports injury? Want to find a massage gel which can help both before and after training? Visit the Albmaleaf page. Albmaleaf is now available to be ordered online via this site.

ENTER ONLINE **Thinking of online entries for your event?** Race Organisers, you can now accept your **online entries** inexpensively (or for free!) and flexibly via ***ukresults*** - contact me to discuss your requirements. I can also accommodate your event's requirements with regard to **full entry management** (postal or online entries, database compilation and submission to you, posting race packs etc.)

Runners - postage costs and envelope sizes causing you a headache with your race entries? Use my service and beat the Mail - postage charges went up again in April 2009!! Always use C5 envelopes - 1st class stamp is now 39p and a large letter stamp (for those bigger envelopes) is 61p - as you will need 2 of these, it makes more sense to enter online!! *Click here for information about using Online forms and registration of your details at UKResults* ALL ONLINE ENTRIES ON THIS SITE ARE GENERALLY CHEAPER THAN RUNNERS' WORLD, ACTIVE EUROPE ETC. The problems which have recently affected Runners' World entries don't affect my site - all your entries are handled personally by a real person so I can deal with any problems which might crop up! None of your email addresses and other information will be released to anyone other than the race organiser without your consent.

Click here to see the full list of Online Entry Forms available on this site

Freckleton Half Marathon 2010 - online entry now open exclusively on UKResults - no postal entries for 2010!

Online entry for some races in November will close on Monday evening, 2nd November, as I will not be able to fully manage entries for the next couple of weeks. Sorry if this causes you any inconvenience. PRESTON 10 AND EAVES WOOD ENTRIES ARE BEING PROCESSED AS NORMAL THOUGH! THE AUTOMATED REPLY YOU GET IS A GENERIC ONE SO DON'T PANIC THAT YOUR ENTRY WILL NOT BE INCLUDED IF YOU HAVE MADE A COMPLETED PAYMENT.

Now Accepting Payl

Nochex Online Payment Services
Payments by Nochex Merchant Account

UcanLearn
Want to learn to drive? Around Accrington, Blackburn or Darwen? Contact UCanLearn2Drive.c

Albmaleaf

Visit Tulloh Books

Which way did they go?

1 Find four services the webmaster is offering.

1 ______________________________

2 ______________________________

3 ______________________________

4 ______________________________

(4 marks)

2 How effective is the layout of this web page? Give reasons for your views.

(8 marks)

3 How persuasive is the language used?
Find four examples and comment on them.

(8 marks)

If there is a review in the exam, is it likely to be a review of a book?

If you are asked to read a review – or write one in Section B of the exam paper – it could be a review of anything: a trip, a CD, a concert…

Read this book review.

The Beacon
Susan Hill

Vintage £6.99

Best known for her ghost stories, Susan Hill tackles a different kind of spectre in this gripping tale. The Prime children – Colin, May, Frank and Berenice – have an uneventful childhood living in a secluded farmhouse called the Beacon. May goes off to university, but she experiences terrible hallucinations and returns home. Frank, the mysterious one, distances himself, moving to London and becoming a journalist. Then he writes a memoir, detailing the horrific abuse he suffered as a child at the hands of his parents and siblings. The book's publication changes all of their lives forever, raising questions about truth and memory. Short and spare it might be, but Hill's novel is expertly structured, her beautifully written prose as haunting as the best ghost story. **SOPHIE MISSING**

Observer, 01.11.09

1 Find four examples of language linked to a sense of ghostliness and haunting.

1 ________________________________

2 ________________________________

3 ________________________________

4 ________________________________

(4 marks)

2 Are we supposed to think *The Beacon* is a good book or not? Find information to support your ideas and explain your views.

(8 marks)

3 Why are the opening and ending sentences particularly effective?

____

____

____

____

____

(4 marks)

This is a review of a television programme.

When A Mother's Love Is Not Enough, Rosa Monckton's film aboput the pressures that bear down on the parents of disabled children, was deeply moving and sometimes uncomfortable viewing. Having children of any kind has its tough moments, but recalling one's own grumbles about fatigue and mess and tantrums in the light of the ordeals faced by some of these parents was a shaming business. Monckton spoke from personal experience as the mother of a Down's syndrome daughter, and was bravely candid about the points at which fatigue and grief overwhelms you. She'd also captured a very touching moment when David Cameron struggled with his emotions on recalling the challenges of living with his disabled son. But it was hard not to feel that something had been left out in her calls for better support for such parents. "What is missing from the state is the help," she concluded, "What is missing is the compassion and the common sense." Surely what is missing is the money that would render state compassion effective?

Independent, 11.11.09

4 What is the writer's opinion of parents who care for disabled children? Support your ideas with details from the text.

____

____

____

____

____

____

____

____

(8 marks)

5 What conclusion does the writer come to after watching this television programme? Give supporting evidence in your answer.

____

____

____

____

____

____

____

____

(8 marks)

Analysing text

How do we analyse?

In the exam, this means looking beyond one straightforward meaning and giving an extended, detailed explanation instead. If you show you understand layers of meaning in the text, you will get more marks.

Read this sports article.

Murray's down and out in Paris

A LONG season and a short night took their toll on Andy Murray with a 1-6, 6-3, 6-4 defeat to Czech Radek Stepanek in the Paris Masters third round. The world No.4, who battled for over two hours to beat James Blake on Wednesday night, finishing well into the early hours, started well, relying on his strong serve, but then collapsed after too many unforced errors. The 22 year old Scot, seeded fourth, joined Roger Federer on the indoor event's casualty list. 'Obviously, I was not at my best but I was not expecting to [be],' Murray said. 'It was four o'clock by the time I got to bed and that's not the ideal preparation.'

Metro, 13.11.09

1 What impression of Murray's performance do we get from the following words? Offer more than one simple explanation.

- 'battled'

- 'collapsed'

(4 marks)

2 Look at the picture. What does it make us think about Andy Murray?

1

2

(4 marks)

Read this text from a school newsletter.

On Thursday 26 November 2009, Ossett School is organizing a Careers Information Event for all students, and their parents, in Years 10, 11, 12 and 13. The world of work and Higher Education is becoming more complicated and competitive. It is essential that your child attends so that they have a chance to explore the many opportunities available to them. With higher levels of skills and knowledge being needed by all workers in the future, it is important for your child to have the chance to learn more about their future options so they can make the right choice for their future.

I would like to stress the importance of this event to members of the Sixth Form – it is a valuable opportunity to meet people from local universities and national gap year providers. For Year 12 it is crucial that they start their planning for after Year 13 early, as Higher Education is becoming much more competitive. Visiting the universities in the sixth form centre will give them an insight into what they need to be doing and what is available. For students in Years 12 and 13 who are looking to go into work and training our exhibitors in Kendal Hall have a wealth of opportunities aimed at students leaving sixth form. Finally, I would recommend that students sign up for talks so that they can find out more about a specific career or learning opportunity.

3 Analyse the ways in which this school is trying to stress the importance of the evening. Select four pieces of language and comment on them, making more than one comment on each.

____

____

____

____

____

____

____

____

____

____

____

____

(8 marks)

4 What is the effect of this phrase: 'our exhibitors… have a wealth of opportunities aimed at students leaving sixth form'?

____

____

____

____

(2 marks)

Extending analysis

What does 'extending analysis' mean?

If the exam question encourages you to develop your ideas, do this, perhaps by linking different parts of the text, and you will be rewarded.

Look carefully at this text from a newspaper.

Ronnie steps in...

Ronnie Corbett stepped into Bruce Forsyth's shoes on BBC1's *Strictly Come Dancing* last night after a bout of 'flu kept the veteran host in bed. "If anyone can help out at short notice, it's me," joked the 5'1" comedian, who was towered over by his co-host, Tess Daly. After *EastEnders* actor Ricky Groves and Phil Tufnell were left in last night's dance-off, it was the former England cricketer who lost out in a close judges' vote.

Observer, 15.11.09

1 What do you think about the presenters when you look at the picture?

____

____

____

____

____

____

(4 marks)

2 How is your initial impression developed or confirmed when you read the text?

(4 marks)

This is the opening of an article about Smart cars.

Squeezy living

You can fit 14 cheerleaders into the new Smart – or two adults. Martin Love stretches out in style

SMART FOR TWO £7,748
MILES PER GALLON: 85.6
CO2 PER KM: 88 GRAMS
GOOD FOR: CONURBATIONS
BAD FOR: CONTORTIONS

What's the first thing you think about when you see a very, very small car? Safety, probably. Or fuel consumption, or maybe its ability to sniff out a parking space in the most uncompromising cul-de-sac… But if you are an Ascension Eagle cheerleader your mind will turn to car cramming. Four years ago they set the world record and squeezed 14 into a Smart. Clearly only two wore seat belts, and there was no room for their pom-poms. Six months ago a party of girl guides in Germany had a crack – they must have been bigger as they only managed 13. But they were quicker, all 13 managed to get into the car in under 20 seconds. Inspired by these girls, I had a go at car cramming myself. I fancied my chances. The new Smart is 3cm longer, after all, and I was using a group of under 8s. We called it quits at seven, plus me as the driver…

Small car, big heart: the Smart is the most efficient production car on the road, doing over 80mpg

The Observer Magazine, 15.11.09

3 How does the writer use humour to interest the reader?

(8 marks)

Dealing with inference

What is inference?

Both the Foundation Tier and the Higher Tier papers will expect you to look at inference in a text or texts. This means deciding what is being suggested, perhaps by the images, presentational features or by the language. You do not just write about 'what is there' but also about 'what the thoughts are *behind* what is there.'

Read this newspaper article.

Beat stress 'with daily chocolate'

By **Jo Steele**

THE train was late. Your umbrella collapsed in the rain. The boss has been giving you a hard time. You can't think straight and the steam is beginning to come out of your ears.

What do you do?

You take five and nibble some chocolate. That's what you do.

Stressed people have long known that a little bit of chocolate is much like getting a hug but new research claims ten squares of dark chocolate a day for two weeks can cure stress.

A regular helping of the treat rebalances chemicals in the body during times of high anxiety, according to a study by Dutch and Swiss scientists published by the American Chemical Society.

Dark chocolate is being described as the latest superfood because of its anti-oxidants and health-boosting compounds called flavinoids.

These reduce the risks of heart disease and lower blood pressure. People with high levels of stress hormones, such as cortisol, also have lower levels of other 'markers' which are meant to correct stress.

The dark chocolate brought these back into balance, said researchers.

'The study shows that a daily consumption of 40 grams over two weeks can modify the metabolism,' said Nestlé researcher Sunil Kochhar.

Next they'll be telling us it can help you lose weight and clean your teeth…

Metro, 13.11.09

1 Read the opening, down to 'That's what you do'. What is the tone of the writer? Does she sound serious or jokey? Give evidence for your opinions.

(4 marks)

2 How might we react to the penultimate paragraph, which begins 'The study shows…'? Explain why.

(4 marks)

3 What is being suggested in the final paragraph?

(2 marks)

These pictures of Barack Obama appeared in an article about him.

Picture 1

Picture 2

Picture 3

4 What impression of the President do we gain from each picture? In each case support your ideas with detail.

Picture 1

(4 marks)

Picture 2

(4 marks)

Picture 3

(4 marks)

Dealing further with inference

Why is there more practice on inference?

Dealing with inference is a skill that needs to be practised and so in this further section, you will be finding the details yourself which you need to write about, rather than having them identified for you. This is likely to be what you are asked to do in one question in the exam.

Read this advertisement.

Throw away your kettle! There's a revolution in kitchens! 100°C boiling water is now on tap - from the unique Quooker. Ultra-convenient, ultrasafe with a built-in child-proof safety mechanism and brilliantly energy-efficient, Quooker's unique compact under-sink tank still leaves ample space for a waste disposal and ancillary storage. The Quooker also offers a wide range of height and handing adjustable tap designs for contemporary and traditional kitchens. The stainless steel tank has revolutionary vacuum insulation and thermos technology, making it highly efficient to run, cool to the touch and allowing delivery of boiling water at 100 degrees unlike any other hot water system in the world today. Uses for the Quooker don't stop at hot drinks. Its filtered boiling water blanches vegetables, prepares instant soups, sterilises baby bottles and food containers and fulfills a myriad of cooking uses once catered for, slowly, by the space and energy-greedy kettle.

Find true boiling water on demand at www.quooker.co.uk, call +44 (0)207 9233355 or mail info@quooker.co.uk

Quooker®
THE BOILING WATER TAP

1 Find four 'selling points' for the Quooker and explain their appeal.

(8 marks)

This is an extract written by a young Sudanese girl. She has been left alone to keep birds off the newly-sewn seed.

Suddenly I saw a movement amongst the trees, and out stepped a wild dog. I watched transfixed. I knew the rest of the pack would be somewhere nearby. I was scared that if I made a move he would hear me and come after me. But I also knew that if I stayed where I was, he would eventually smell me out. Finally, terror forced me to run for the big tree in the middle of the field.

I jumped up into the lowest branches and quickly climbed to the top. I could feel my legs shaking uncontrollably: I was still scared that the dogs had heard me or seen me. Although I knew they couldn't climb trees, I imagined them waiting for me to fall out when I dropped asleep.

I turned and caught sight of the wild dog stalking slowly across the field towards me, its belly to the ground. Then, when it was quite close, it suddenly pounced. I heard a bird making a sickening, squawking sound, as the wild dog sank its teeth into its neck, holding it down with its paws. It was a big forest chicken. Then the wild dog ran off, jumped the fence and disappeared into the forest with the bird in its mouth. That could have been me, I thought.

2 How is the girl's fear presented?

(8 marks)

Analysing language

Will we always have to examine language?

There will always be a question in the exam that focuses on the language used in texts and its effects.

Read this news report.

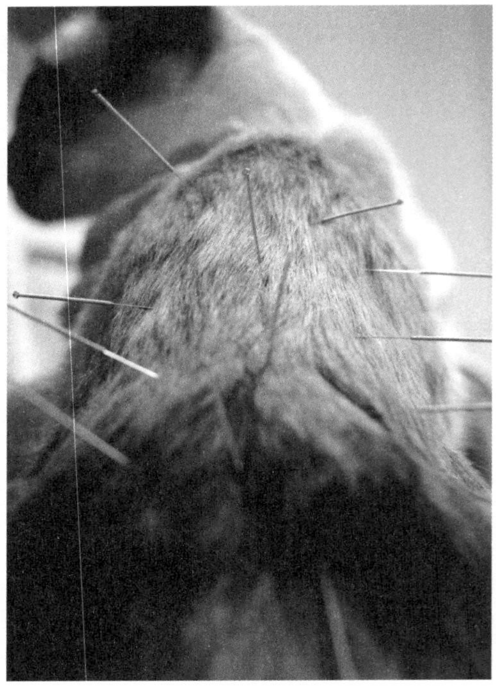

It's catupuncture..

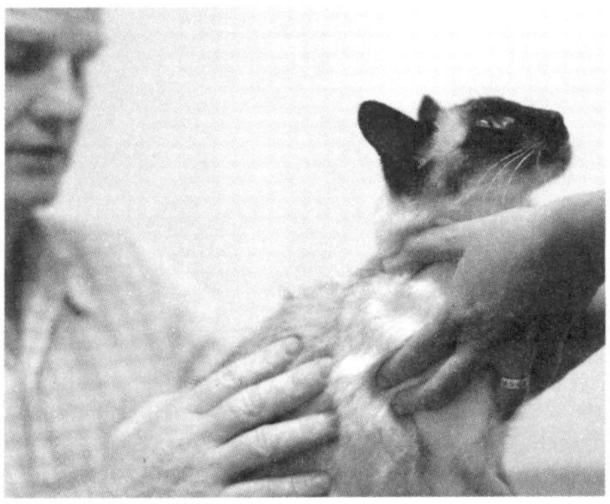

▲ **TO THE POINT Therapist assess the sick feline**

▶ **FELINE PRICKLY Kiki bristles as needles are in place**

NEEDLES give most people paws for thought but Kiki the cat seems to be enjoying her acupuncture session.

The 11-year old has suffered asthma and a cough for three years.

Traditional medicine did not help, so owner Virginia Sanders of Western Cape, South Africa, tried the alternative therapy – and three sessions later Kiki was feline much better.

It has been used on animals for thousands of years in China and India, so it's a furly old remedy...

Daily Mirror, 17.12.08

1 What is the effect of the headline and the captions?
'It's catupuncture'

___

___

___

(2 marks)

'TO THE POINT Therapist assesses the sick feline'

___

___

___

(2 marks)

'FELINE PRICKLY Kiki bristles as needles are in place'

___

___

(2 marks)

2 How are the following sentences intended to appeal to the reader?

'Needles give most people paws for thought...'

(2 marks)

'It has been used on animals for thousands of years in China, so it's a furly old remedy.'

(2 marks)

Look at this advertisement.

3 Why is the following language used?

'an experienced advisor'

(2 marks)

'maximum compensation'

(2 marks)

'fast and hassle-free'

(2 marks)

4 What effect are Cornelius' words intended to have? Analyse what he says and how he says it.

(8 marks)

Read this news article.

If there were a device that could measure toughness – an adrenalin radar scanning the planet for nutters in harnesses – hardcore hotspots would probably include the Himalayas and the Alps. But the sick-ometer (as in "dude, that was like the sickest jump ever") is at risk of blowing up over a grey corner of northern England later this month when some of the world's greatest daredevils gather for the Kendal Mountain Festival.

If you like mountains, or films about mountains, or doing dangerous things on mountains on film, then Kendal is your Cannes. Just swap red carpets for cobbles, and canapés for mint cake. "It's a tribal gathering for mountain lovers," says the festival's director, Clive Allen. "We get at least 7,000 people over the weekend and put on screenings and exhibitions and family events. It's a big deal for a small town."

Independent Life, 11.11.09

5 How does the language used in the first paragraph aim to interest the reader?

(8 marks)

6 What is the reader's reaction when she/he reads the following? Explain the effect of the language.
'If you like mountains, or films about mountains, or doing dangerous things on mountains on film…'

(4 marks)

'swap red carpets for cobbles and canapés for mint cake'

(4 marks)

'it's a tribal gathering for mountain lovers'

(4 marks)

This is an extract from an autobiography by the actor, David Niven. His father sent him away to a boarding school run by an old navy Commander.

> He and his thin-lipped, blue-veined, tweedy, terribly 'refained' wife added to his meagre pension and indulged their mutual passion for pink gin by taking in a dozen or so boarders.
>
> We were treated like young criminals and soon began to feel that we might as well behave like them. The house was a three-storeyed rabbit warren and terribly over-populated, but oh! it was clean. We scrubbed and re-scrubbed every inch of it daily. Oil lamps had to be spotless too – there was no electric light – and an ill-trimmed wick was evil-smelling evidence of highly punishable inefficiency. We did not sleep in hammocks but on wooden shelves, four to a room. The Commander and his wife prowled around at night in stockinged feet hoping to catch us talking.

7 What impression is given of the Commander's wife and how is the impression created?

(4 marks)

8 Why are the following phrases used?
'like young criminals'

(2 marks)

'three-storeyed rabbit warren'

(2 marks)

'prowled around'

(2 marks)

Presentational features

Why are 'presentational features' important?

You will be asked to examine the **visual features** of at least one text – perhaps the pictures or illustrations, headings, text boxes, colours and so on. You could also be asked about the general **layout** – how the text and features have been arranged on the page.

Look carefully at this advertisement.

1 How are the pictures used in this advertisement?

____

____

____

____

____

____

(8 marks)

2 What other presentational features are used and how effective are they?

____

____

____

____

____

____

(8 marks)

Read this short text from a magazine.

Time for tea?

If you're increasing your number of tea breaks in the hope it might reduce your risk of diabetes, you may be wasting your time – despite recent reports telling us tea can cut our risk by 42 per cent. "So far, the evidence that it can cut your risk of developing type 2 diabetes is inconclusive," says Dr Iain Frame, research director at Diabetes UK. "We all want to find a way to stop the epidemic, but until solid scientific eveidence proves otherwise, the best way to prevent the condition remains keeping active and eating a healthy, balanced diet that is low in fat, salt and sugar, and with plenty of fruit and vegetables."

Best, 06.10.09

3 Who are the presentational features designed to attract here, and how?

____

____

____

____

(4 marks)

4 Decide what different effect this text would have if:

- the background were green and the girl's top beige

____

____

____

(2 marks)

- the background were pink and the girl's top orange.

____

____

____

(2 marks)

5 Imagine you were given the task of re-designing the 'Time for tea' text. Say what presentational features you would use and why.

____

____

____

____

____

(4 marks)

Read this newspaper article.

MAIN ATTRACTION: WHY ENCOUNTER IS NOT WHAT IT SEEMS

THEY may have a lion on their bonnet, but the occupants of this jeep can see the funny side. They are enjoying an optical illusion on a vist to the Werribee Open Range Zoo in Victoria, Australia, where their "broken-down" truck is one of the main attractions of the lion enclosure. Its bonnet is on one side with the big cats, while the visitors sit on the other side, protected by a wall of glass in front of the dashboard. No wonder they can afford to roar with laughter.

Evening Standard, 06.11.09

6 How does the headline link with the picture?

____

____

____

____

(4 marks)

7 Why has this picture been used? Explain.

____

____

____

____

(4 marks)

8 What effect do we get from the expressions on the people's faces? Use precise detail in your answer.

____

____

____

____

(4 marks)

Look carefully at this magazine cover.

Best, 08.09.09

9 How is the magazine cover trying to appeal to the reader?

(8 marks)

10 How has the designer prioritised the stories and how effective is this layout?
(Which story comes across as most important, which is next important, etc? Would the reader respond positively to the way the cover is set out?)

(8 marks)

Comparing presentation: Foundation Tier

Why is this section targeted specifically at Foundation Tier?

The final question in Section A of the Foundation Tier paper will ask you to compare the presentational features in two texts. This type of comparison will not be required for the Higher Tier.

Look carefully at the following two adverts.

Compare how the advertisers use presentational features to try to sell their shoes in these adverts.

Write about:

- the target audiences
- how the Ethletic shoes are presented
- the methods Brantano use to draw the consumers' attention
- the essential differences in the advertisements.

Tread Softly
in the Worlds first Fairtrade certified footwear
ETHLETIC shoes may look like an iconic American brand but the ETHLETIC logo tells a very different story. These Organic canvas sneakers will be the first shoes in the world to carry the official Fairtrade label under new Fairtrade composite rules that allow products containing Fairtrade certified cotton to bear the famous Fairtrade mark. They also have rubber soles that carry the logo of the Forest Stewardship Council meaning almost every every material part of the sneakers is Fairtrade or ecologically certified. Even the final construction of ETHLETIC sneakers is covered by a fair trade project that supports workers and their families in Pakistan, making these perhaps the world most ethical shoes.
They come in a range of great colours and are available in both low and high cut style models. The arch supports make for a cushioned and comfortable sneaker that rivals the major brands for shear wearability and with prices starting from £36.50 positive minded shoppers can convert to Fairtrade and Organic without hitting their pocket.
www.fairdealtrading.com
Enquiries to
contact@fairdealtrading.com
or call 0845 094 4746
Ethical Manufacture
Fairtrade Certified Cotton
ETHLETIC
100% Vegan
Arch Supports
0% Plastic
Organic Cotton Canvas
FSC Certified Rubber Soles
Fairly Traded Rubber
ETHLETIC
FAIRTRADE
Certified Cotton
THE ETHICAL ALTERNATIVE
FSC
100%
LATEX

Write your response to the question below.

Continue on lined paper if necessary.

(12 marks)

Comparing language: Higher Tier

Why is this section targeted at Higher Tier?

Foundation students will just write about language in one text; for the final question in Section A, Higher Tier students will be required to compare the language used in two texts.

This film review is from *Sky Movies Magazine*:

TAKEN 18

DIRECTOR PIERRE MOREL **STARRING** LIAM NEESON, MAGGIE GRACE, LELAND ORSER

A muscular action thriller that packs a political punch, *Taken* sees Liam Neeson cut up rough as a retired CIA operative out to rescue his daughter from evil Arabs. It's Bourne in middle age: a straightforward shoot-em-up given a little heart by the regret and redemption of a hard-working professional trying to re-connect with his alienated sprog.

There's also the dubious but undeniable pleasure of watching bone-crunching scraps involving an Oscar nominated actor soon to play Abraham Lincoln in Spielberg's biopic of the revered American president. Neeson makes for a surprisingly credible action hero, adding brawn to his usual brooding gravitas, delivering well-practised beat-downs and stone-faced ultimatums.

The story's as simple as it sounds. After a half hour of scene-setting – Neeson's a deadbeat dad who has put his country before his family; his ex-wife (Famke Janssen) doesn't understand; his daughter (Grace) is spoilt but, y'know, adorable – we're off to Paris, where Grace is half-inched. So Neeson decides to get her back… by killing everybody.

Then we're into a string of set-pieces of varying degrees of brutality, as Neeson storms through the French capital on his bloody, one-man revenge mission. Visually, Pierre Morel – director of *District 13* and cinematographer on Louis Leterrier's *Unleashed* – opts for fast-cut camera work and relentless energy to keep you going once your disbelief hasn't so much been suspended as hung, drawn and quartered.

Daniel Webb

10.09

This is the start of a review from the London *Evening Standard*.

Now that's poetry

Jane Campion's biopic of John Keats is a love story that achieves the rare feat of making verse captivating on screen

Andrew O'Hagan

Film of the Week

Bright Star

Cert PG, 119 mins

★★★★☆

Films about poets are under a lot of strain to prove themselves poetical. Jane Campion's *Bright Star* manages to avoid this in some old-fashioned ways: first, by being full of confidence about its artistic vision and second, by being genuinely poetic. Anybody who thinks 'poetic' should mean limp, airy, or flouncy is either not reading enough good poetry or is reading good poetry badly.

Bright Star is poetic, but that is because it is tough, replenishing, beautiful and true – a film about John Keats that conjures the strange spirit of the man.

Based on Andrew Moon's brilliant biography, the movie seeks to express itself by a series of fine discriminations. We first meet the young Fanny Brawne (Abby Cornish), Keats' first love, in 1819, when he was 24 and she is 19.

The Keats who begins his love affair with Fanny is different from the mythical one. Living in Brawne's house, he is given to laughter and to boyish excesses of both laziness and torment, though Keats (Ben Wilshaw) conveys such gentle thoughtfulness at all times that you never doubt the poet is a special soul.

The film is an artist's work about an artist – which the best biopics and biographies always are…

6.11.09

Compare the language used in the two texts.
Comment on:

- how it is appropriate for the audiences
- the effect of words and phrases
- the differences in the style of the two texts.

Continue on lined paper if necessary.

(16 marks)

Exam practice Higher Tier: Section A Reading

Should I treat this as practice for this part of the exam?

This section contains texts of the kind you might well be faced with in the Higher Tier exam itself. These are followed by exam-style questions for Higher Tier. Ideally, you should take an hour to read the texts and respond to the questions. This will offer you an opportunity to answer typical questions in the time you will be allowed when you sit 'the real thing'.

Higher Tier texts

Source 1: an advert for a holiday

AMERICA

Enjoy the award-winning escorted tour of your life in 2010

Expert Tour Managers • Quality hotels • Select Excursions Included

Wherever you want to travel, there is one operator that stands head and shoulders above the rest - Titan HiTours. Nowhere is this more true than to the USA, whose delightful highways and byways and stunning sights we've been revealing to clients for over thirty years. Having been voted many times best tour operator by newspaper readers as well as topping leading consumer surveys, we know that travellers continue to expect the best organisation, service and quality from us. Our philosophy is that your holidays are among the most important investments you make in your life. Our job is to make them perfect and with Titan HiTours' unique VIP Home Departure Service® included on every date from every address in mainland England and Wales, your escorted holiday begins and ends at your front door. So try us and experience the difference for yourself. Call us now for your FREE copy of our new Worldwide 2010/11 brochure featuring 34 unbeatable itineraries to America including those shown below.

California and the Golden West - 16 days from £1295
The Awe-inspiring National Parks - 17 days from £1895
Las Vegas - 7 days from £995 (Dec 2009)
Southern Sights and Sounds - 14 days from £1695
Eastern Extravaganza - 15 days from £1695
Heart of New England and Niagara Falls - 10 days from £1295
USA Coast to Coast - Classic Rail Journey - 21 days from £2795

including the unique Titan HiTours VIP Home Departure Service® from every home in mainland England & Wales. Or take advantage of complimentary regional flights, now with FREE private transfers from many postcodes*

PAY IN FULL AND SAVE UP TO 5% - CALL US FREE

0800 988 5816

Titan HiTours
Our Service Makes a World of Difference!®

BOOK ONLINE www.titanhitours.co.uk

ABTA V4585 • ATOL 2850

*Calls free from BT landlines, mobiles may vary. *Conditions apply.* NOW OPEN ON SUNDAYS 10am-4pm DMUSA

Source 2: a travel article from a newspaper

THE TRUE PERU

From soaring condors to plunging gorges, the little known Colca Canyon will take your breath away

by Chris Leadbeater

THE ROAD from Arequipa to Chivay leaves you breathless. Literally. As the bus carrying my tour group inches up this highway in the southern Peruvian Andes, I can feel the air thinning with each mile.

By the time we hit the hamlet of Canahuas, 4,000 metres above sea level, I am having to focus on the simple ins and outs of breathing.

This is just the start. An hour later we break the 5,000 metre barrier – higher than Mont Blanc, the roof of Europe – and the world changes. The landscape has gone lunar, a plain of rocks and dust. And the oxygen seems to have gone entirely. I tilt my head back, open my mouth as wide as possible, and suck at the meager atmosphere. Happily, there is good reason for this madness – as becomes clear as the road dips towards the relative sanity of 3,000 metres. In the valley below, the town of Chivay, all white walls and low houses, glints in the sunlight. Beyond is the geological scar that has lured us to this distant corner of South America.

Highlight: Peru is packed with mountainous beauty

Thirty-five miles long and 3,269 metres deep at its most vertigo-inducing point, Colca Canyon is undoubtedly worth a flirtation with the side effects of altitude.

Even at first glance, it is a marvel. Snow-capped peaks rise on either side. Agricultural terraces that pre-date the Incas cling to its sloping flanks. Pale churches, evidence of Spanish conquest, act as centerpieces to tiny villages that hover near the edge.

It is proof that there is more to Peru than its poster image – Machu Picchu. Every year, half a million visit this 'lost city' and no other Peruvian site can compete on fame or publicity.

Little known outside Peru, Colca Canyon certainly cannot. But any doubts I'd had that it could compare as a spectacle are banished when we reach 'Condor Cross'. At this point, the canyon is 1,207 metres deep, its wall plunging to shadow.

Yet the main attraction here is not the drop. It is the birds of prey that soar overhead, searching for carrion.

Daily Mail, 05.09.09

Source 3: an account of visiting Rome from a travel book by Bill Bryson

On my final morning I called at the Capuchin monks' mausoleum in the church of Santa Maria della Concezione on the busy Piazza Barberini. This I cannot recommend highly enough. In the sixteenth century some monk had the inspired idea of taking the bones of his fellow monks when they died and using them to decorate the place. Is that rich enough for you? Half a dozen gloomy chambers along one side of the church were filled with such attractions as an altar made of rib cages, shrines meticulously concocted from skulls and leg bones, ceilings trimmed with forearms, wall rosettes fashioned from vertebrae, chandeliers made from the bones of hands and feet. In the odd corner there stood a complete skeleton of a Capuchin monk dressed like the grim reaper in his hooded robe, and ranged along the other wall were signs in six languages with such cheery sentiments as WE WERE LIKE YOU. YOU WILL BE LIKE US, and a long poem engagingly called 'My Mother Killed Me!!'. These guys must have been a barrel of laughs to be around. You can imagine every time you got the flu some guy coming along with a tape measure and a thoughtful expression.

Four thousand monks contributed to the display between 1528 and 1870 when the practice was stopped for being just too tacky for words. No one knows quite why or by whom the designs were made, but the inescapable impression you are left with is that the Capuchins once harboured in their midst a half-mad monk with time on his hands and a certain passion for tidiness. It is certainly a nice little money spinner for the church. A constant stream of tourists came in, happy to pay over a stack of lire for the morbid thrill of it all. My only regret, predictably, was that they didn't have a gift shop where you could purchase a boxed set of vertebrae napkin rings, say, or back scratchers made from real arms and hands, but it was becoming obvious that in this respect I was to be thwarted at every turn in Rome.

Questions: Higher Tier

Section A: Reading

Answer **all** questions in this section.

You are advised to spend about one hour on this section.

Read **Source 1**, the advertisement headed *America*.

1 According to the advertisement, what would make Titan HiTours a good choice if you wished to visit the United States?

(8 marks)

Read **Source 2**, the travel article entitled *The True Peru*.

2 How do the presentational features add to the effectiveness of the text?

(8 marks)

Read **Source 3**, the extract about visiting Rome from a travel book by Bill Bryson.

3 What thoughts and feelings does Bryson have when he visits the Capuchin monks' mausoleum?

(8 marks)

Now you need to refer to **Source 2**, *The True Peru*, and **either** Source 1 **or** Source 3. You are going to compare two texts, one of which you have chosen.

4 Compare the ways in which language is used to interest the reader in the two texts. Give some examples and explain how they are used to interest the reader.

(16 marks)

Total: 40 marks

Exam practice Foundation Tier: Section A Reading

Should I treat this as practice for this part of the exam?

This section contains texts of the kind you might well be faced with in the Foundation Tier exam itself. These are followed by exam-style questions for Foundation Tier. Ideally, you should take an hour to read the texts and respond to the questions. This will offer you an opportunity to answer typical questions in the time you will be allowed when you sit 'the real thing'.

Foundation Tier texts

Source 1: an advertisement for a holiday to America

travelsphere
Discover America's Golden West
12 days from £999
On this great value tour you will visit the famous sights of Las Vegas, Los Angeles and San Francisco accompanied by a friendly and experienced Tour Manager. They will ensure you see all the sights of America's West Coast plus you'll get plenty of free time to relax or make your own discoveries.
Highlights:
✓ Grand Canyon ✓ Las Vegas ✓ Palm Springs ✓ Hollywood ✓ Stunning Pacific Coast ✓ San Francisco
Fly from your local airport - Flights available from Heathrow, Gatwick, Birmingham, Bristol, Glasgow and Manchester
Our holidays include all this:
✓ Services of a Travelsphere Tour Manager
✓ Sight-seeing tours of Las Vegas, Los Angeles and San Francisco
✓ Return scheduled flights & transfers
✓ Ten nights room only accommodation
Add on:
✓ Extend your stay in San Francisco from only £48 pp per night
✓ Add-on 6 nights in Hawaii from only £699
Please speak to a Holiday Advisor for further details
Departures throughout 2010
To book or to speak to a friendly Holiday Advisor call:
0800 987 5011
or visit travelsphere.co.uk for our full holiday range. quoting ref: VWC
We're open 7 days a week: Mon - Fri 9am - 8pm / Sat 9am - 4pm / Sun 10am - 3pm
ABTA
ABTA No.V5874

Source 2: an article from a weekend newspaper supplement

Holiday Disaster

Turkey is for Christmas, not for holidays, writes David Donald

My wife loves cats. Cats in general, but not Turkish ones. She has good reason. We visited Turkey, once.

She and I were enjoying a tasty lamb meal in a restaurant in Datca, away from the usual tourist routes, when she laughed suddenly and swept her arm from her side to her mouth, and a cat beside her chair bit her. Its teeth dug deep.

Next morning, the hand was swollen. We went to the local doctor, who sent us to the hospital. The rooms there had blood on the walls, used syringes just lying around, and flies everywhere. My wife was examined and the doctor, who spoke next to no English, said she might have 'rubies'. 'Rabies?' I asked. 'Yes – rabies,' he said.

My wife panicked but we had to face the treatment. She was braver than me. I was sick outside the room because the doctor had told me what was to come: 'Injection … umbilical,' said the doctor. We went to the chemist's and got syringes, then returned to the hospital. My wife lay on a table and had an injection into her stomach. Two days later, she had another. Then another. Six injections over eleven days. Her stomach was bruised and swollen. Apparently, the needle going in was painful: the serum going in was worse. A male orderly stroked her hair; the nurse who gave the injections was efficient, but the flies buzzed all the time and no one spoke English to make it all any better.

On our last visit, the orderly got out his guitar and sang and the nurse offered us food. All we wanted to do was escape.

The individuals there were lovely and the waiters from the restaurant where it all started even came onto our coach when we were leaving and gave my wife flowers. Even so, we will not be returning to Turkey …

Source 3: an account of visiting Paris from a travel book by Bill Bryson

This is what happens: you arrive at a square to find all the traffic has stopped, but the pedestrian light is red and you know that if you venture so much as a foot off the kerb all the cars will surge forward and turn you into a gooey crêpe. So you wait. After a minute, a blind person comes along and crosses the great cobbled plain without hesitating. Then a ninety-year-old lady in a motorized wheelchair trundles past and wobbles across the cobbles to the other side of the square a quarter of a mile away.

You are uncomfortably aware that all the drivers within 150 yards are sitting with moistened lips watching you expectantly, so you pretend that you don't really want to cross the street at all, that actually you've come over here to look at this interesting fin-de-siècle lamppost. After another minute 150 pre-school children are herded across by their teachers, and then the blind man returns from the other direction with two bags of shopping. Finally, the pedestrian light turns green and you step off the kerb and all the cars come charging at you. And I don't care how paranoid and irrational this sounds, but I know for a fact that the people of Paris want me dead.

Questions: Foundation Tier

Section A: Reading

Answer **all** questions in this section.

You are advised to spend about one hour on this section.

Read **Source 1**, the advertisement headed *Discover America's Golden West.*

1 What are the attractions offered on this holiday package?

(4 marks)

2 Why might the reader imagine this is a good value holiday package?

(4 marks)

Now read **Source 2**, the article from the weekend magazine headed *Holiday Disaster*.

3 What is the writer suggesting about Turkish health care?

Write about:

- the hospital
- the people.

(8 marks)

Now read **Source 3**, an account of a visit to Paris by Bill Bryson.

4 How does Bill Bryson use language to make his story clear and interesting for the reader?

(12 marks)

Now look again at all three **Sources**. They have each been presented to attract the interest of the reader.

5 You are going to compare the presentational features of two of the texts. Choose two of the **Sources** and compare them, using these headings:

- pictures
- headings and any other presentational features

(12 marks)

Total: 40 marks

Exam Section B: Producing non-fiction texts

What questions will I face in Section B?

Whilst Section A of the exam tests your Reading skills, Section B tests your Writing skills.

You could be asked to write in almost any form, so you need to be prepared for all eventualities.

You will have 60 minutes to complete two writing tasks.

The **first writing task** will be shorter and should take you about 25 minutes.

It is worth up to 16 marks.

You will be expected to write 1–1½ sides of A4.

You could, for example, be asked to write a letter or an e-mail.

You might have to write to inform or explain.

It is likely to be a more 'functional' task, such as writing to apply for a job or telling new students how to behave in your school.

The **second writing task** should take you about 35 minutes.

It is worth up to 24 marks.

You are likely to write 1½–2 sides of A4.

In this case, you will have a little more time to develop ideas.

You might have to write to argue or persuade.

For example, this might be an article for a newspaper or magazine, encouraging readers to support a charity or arguing that we should or should not bring back the death penalty.

If no particular audience is prescribed, you will be writing for the examiner. However, if you are asked to produce a text form which is more specific, such as a letter or an article, your audience will also be provided. For example: 'Write an article for a local newspaper in which you argue that…' or 'Write a letter to a relative living abroad to explain…'.

For both tasks you will be expected to write appropriately to:

- meet the purpose you have been given
- appeal to your particular audience
- produce any form that has been specified.

Will both my written responses be marked in the same way?

Essentially, both pieces of writing will be marked in the same way. In each case, you will receive one mark for Organisation and Communication and another for Accuracy. However, because the first one has to be written more quickly and is likely to be shorter, there are more marks for the second piece.

Organisation and Communication

This mark will be awarded for:

- how well you deal with purpose and audience
- how well you communicate your ideas
- how interesting your ideas and your expression are
- how well you use paragraphs and structure your writing.

Accuracy

This mark will be awarded for:

- how well you vary your sentences
- the accuracy of your spelling
- your ability to write in standard English.

If you do well on one set of skills, it can compensate for any slight weakness elsewhere. So, for example, if you use good expression but fail to use paragraphs properly, the examiner will decide on a mark that balances both aspects; and if your punctuation is good but your spelling is less secure, both abilities will be considered so that a fair mark is awarded.

Writing skills

Isn't writing in the examination just like any other essay you write in school?

Writing skills are transferable, and you use them in different situations. In fact, you will use them for the rest of your life. However, to be successful in the exam, you need to know exactly what is required so that you can respond appropriately.

Timing

The time constraints are a vital consideration when performing in the exam. You need to be able to produce:

- the right material
- in the time available.

This means being able to write a **shorter response** in just **25 minutes** that reveals your abilities and the skills that the examiner expects to see; and to write a more detailed, **longer response** in **35 minutes**.

Practice is the key to success: the more time you invest in practising the skills that will be rewarded and the more opportunities you can find to write for just 25 minutes and 35 minutes, the better your final grade is likely to be.

A routine for writing

If you adopt a regular routine for writing, then you will learn techniques to support you in the exam itself.

Consider spending:

- 5 minutes planning a response
- 16–17 minutes writing (shorter response) or 25 minutes writing (longer response)
- the remaining time checking and improving what you have produced.

Planning

Aim to produce a detailed plan, because that will make the writing much easier. Planning is not just a case of collecting some random ideas, because that does not necessarily result in the best structure for your response. It helps if you can put the ideas into a numbered order, so you have something like a route map which you can follow as you write. Each numbered section can even be the basis for a paragraph, when that is appropriate to the form you are writing in.

Here is one possible planning approach.

1 Underline the significant words in the task title, so you produce exactly what is required.

For example:

Write an <u>article</u> for a <u>local newspaper</u> in which you <u>argue</u> that <u>local transport needs improving</u>.

2 Produce a spider diagram of ideas.

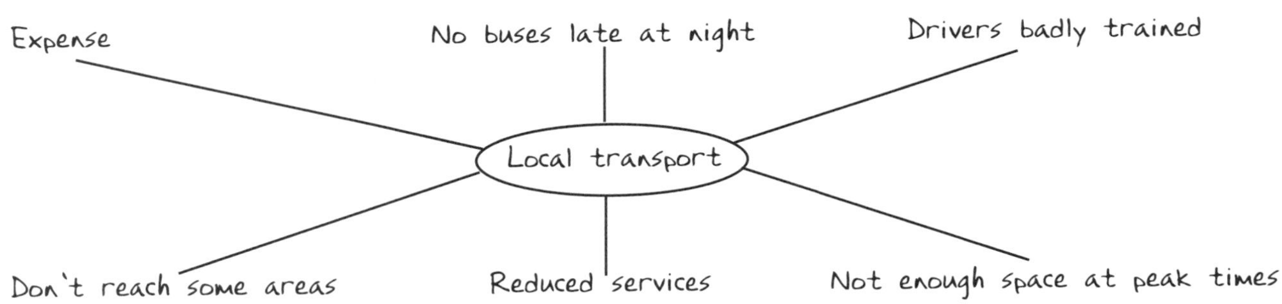

3 Put those ideas into the order you will use them: but leave a couple of empty lines beneath each idea or sub-heading.

Put extra thoughts into the spaces you have left: these will become the detail you will use in that section. For example:

> 3 Drivers badly trained
>
> not just prices/ some drivers have no manners/ drive erratically/ no consideration for public (grandma actually fell off when bus started suddenly)/ treat teenagers as if they are all hooligans

4 List words and phrases you know you are likely to use – such as connectives (however, nevertheless, on the other hand, etc).

When you are writing, you can then use these to join ideas, expand your thoughts and so on, but choose a different one to use each time to offer variety.

Writing

As you write, remember:

- your response must be in the form specified by the task (for example, letter, article…)
- you must argue or persuade or do whatever is requested
- your ideas must come in a structured, logical order
- your responses should be in paragraphs
- you need to demonstrate a range of punctuation
- your language should be varied and appropriate for the audience
- your spelling should be as accurate as possible
- you are aiming to keep the examiner interested in what you have to say.

Checking

Checking your work is vital, so that you can correct and improve it. Alterations are a sign that a candidate has made every effort to do his or her best. Importantly, there are no marks for neatness: so long as the examiner can read what is there, there is no problem.

Planning

Do we have to plan our written responses?

It is not compulsory, but you are advised to plan your writing. Plotting your essay's development makes its structure more logical. Without planning, ideas tend to be presented in a random order, and it is be easy repeat yourself, omit vital ideas or use paragraphing less effectively.

Write a newspaper article in which you argue **either** for **or** against the idea that students should set the rules in school.

1 Identify the most important ideas in the title.

Purpose ____

Audience ____

Form ____

2 Produce a spider diagram of your ideas, using the outline below.

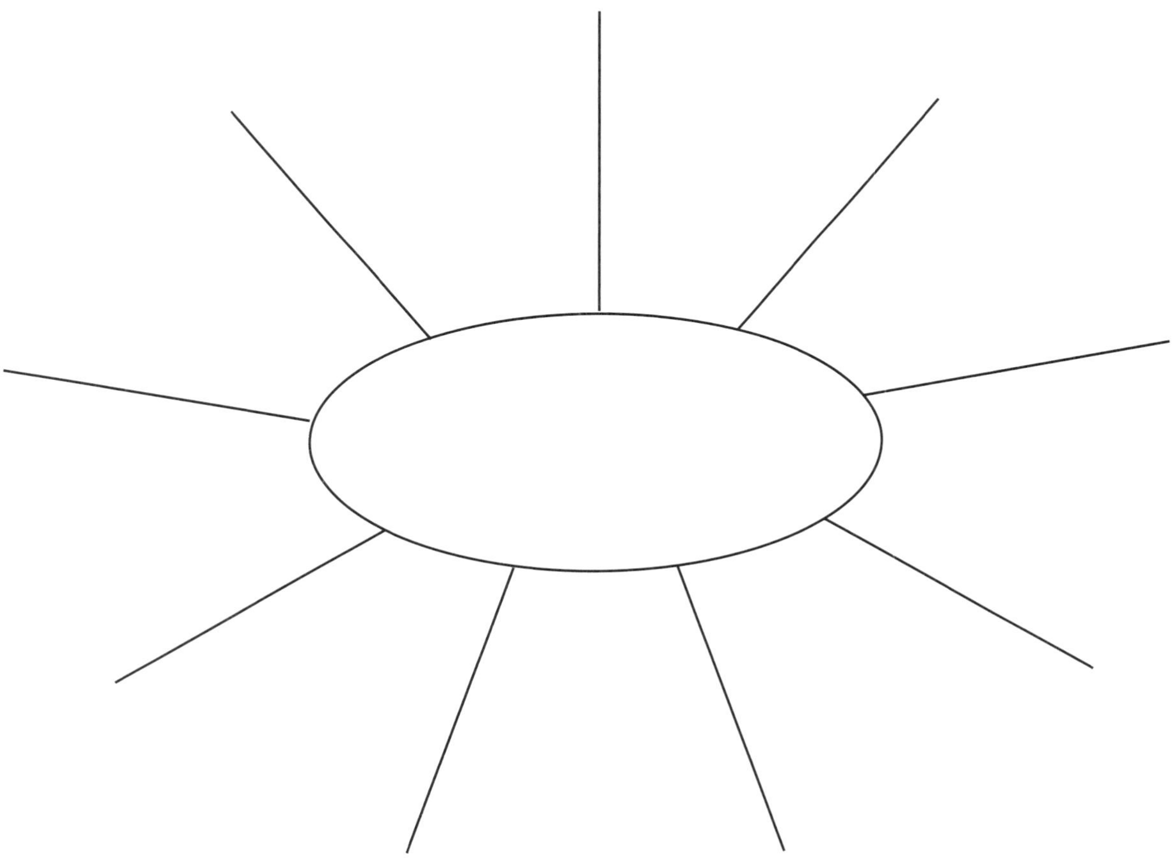

3 Put your ideas in order, adding detailed notes under each idea or sub-heading. Remember to include an introduction and a conclusion.

4 Write down some of the words and phrases you might need for this response, for example, connectives.

Further practice

Plan a response to this task:

Write an essay in which you try to convince the reader that love is – or is not – the most important thing in life.

Paragraphing

Are paragraphs really important?

Paragraphs are very important when examiners are deciding what mark to give you for Organisation and Communication. If you can use topic sentences but then vary your paragraph length, you can add extra impact and meaning to your writing. This will help you achieve a higher grade.

1 Write a section of a response in which you review a recent book you have read or programme you have seen. Try to write logically linked paragraphs in this order:

- a paragraph of about 8-10 lines explaining what the book or programme was about
- a longer, descriptive paragraph about the main character or presenter
- a short, punchy paragraph giving your opinion on how successful the book or programme and its main character or presenter was.

Continue on lined paper if necessary. *(16 marks)*

2 Write the opening of a response in which you explain what is wrong with the world today. Produce:

- an introduction of 8–10 lines, in which you set out your ideas
- a short paragraph in which you identify one as particularly important
- a longer paragraph in which you give much more detail about that idea.

(16 marks)

Sentences

Why are sentences so important to my writing?

Since sentences carry our meaning, it is essential that they work effectively. In addition, varied sentence structures offer more interest to the reader and can add extra meaning to what you say.

1 Combine the following short sentences to create complex sentences – sentences with a main clause and sub-clauses:

> You should move out of the house. Your mother is treating you in an unacceptable way. You are a teenager now, not a child. You don't have to accept what is happening. Find another place to live and leave before it is too late. Your mother is like a brutal jailor.

(2 marks)

2 Complete this paragraph with a short, effective sentence:

> With unemployment so high in this area, it is tragic that the government and the local authority can find no extra funding to support the people out of work. When you walk though the estates right across the town, you see men leaning on walls, you hear women complaining to their neighbours about how they can't afford even simple treats for their children and the children themselves seem to be just running wild.

(1 mark)

3 Using an ellipsis (…) leaves a sentence unfinished and allows the reader to imagine what might have come next. This can add humour or mystery, for example, and can engage the reader more fully in the ideas or the situation.

- Add an unfinished sentence here to add humour:

> He had a head that was big, in more ways than one.

(1 mark)

- Add an unfinished sentence here to make the reader wonder what might come next:

> His reputation spread widely, so that he was recognised wherever he went.

(1 mark)

- Add an unfinished sentence here, so that the reader will not immediately know which side you are on:

  The newspapers would have us believe that he is the most over-rated player to ever set foot on a pitch; his manager claims to have rate him more highly than any other member of the team and says his skills go largely unnoticed.

(1 mark)

4 Very short sentences can add impact to your writing if used occasionally. They can also be used show emotion.

- Add a short 'sentence' (perhaps of just one word) or two short 'sentences' to the following paragraph – to show an emotional response to what has happened:

  The posters were all taken down within hours and the graffiti was removed and it was as if there had never been a protest or a baying crowd of people complaining at what was being proposed. It was a heartbreaking end to a day that had begun with hopes high and resolution strong.

(1 mark)

Further practice

You have been asked to describe the most important event in your life so far.

Write a paragraph in which you include:

- at least two complex sentences
- at least one short sentence
- an ellipsis.

(6 marks)

Punctuation

When we are writing, isn't it just a matter of punctuating accurately?

Since your punctuation will be assessed, you do need to be as accurate as possible. However, varied punctuation helps create more interesting sentences; and, as the examiner does not know how good your punctuation is, it will help if you can demonstrate all your punctuation skills when completing your responses.

1 Add the commas, question marks and an exclamation mark into this opening paragraph.

> Why is it that some schools have some teachers that are far from perfect. Why is it that some students do not as a consequence reach the grades of which they should be capable. It simply is not fair. In my own case the teachers in my school most of whom have been here for many years seem excellent. How lucky am I. What a relief it is to be here.

(8 marks)

2 Re-write this extract, adding correct speech marks and commas.

> As soon as I walked into the classroom Mrs Reynolds saw me. Just the young man I was looking for she said. I would like a word with you. I immediately feared the worst. I don't think I said that I have done anything wrong yet today. No. I just want some information she said smiling like a rattlesnake.

(10 marks)

3 A colon can be used, following a general statement, to introduce a list.
A semi-colon can be used to separate the parts of a complicated list with lengthy items.
Re-write this extract, making the punctuation more adventurous.

> Each of the schools in this area has been improved massively in the past few years. There are new buildings with state of the art computer facilities. Two schools now have their own swimming pools. And in every school the libraries have been completely replaced.

(4 marks)

4 Colons can also be used to introduce quotations; and semi-colons can be used to connect closely-related ideas, replacing a full-stop.
Complete each sentence below, adding colons or semi-colons and additional ideas as appropriate.

The headteacher was clear about what he expected ______________________________

____

I had to tell the truth about what happened ______________________________

____

My friend was excluded ______________________________

____

It shows that you cannot just behave any way you want ______________________________

____

(4 marks)

5 Add apostrophes of possession and of omission to this short extract.

> The schools security measures werent perfect, thats for sure. Some of the boys lockers were ransacked and one girls bag was stolen.

(5 marks)

Further practice

Write a paragraph which informs the reader about what is best about your school. Include:

- commas
- at least one question mark and an exclamation mark
- apostrophes
- speech marks
- a colon and semi-colons.

____

____

____

____

____

____

____

____

____

____

____

____

(6 marks)

The use of language

What affects my choice of language?

It is essential that you use language that is appropriate for your audience in your written responses. In some cases the language you use might also be affected by the purpose of the writing.

1 Re-write this chatty extract so that it is suitable for a newspaper audience.

> Kids these days! They've no idea what's happening in the world – nor how it's got to where it is. Something for nothing, that's all they're after. Whether it's right or not, they don't know and don't care. Tragic, isn't it? No values, no sense of right and wrong and knowing nothing about our tradition of duty and fair play and fighting for what's right. Get 'em in the army. That'd sort them out…

(6 marks)

2 Find more interesting words or phrases to replace the casual ones in italics.

Original	Replacement word or phrase	
	Alternative 1	Alternative 2
It was a *good* night out.		
We started in a *lovely* restaurant		
which had the *best* waiters		
I have ever *had*		
and the food was *great*.		
It was *fantastic*.		

(12 marks)

3 Re-write this set of instructions for new employees in a hotel complex so that they form an effective paragraph in a health and safety manual for hotel workers.

Make sure your paragraph:

- is suitably organised
- uses appropriate language
- includes effective connectives.

1 When by the pool, stay alert.
2 Make sure all children are accompanied by an adult.
3 No diving is permitted: if necessary, warn guests of the dangers.
4 Stop any silly behaviour, to prevent serious accidents.
5 No one under the influence of alcohol is allowed to use the pool.
6 Remove any dangerous objects, such as glass bottles.
7 Tell anyone who is not behaving appropriately to leave the pool area.
8 If you are in need of any assistance, contact the site manager.

(6 marks)

4 Write the opening of a speech to a group of MPs, in which you argue in favour of free bus travel for the young.

Make sure you use:

- language which avoids slang and casual expressions
- vocabulary to impress the listeners.

(6 marks)

Rhetoric and humour

Do we have to include rhetoric and humour?

Rhetorical questions challenge the reader and usually involve them more in what you are saying. Humour, if used appropriately, will enliven your writing. If you can make the examiner stop and think or if you can bring a smile to his or her lips, it is usually a good sign.

1 Write the opening paragraph of an article for a local newspaper, to persuade the readers to support your plan to raise money for a new skate park. Begin with one or two rhetorical questions (e.g. Surely, anyone can see that a skate park would mean fewer teenagers on the streets causing trouble?).

(6 marks)

2 Write the concluding paragraph of a letter in reply to the newspaper article from an angry local resident, arguing that there is no suitable area available and no real need for a skate park.
Conclude with two rhetorical questions.

(6 marks)

3 Exclamations are another feature of rhetoric: language used for particular effect.
Write a paragraph from a blog in which you react to news that new drivers will not be able to take their test until they reach the age of 21.
Use two exclamations in your response.

4 Complete this paragraph, describing a package holiday to Spain, continuing its sarcasm. *(6 marks)*

What a wonderful hotel we had booked! It had been beautifully decorated in the primitive style which excites us so much when we go to see cave paintings produced thousands of years ago. The pool area

As for the staff they

Breakfasts were a treat too

5 Use a funny anecdote to illustrate how dreadful conditions were on the beach during the holiday to Spain. An anecdote is a brief story which adds detail and creates interest. *(6 marks)*

6 Try to make the reader smile by using exaggeration to say how pleased you were to arrive home from Spain. *(6 marks)*

(6 marks)

Similes and metaphors

Should we only use similes and metaphors when we are writing to describe?

Using similes and metaphors will help make any response more interesting, for example, even if you are reviewing or arguing.

Similes make a comparison using 'like' or 'as'. **Metaphors** say things which are not literally true. For example: 'he was all alone in the world'.

1 Explain why we should consider giving money to 'Children in Need'. Consider three original similes you might use to complete this opening:

It is tragic when you see people living in real poverty. Those living on the street are like…

1 ______________________________

2 ______________________________

3 ______________________________

(3 marks)

2 Add similes to this extract, to show clearly why these people are in need of help.

When you visit some homes in the inner cities, you understand how desperate they are for some kind of assistance. Living rooms can be like ______________________________

______________________________;

and often the cramped sleeping area is like ______________________________

____

(2 marks)

3 Here, a student has decided to include similes, but has only managed to use well-worn examples he has come across before. Change the similes, offering more original ideas.

I needed this new problem like <u>a hole in the head</u> ______________________________

____

I didn't know what to do, and I felt like <u>an idiot</u> ______________________________

____

(2 marks)

4 Write a paragraph from a letter in which you try to persuade your headteacher to make the lunchtime break longer. Include two original similes.

____

____

____

____

____

____

(6 marks)

5 Write the opening section from a report on a sporting or musical performance. Include three metaphors.

(6 marks)

Further practice

Continue your report on the sporting or musical performance by writing:

- a paragraph describing one of those involved and how they performed
- another paragraph describing the crowd.

Use at least three similes and three metaphors in your answer.

(10 marks)

Using evidence and quotations

Don't we only use evidence in the Reading section of the exam?

Any response you produce is likely to be more convincing if you include evidence, an anecdote or quotation. Supporting your points will help you argue, persuade, explain or inform more successfully. In the exam, you are free to invent any evidence you need, because you do not have books or search engines to help you.

1 If you had to support these points, what evidence would you use?

Statement	Evidence
I live in a country I can be proud of.	
There are some things in this country that need to be improved.	
My friends value some aspects of life here that I don't.	
My mother/father/carer gets excited about some elements of life that I find very unimpressive.	

(4 marks)

2 In a letter, you are informing your pen friend about the things in daily life that can make you angry. Write a paragraph about one of these things. Include some evidence to show why it annoys you. (Consider using statistics, facts or relevant examples.)

(6 marks)

3 Write another paragraph, using an anecdote to show, in contrast, what appeals to you or makes you happy in life.

(6 marks)

4 Add a name and quotation to support this statement and conclude your letter.
(Remember: you can invent this quotation but try to make it sound convincing.)

I have to say that, overall, I am pleased to be living in this country.

As ________________ once said: '________________

____

________________'

(2 marks)

Further practice

Write a short response (three or four paragraphs long) to argue that young people work quite hard enough in school: more should not be expected of them and homework should be banned.
Use evidence to support your views.

Continue on lined paper if necessary.

(16 marks)

Emotive language

What, exactly, is emotive language?

Emotive language affects us emotionally. It is designed to make us feel sympathy, inspire us to act or make us feel happy, angry, guilty, etc. For example: 'Imagine the pain: bleeding feet, burnt skin and a stomach which has been empty for many days…'

1 You have been asked to explain the attractions of the most amazing place you have ever visited. Write a general description of the place, using emotive language where appropriate. For example: 'It was so beautiful, I could have cried with joy…'

(6 marks)

2 Explain what stands out most about the place. Try to blend facts with some emotive language.

(6 marks)

3 Write a paragraph about something that has happened to you there which was not totally positive. Include emotive detail.

(6 marks)

Further practice

Write the text of a letter informing the Prime Minister about three key things the government should concentrate on improving.
In no more than 25 minutes, write three paragraphs and use some emotive language in each.

Continue on lined paper if necessary.

(16 marks)

Openings and endings

Why are openings and endings particularly important?

The opening is the first thing the examiner reads – it presents an immediate impression of your writing abilities. The ending is the last thing the examiner reads before putting a mark on your work: it makes a final and probably lasting impression.

1 Your cousin is about to move abroad. Write the first paragraph of a letter to advise them about what their first few weeks might be like and what they should do to settle in.
Remember the high-quality writing features you have been practising (pages 162–177) and try to include some that are appropriate.

(6 marks)

2 Write the ending of the letter. You might wish to explain why they are especially lucky and wish them all the best as they settle in.
Use some high-quality writing features you did not use in the introduction, to further impress the examiner. Also make sure that you link your ending with your opening – often a quality found in excellent responses.

(6 marks)

3 Write the opening paragraph for a broadsheet newspaper, in which you argue that we must act immediately to save the environment.

(6 marks)

4 Write an opening paragraph on the same topic for a magazine aimed at young teenagers. Adapt your content and tone to match this different form and audience.

(6 marks)

5 Write the concluding paragraph to either of the openings. Link it back to what you said in your opening.

(6 marks)

Writing letters

Aren't letters basically the same as emails?

Letters and emails can be very different. Letters need to be set out more formally and generally have a more formal structure throughout; emails can be more in note form – though in the exam if you are asked to write an email, you will certainly be expected to include a good deal of detail, paragraphing and effective structure.

1 Write a letter to an elderly relative, persuading them to install security equipment around their home. Make sure you:

- set out the letter correctly
- adopt an appropriate tone
- include detail
- end the letter correctly.

Continue on lined paper if necessary. *(16 marks)*

2 Write a short letter to a security firm, asking them to install security equipment for your elderly relative and informing them of what he or she will require.
Use the conventions and layout of a formal letter, as shown below. Take no more than 25 minutes.

your address

____
____
____
____

date ______________________________

Name and address: person and firm

____
____
____
____
____

Dear ______________________________

____
____
____
____
____
____
____
____
____
____
____
____

Yours ______________________________

____

(16 marks)

REMEMBER

- 'Dear Sir/Madam' ends 'Yours faithfully'.
- 'Dear Mr/Mrs/Ms…' ends 'Yours sincerely'.

Writing news reports

Isn't writing a news report just the same as telling a story?

A report will tell the story, but give it emphasis and structure, so the focus is on the central point(s). The basic events are presented in the opening, then detailed later; the story will be filtered so that only the important people are named; and the ending will sum up the situation or, sometimes, predict what might happen next.

1 You have been asked to write a report for a school magazine about:

- a trip you have been on
- a match or competition or
- an unusual event that has happened.

Write your opening paragraph in three or four sentences summing up what happened.

(6 marks)

2 Write a paragraph explaining what happened at the start of the event.

(6 marks)

3 Move on to write about the main person or persons involved in what happened.

(6 marks)

4 Develop your explanation of what happened, remembering not to confuse the reader with too much detail.

(6 marks)

5 Write about the climax of the event.

(6 marks)

6 End your report in a memorable way: summarising what happened or hinting at what was to come. If appropriate, comment on the effect it had on the individual(s) involved.

(6 marks)

Writing to argue

What is it most important to remember when writing to argue?

Your argument needs to be convincing. It is usually easier to put together a line of argument if you have something to argue against, so it helps to include the opposite viewpoint. The two sides do not have to be equally matched – you might just mention the alternative viewpoint in passing as a way of introducing or balancing your arguments.

You are going to write an article to argue that the death penalty **should** or **should not** be re-introduced for the most serious crimes.

1 Make a list of points for and against the re-introduction of the death penalty.

For	Against

(4 marks)

2 Read this opening paragraph then re-write it, maintaining the viewpoint but including:

- a topic sentence
- variety in the expression
- additional or different detail as appropriate
- at least one feature to attract the reader's interest.

There are too many murderers walking the streets. Other people should be arrested and executed too if they do terrible crimes. My brother got beaten up only a couple of weeks ago. Old people aren't safe in their beds at night. The world would be a better place if we got rid of all the bad people. Hanging might be too good for them.

(6 marks)

3 Write a paragraph in which you run through your points for and against the death penalty, but end by choosing which view to support.

(6 marks)

4 Write a paragraph supporting your own viewpoint, in which you provide evidence (either quotation, example, anecdote and/or statistics).

(6 marks)

5 Write a concluding paragraph which is linked to the previous one but finishes off your argument convincingly.

(6 marks)

Practice essay title

Write the text of a speech in which you argue that 'There is no place like home': either because it is the best place or, perhaps, just because there could not be another place like it. *(24 marks)*

Writing to persuade

What are the differences between arguing and persuading?

Sometimes we persuade by arguing effectively. However, often we persuade by putting forward just one point of view. We can use a range of techniques to support our ideas, such as emotive language, convincing examples and appropriate anecdotes.

You are going to write a letter to your local council to persuade them to provide a good range of leisure facilities for young people.

1 List at least five facilities you would like to see provided, reasons why they are needed and how they would improve life in your area.

Facility	Why needed	How life would improve

(5 marks)

2 Begin your letter, setting it out appropriately and including a persuasive opening paragraph. (For a reminder about letter layout, see page 181.)

Continue on lined paper if necessary. *(8 marks)*

3 Write a second paragraph, outlining one or two of your suggested facilities. Use some emotive language, which touches the reader's emotions.

(6 marks)

4 Write a third paragraph about another facility. Try to win round the reader by using humour, exaggeration or an anecdote.

(6 marks)

5 Sum up your reasons for wanting these changes in a conclusion. End with an effective point or a final plea – perhaps using a rhetorical question.

(6 marks)

Practice essay title

Write an article for a national newspaper, persuading the readers to watch less television and, instead, to do things which are more productive or creative.

(24 marks)

Writing to inform

Isn't it easy to write to inform?

Presenting information can be straightforward, but in the examination, the marker will be looking for detail and relevance and will be expecting the information to be well-structured. Of course, what you write will also need to be suitable for the purpose and audience.

You are going to write a section of a guide book for your local area to inform visitors about what it has to offer.

1 List the local features you intend to include. Try to offer a range that would appeal to different sorts of people.

(3 marks)

2 Write the opening paragraph. Indicate the range of attractions and aim to engage the reader.

(6 marks)

3 Write the next paragraph, including details such as facts or statistics and a quotation. (Remember: you can invent details like this but try to make them sound convincing.)

(6 marks)

4 Write the final two or three paragraphs, including a touch of humour if possible and any other features to interest your audience.
Make you ending memorable if you can.

(12 marks)

Practice essay title

An older couple you like and know well have recently moved abroad – it could be your grandparents. Write a letter to inform them about what has been happening locally since they moved away.
Aim to include information which will interest them and write in a way that will entertain them.

(24 marks)

Writing to explain

What is the difference between informing and explaining?

When you inform, you give facts and interpretations of them; when you explain, you are saying why something happens or how a situation arose. You move beyond the obvious to give reasons or causes for things.

You are going to write an article in which you explain how to lead a healthy life.

1 Produce a spider diagram of ideas for your article.

Now, structure your ideas into a logical sequence.

Idea for a healthy lifestyle	How this will make you healthy
Example: run regularly	Explanation: improves fitness, strengthens lungs
1 ________________	________________
2 ________________	________________
3 ________________	________________
4 ________________	________________
5 ________________	________________
6 ________________	________________

(6 marks)

2 Write a first paragraph, to introduce the readers to your ideas for a healthy lifestyle.

(6 marks)

3 Write a second paragraph, linked to the first but explaining one or two of your ideas in more detail. Try to introduce some facts and figures. It may be appropriate to use some emotive language to reinforce your reasons.

(6 marks)

4 Omit the rest of the central section of your response which might take up several more paragraphs. Write the conclusion for your article.

Continue on lined paper if necessary.

(6 marks)

Practice essay title

Write an article for a teenage magazine, explaining how to be fashionable. You can choose to write about clothes, music or lifestyle.

(24 marks)

Writing to review

What is special about review writing?

In a review, you are likely to give your opinion of whatever you are reviewing, describe important elements of it, probably judge some of the people involved and try to entertain the reader.

Write a review of your least favourite television programme.

1 As an introduction, describe an incident from the programme and what was wrong with it.

(6 marks)

2 Move on to a second paragraph in which you offer your opinion of the programme as a whole but also give more objective details about it.

(6 marks)

3 Choose an individual or individuals from the programme and write about how good or bad they are and why.

4 Analyse the storyline, filming or staging – whatever is appropriate to the type of programme. Give precise details but also a personal interpretation of what happens, saying why it is disappointing/repetitive/how it could be improved, etc. *(6 marks)*

5 Comment on others' opinions of the programme. Consider using one or more quotations. *(6 marks)*

6 Conclude with your summary of the programme, offering some final opinions in an entertaining way. *(6 marks)*

(6 marks)

Practice essay title

Write a review of the most memorable holiday you have had. Summarise the main events and give your opinions on any high and low points.

(24 marks)

Writing to advise

What is the key to successful advice?

You need to convince the reader to take your advice. To do that, you need to present a logical response, using effective detail and supported opinion. You might choose to include anecdote, rhetoric, emotive language or other high-quality writing features to persuade the reader that your advice is sound.

You are an agony aunt for a national newspaper. A reader has written asking you for advice on how to make sure her teenage son or daughter does not get into any trouble. They seem to be mixing with the 'wrong sort' of friends…

1 Complete this planning grid, listing the problems of getting in with the wrong group of friends and how to avoid each one.

Problem	Advice

(6 marks)

2 Write an opening paragraph of your 'reply', addressing the reader who has written in. Show that you are well aware of the problems and that you have possible solutions to offer.

(6 marks)

3 Choose one of the problems and offer advice. Use an anecdote to support your ideas.

(6 marks)

4 Deal with a second problem. This time, use emotive language to convince the reader.

(6 marks)

5 Choose another problem. Use humour or rhetoric or both in your advice.

(6 marks)

6 Write a concluding paragraph, addressing the same reader directly and demonstrating confidence in your opinions.

(6 marks)

Practice essay title

Write an article for your local newspaper, advising readers how to cope if they lose their job: how to make money go further; how to find another job; or how to use any spare time they might have. *(24 marks)*

Checking your writing

Is checking what we have written really important?

There are no marks in the exam for neatness. What matters is the quality of what you produce. So, as long as the examiner can read your work, the number of alterations does not matter. This means that you can change as much as you like without fear of losing marks: and every correction you make might well help to improve your final grade.

1 Improve the punctuation in this extract.

I did not know where to turn. I had bills to pay, the car had broken down and my sister said its no good we will have to leave here. The rent is too high. What an awful day that was.

(3 marks)

2 Correct the incorrect spellings in the following paragraph.

Unfortunatly, the rise in global temprature is likely to continue. Siting in Britain, it's easy to forget that unpresedented numbers of people are being made homeless as sea levels rise and storms decamate frajile comunities. It will take a huge effort from govenments and a change in lifestiles before we can even begin to think that there might be a future for the world as we now it.

(10 marks)

3 Re-write this extract from a teenager's email, to make it suitable for older people.

I hate school and nothing will change that. A lot of the other kids are minging and the lessons are just *****. I used to be in a better school. I'd still have been better lying in bed with my ipod but I had some OK times and a couple of teachers there were well fit. Mind, even there I got stuck with some chavs in music and they were like, 'This is banging' but it wasn't. They didn't know nothing.

(6 marks)

4 Read this response and make changes to improve it.

- Decide where paragraphs might go.
- Correct the spelling/grammar/punctuation.
- Improve the vocabulary/sentences/phrasing whenever necessary.

My next door neghbour is the most boring person I have ever met for a start he loves basketball and I hate it but he spends hours hamering a ball against the wall of his house and we get the noise in our's. When hes not bounceing the ball around hes talking about basketball or watching basketball or dreaming about basketball I guess When he first moved in I though he could be a good mate and I tried to be friendly with him but he didn't want to know 'Yeah we can go out' he said. There's a basketball game on Sunday at the leisure centre we could go there and that was that. I could just see him sat there eating a burger or something and drinking coke like it were a proper meal or something and then jumping up and spilling chips or fries as that's probably what they are at a basketball match all over the place. I just don't get it at all. I never went and you wouldn't of either would you. His sister must lead a terrible life cos she has to be around him like all day long she seems nice but what a sad life, eh? It's not nice being next door so it must be very not nice in the same house. His parents never seem to come out at all. I don't know what they look like. They probably look like him really tall with a baseball cap on all the time and a basketball in their hand all the time and there might be pictures of basketball players on all the walls and framed ones on top of the telly. Like a museum, sort of. I just don't get it. How boring can you get?

(10 marks)

Revision advice

Working through the sections in this book will have helped you to focus on the important elements in each part of the exam.

You can extend your revision and preparation in various ways.

Section A

Spend five minutes every day reading and analysing a text. For example, read newspaper articles, reports, or advertisements.

Try to look at a different type of text each day. Read anything and everything, from broadsheet newspapers to the back of cornflake boxes.

You could follow this kind of routine.

Day 1: purpose and audience – what form is the writing in, is there a specific audience and how do you know?

Day 2: presentational features – what effect do these have on the reader and how does this fit with the purpose of the text

Day 3: language features – what stands out about the language and what is its effect?

Day 4: the writer's main message and how the parts of the argument or story fits together – how is the writing structured?

Day 5: what the writer wants the reader to think and how that effect is created – which presentational or language features are chosen to achieve this?

And then begin again.

Section B

The more you practise the vital skills, the better you are likely to perform in the exam.

Consider:

- setting your own titles and producing detailed plans
- writing openings and endings or central sections of responses
- using high-quality features like rhetoric, anecdotes, humour, similes and so on
- writing whole responses in 25 minutes and 35 minutes, to become familiar with the exam timings
- checking your work for errors and making appropriate improvements.

Students who invest time like this preparing for the exam paper generally make the greatest improvements.

It is also true that in English exams students usually get what they deserve. This means that your hard work will be rewarded!

Index

Answers

Understanding non-fiction texts

Most of the answers that follow are not 'the correct answers' but should help you to see the sort of answer you need to write in order to get a Grade C.

As a reminder, here is an outline of the skills you need to show at different GCSE grades. You should refer back to this, and use the grids provided with some answers, when working out your mark and grade for a question.

Grade	Skills demonstrated
A*/A	• has thorough understanding of the text and able to apply it fully to the question • engages with the text showing perception throughout • selects and uses apt quotations to support detailed understanding • makes perceptive and analytical comments
B/C	• has a clear and focused understanding of the text and is able to handle the question with confidence • engages with the text and is able to interpret it clearly • uses relevant quotations to support understanding • makes clear and relevant comments
D/E	• has some understanding of the text and attempts to respond to the question appropriately • attempts to engage with the text • uses quotations to support understanding • some focus on what is required
F/G	• shows limited understanding of the text with random comments in response to the question • is aware of the text, but unable to respond in detail • may copy sections • offers little relevant material
U	• offers nothing relevant

pages 110–111

1 Some likely responses:
- to interest the general reader
- to inform about the situation
- because it is such an unusual occurrence
- possibly to publicise the efforts of Loganair

A/A*: 4 marks – likely to offer three or more reasons, with detailed support
B/C: 3 marks – likely to offer two or three reasons, with convincing support
D/E: 2 marks – likely to offer two or three reasons, with some convincing support
F/G: 1 mark: – likely to give one or two reasons and offer general comment

2 Likely answers:

Extract 1: advice column, perhaps from newspaper (1) – clearly a response to the first statement (1)

Extract 2: perhaps article on conservation (2) or advice column again (2) or anything appropriate (2) – it is telling the reader what to do (using imperative) (1) and sounding superior/knowledgeable (1)

Extract 3: an article (1) or speech (1) or textbook (1) or anything suitable (1) – offering an opinion on nurses and how they are seen by the public (1)

A/A*: 8 marks
B/C: 6–7 marks
D/E: 4–5 marks
F/G: 1–3 marks

3 Likely responses:

Audience: older people who need cash or have debts;

How: picture suggests the deal will make people happy, 'FREE' to attract people, idea you will then 'enjoy life; language like 'unique', 'up to 100% of the value', 'absolute discretion', 'all costs will be covered'

A/A*: 7–8 marks
B/C: 5–6 marks
D/E: 3–4 marks
F/G: 1–2 marks

pages 112–113

1 'response was staggering' (1); more than 100 individuals and organisations put forward (1)

2 Any four from:
- can vote in different categories (1)
- categories named (1)
- can go on line to vote (1)
- can read details and make informed choice (1)
- can vote as many times as you like (1)

3 Any four from:
- a £30 ticket really costs £34.50 (1)
- the 'hidden charge' is a kind of deception (1)
- booking fee added 40% to the ticket price (1)
- the price of a Leonard Cohen ticket has rocketed (1)
- you used to be able to get Leonard Cohen tickets without paying a booking fee (1)

4 Possible words and phrases:
- extortionate (1)
- this kind of deception (1)
- corporate avarice (1)
- eye-wateringly pricey (1)

A/A*: 14 marks
B/C: 11–13 marks
D/E: 7–10 marks
F/G: below 7 marks

pages 114–115

1 Any two from:
- to report on what happened (1)
- to interest a tabloid newspaper reader (1)
- to highlight Lambert's foul play (1)
- to surprise readers because she is not like a typical female stereotype (1)

C/A*: two purposes, with explanations
D/F: two purposes, perhaps with attempted explanation
G: one purpose

2 Any four from these details likely to be mentioned:
- pictures (1)
- headings (1)
- alliteration (1)
- dramatic opening (1)
- vocabulary like 'dirtiest', 'violent', vicious', etc (1)
- list of Lambert's fouls (1)

A/A*: 4 marks
B-C/A: 3 marks
E/F: 2 marks
F/G: 1 mark

3 Likely comments, with explanations of effects:

headline – play on 'Beauty and the Beast'; alliteration

sub-heading – alliteration continued; focus on 'blonde', to link with 'beauty'; metaphor ('kicks up storm') to link with 'Booty'

captions – 1. 'Head case' double meaning; alliteration 2. 'Take that' as if from comic; 'boots' repeated

A/A*: 6 marks
B/C: 4–5 marks
D/E: 2–3 marks
F/G: 1 mark

4 Possible points of focus:

'football babe', 'sticking the boot in', 'blonde bruiser', 'dirtiest player in women's game', 'violent', 'yanked, punched, lunged', 'knee-high tackles', 'booting the ball into the face…', 'vicious', 'suspended' and 'banned', 'deeply regretful'

Better answers will include mention of her remorse at the end.

A/A*: 7–8 marks
B/C: 5–6 marks
D/E: 3–4 marks
F/G: 1–2 marks

5 Extract from a Grade C response

The impression we get of Elizabeth Lambert is that she plays football like an animal. She is very violent. She is described as a 'blonde bruiser', like a boxer, and she sticks the boot in. This can be good in a football defender, but not if you are setting out to hurt someone. The writer picks out the fact that she committed 'a series of violent fouls in one match', so it is not just the odd incident. Also, her fouls seem particularly bad because she pulls hair and performs knee-high tackles …

pages 116–117

1 Two marks for purpose(s):

Answers might include: Botham presented as hero/shows sports stars can do more than just perform in sports/show what is good about Britain, etc.

Two marks for audience:

Answers might include: newspaper readers/those attracted by headings and pictures/fans of Botham, etc.

A/A*: purposes and audience(s) with detailed explanation – 4 marks
B/C: purpose(s) and audience(s) with clear explanation – 3 marks
D/E: purpose and audience explained – 2 marks
F/G: attempt to identify purpose and/or audience – 1 mark

2 Any four from:

- 'Heroes leading from the front' (1)
- 'His … performances inspired a nation' (1)
- 'relentless charity walks' (1)
- 'the aura and invincibility' (1)
- 'looks to build on the £10m that he has already raised for charity' (1)
- 'his latest marathon effort' (1)
- 'such determination' (1)

C/A*: 4 details – 4 marks
D/E: 3 details – 3 marks
F: 2 details – 2 marks
G: 1 detail – 1 mark

3 Possible language to be commented on:

'Facebook generation'; repeat of 'pressures' and phrasing ('in lofts', 'in universities', etc); question and answer; humour – 'they gather to knit'; the unexpected - 'modern life is stressful, let's make chutney'; lists ('jam-making, crocheting and even…'); quotations from people involved, etc.

A/A*: 7–8 marks
B/C: 5–6 marks
D/E: 3–4 marks
F/G: 1–2 marks

4 Possible points:

Opening: apparently 'everyday' first sentence, then the sarcasm (updating the Facebook profile); introduction of the unexpected (the Women's Institute as a solution); repetition of phrasing in third paragraph to make it sound as if it is happening everywhere; and the joke to end the paragraph, poking fun at the women.

Ending: quotations to make it more real; ridiculous idea that these groups have to exist so people talk to each other; novelty stressed; 'Young Conservative' – joke, poking fun at the women and their old-fashioned pursuits; final paragraph perhaps showing that normal young women are involved in these activities.

A/A*: 7–8 marks
B/C: 5–6 marks
D/E: 3–4 marks
F/G: 1–2 marks

Extract from a Grade C response

The writer begins by telling us how hard life is for young women, so we feel sorry for them. He explains that they have pressures at home and at work and still have to update their Facebook pages. This must be to make us smile, because that is never a hard task. They must be exaggerating what they have to do. However, in order to make their lives easier, they are joining the WI, which is strange because that must take even more of their time. Not only that, they meet in bedrooms and lofts, so the writer must expect us to see these people as really weird…

pages 118–119

1 Possible points:

Fostered children will be 'fun' (face and action); they will be attractive; they will be fit and healthy, so good to have around; you will make them jump for joy; she is in the sky, so could be like a god-send…

A/A*: 4 marks
B/C: 3 marks
D/E: 2 marks
F/G: 1 mark

Extract from a Grade C response

When we look at the picture, we are supposed to spot the fact that the girl is really happy and it is saying to us that people can bring this sort of excitement to youngsters if they become carers. She looks pretty and is smiling and looks healthy, as if this is what all kids who are fostered are like. This is to persuade people to foster children. There are clouds all around the girl, so she seems to have been sent sky-high with happiness because she has been fostered…

2 Possible language for comment:

'Specialist' – making carers seem valuable; 'highly motivated individuals' – anyone who becomes a carer should feel good about themselves; financially rewarding – 'generous retainer' with 'top-up'; sounds like a profession – 'specialist training', 'part of a professional team; '24 hour support'; appealing for people with 'skills' – makes people feel positive about themselves if they apply; 'make a difference' – emotive appeal

A/A*: 7–8 marks
B/C: 5–6 marks
D/E: 3–4 marks
F/G: 1–2 marks

3 Two marks for each explanation. Answers might include:

1 sense of something different; links to picture and war scenario

2 rhetorical question; metaphor; sense of dealing with dangerous situations; comparison with normal boring life

3 to appeal to people wanting to make a difference/wanting excitement; sense that you will be facing danger; use of cliché

4 making reader think they are special; implies we are all looking for something more exciting

A/A*: 2 detailed explanations of each (7–8 marks)
B/C: 2 clear explanations of 2–3 of them and one clear explanation of the other(s) (5–6 marks)
D/E: explanations showing some understanding (3–4 marks)
F/G: comments, some of which are valid (1–2 marks)

4 Possible comments:

Picture: desk in middle of a war zone; linking of desk job and job of soldier; sense of danger and risk; someone has left the chair to..?; sense of desk job being modern (PC etc) and important – it is in the foreground…

Other features: 'Not exactly…' – in larger font to emphasise it; white on black (goodness coming out of darkness?); upper case stresses importance

'Careers in British intelligence' and 'Cheltenham' put it into context

GCHQ logo and details top left give it credibility and status

A/A*: 7–8 marks
B/C: 5–6 marks
D/E: 3–4 marks
F/G: 1–2 marks

pages 120–121

1 Possible comments:

emotive appeal; pretty but sad baby girl; wet nose for sympathy or suggesting sickness; forlorn look in eyes; no sense of parent; face fills picture, giving importance

A/A*: 4 marks
B/C: 3 marks
D/E: 2 marks
F/G: 1 mark

2 Possible comments:

Stressing togetherness of parent and child to begin ('cried…cried', 'laughed… laughed');

Repetition of 'The first time' to show newness; contrast of 'normality' of parental reactions in the opening with 'The first time she got sick…'

Intended to shock, reveal hopelessness of parent's situation; intended to motivate reader to react and help

Bottom banner: request for support – joining others who care. Simple appeal: 'Will you?'

A/A*: 4 marks
B/C: 3 marks

D/E: marks
F/G: 1 mark

3 Likely points:

picture link, this time focusing on parent/child bond; 'Even my husband' connection; 'we/you' again; questioning reader again; the picture shows a wider view of what is happening in this second text.

A/A*: 4 marks
B/C: 3 marks
D/E: 2 marks
F/G: 1 mark

Extract from a C Grade response

The two parts are linked because we see the same child. In the first picture, we see how sad and ill he is and in the second we see how this is affecting his father, who is holding him tight. We know that the mother can't save the child when he gets sick, but in the second part we are told that the father can't save him either. Also, of course, both parts of the leaflet are asking the reader to do something to help. The first page says 'We Save the Children. Will you?' and the second one asks us to give some money each month…

4 Some possible points:

First page: 'The first time', etc – almost like a song or a lament

Second page: situation simply stated, simple solution, simple appeal; 'We're… We're…' – confident statements; 'How many/fast/up to you' – all made to sound straightforward. Also, brevity makes it easily accessible to any reader.

A/A*: 4 marks
B/C: 3 marks
D/E: 2 marks
F/G: 1 mark

5 Purpose: to raise donations

Success: likely to focus on effectiveness of pictures, presentational features and perhaps layout; and on text and general appeal.

A/A*: 4 marks
B/C: 3 marks
D/E: 2 marks
F/G: 1 mark

pages 122–123

1 Point: the old language was more varied and interesting

How: giving examples from around the country; probably trying to amuse or confuse the reader; making clear comparison with Americanisms; using touch of humour at the end, as a clear contrast in language styles.

A/A*: 4 marks
B/C: 3 marks
D/E: 2 marks
F/G: 1 mark

Extract from a Grade C response

The writer thinks that modern language is not as good as the language there used to be, because it is 'sloppy' and comes from television and from rappers. To make it clear how much better the language used to be, he gives examples of all the words and phrases he used to hear when he was younger. To do this, he picks bits of language from different places in the country…

2 Any four from:

'hod your whisht', 'moidering', 'mithering', 'midden men', 'fever grates', 'scouring stone', 'causer edge', 'apple kipping', 'tusky', 'taws', 'gibbing', 'broddling your lug', 'taldering'

C/A*: 4 examples
D/F: 3 examples
G: fewer than 3 examples

3 Final sentence: colloquial style; first half formal but second half Americanised and less correct, as young people might speak (2)

First sentence: formal throughout; vocabulary unlikely to be used in Americanised context, like 'fascinating' and 'evoke'; use of (presumably) local term 'Leeds Loiner' (2)

A/A*: 4 marks
B/C: 3 marks
D/E: 2 marks
F/G: 1 mark

4

1 'cherubs': simile, suggesting they look like angels; possibly 'they look' suggests this is an incorrect impression

2 'deranged hounds': metaphor, suggesting they work together ('pack') are mad and unpredictable ('deranged') and like animals ('hounds')

3 'Uncontrollable': at start of sentence gives it emphasis; sense of wildness

4 'It's shocking': 3 for emphasis, stressing 'shocking' and 'demoralising' as powerful effects on teacher; 'daily' comes as an unpleasant surprise

A/A*: four detailed analyses – 4 marks
B/C: two or more clear explanations with some analysis and remaining language explained in less depth – 3 marks

D/E: all four explained, with some understanding – 2 marks
F/G: two or more brief comments

5 Any two points from:

we hear the writer's 'speaking voice' / we understand exactly how the writer is feeling / we get exactly what she is thinking and not necessarily in processed sentences, e.g. 'Uncontrollable at times'

C/A*: 2 points
G/C: 1 point

6 Possible points:

- The students (1)
- Students and senior members of staff (2)
- Students with examples, e.g. 'deranged hounds', etc; and senior members of staff (because ordinary teachers are 'left to flounder') (3)
- Above points with explanations (4)

B/A*: 3 points, with valid explanation
C: 3 points, with some explanation
D/E: 2 or 3 points, with attempted explanation
F/G: 1 or 2 points

pages 124–125

1 Any two from:

- Getting the floors washed (1)
- Getting the men's clothes clean (1)
- Suggestion she got the toilets cleaned (1)

E/A*: 2 points
F/G: 1 point

2 Likely points:

Men would not allow their shirts to be washed. Suggestion at start that the doctors had not insisted on important cleanliness. No one took responsibility

A/A*: 4 marks
B/C: 3 marks
D/E: 2 marks
F/G: 1 mark

3 Possible points:

Wants things cleaned / dynamic enough to order what was needed / puts necessary system in place to get shirts clean / natural organiser, leader

A/A*: 4 marks
B/C: 3 marks
D/E: 2 marks
F/G: 1 mark

4 Either of:

Sees him as a deserter, so his suffering is all he deserves /she seems cold in her description, right from the start

Writes about how he is treated with sarcasm, as if it should not be happening like this / the initial description is to show his desperation and the horror of his situation

So, 'This is War' could be interpreted as agreeing that men must die in this way or as showing how terrible war is.

A/A*: 7–8 marks
B/C: 5–6 marks
D/E: 3–4 marks
F/G: 1–2 marks

Extract from a Grade C response

The nurse does not seem to like the soldier. She describes his injuries but does not say she feels sorry for him. She tells us about his eye being shot out and how he is treated afterwards but says it does not matter if he dies because 'he was a deserter'. It sounds as if this sort of thing happens everyday when you are a nurse, even if it is not wartime: 'Things like this also happen in peace time'...

5 Some possible points:

clinical description ('The ball tore out his left eye'); uncaring nature of ambulance men ('bundled'); his pain ('cursing and screaming'); 'if he were bounced to death' and 'breakneck speed' (with play on 'break' 'neck') sounds careless; simple grim reality ('discipline must be maintained') etc.

A/A*: 7–8 marks
B/C: 5–6 marks
D/E: 3–4 marks
F/G: 1–2 marks

pages 126–127

1 Any four services from:

help with events / chip timing / help for charities / help with sports injuries / cheap or free online race entries / entry management for races / online entry for runners / cheaper online entry / list of online entry forms / confidentiality with details / exclusive entry to Freckleton Half Marathon

C/A*: 4 services
D/F: 3 services
G/U: fewer than 3 services

2 Likely points:

dense, small, hard to read / full of detail / lacks clarity in side-bars etc / short of visual elements /

lacks clear heading, sub-heads, etc / useful side-bar with items to click on

A/A*: 7–8 marks
B/C: 5–6 marks
D/E: 3–4 marks
F/G: 1–2 marks

Extract from a Grade C response

The layout is good because it offers many things which can be clicked on, such as the items in the side bar, and also there is bold font which makes the most important phrases stand out, e.g. 'Are you a charity?' There are not many pictures to make it interesting, but there are some books shown and that would be attractive to anyone looking for things to read about running…

3 Any four from:

Possible language: 'Welcome' and 'friendly' / 'expertise' / 'please' / enticing questions / 'Free' / 'click here' / first person approach, etc.

A/A*: 7–8 marks
B/C: 5–6 marks
D/E: 3–4 marks
F/G: 1–2 marks

pages 128–129

1 Any four from:

'spectre'/ 'secluded' / 'terrible hallucinations' / 'the mysterious one' / 'haunting'

C/A*: 4 examples
D/E: 3 examples
F: 2 examples
G: 1 example

2 Answers are likely to consider details in the story: characters and story-line. Also likely to consider final sentence: 'short and spare' – which sounds critical; 'expertly structured', 'beautifully written prose' both offering praise; style of writing memorable – 'as haunting as the best ghost story'.

A/A*: 7–8 marks
B/C: 5–6 marks
D/E: 3–4 marks
F/G: 1–2 marks

Extract from a Grade C response

The reviewer seems to like the book. The story is described in a positive way, with 'terrible hallucinations' mentioned, which seems interesting. Frank is 'mysterious', which is another quality you might expect in a good book, and there is mention of 'horrific traumas', which also seems the sort of thing a reader would be interested in. Towards the end, the writer mentions the fact that it is all in 'beautifully written prose', which must prove it is worth reading…

3 Opening: likely to focus on emphasis on ghostly vocabulary ('ghost stories', 'spectre') and on attraction ('gripping tale').

Ending: returns to idea of ghost stories; and on language as in previous question; and repetition of 'best'

A/A*: 4 marks
B/C: 3 marks
D/E: 2 marks
F/G: 1 mark

4 Likely to mention: 'pressures', 'ordeals', 'fatigue and grief', 'challenges'; and 'touching moment', 'struggled with emotion'… It is a sympathetic picture, recognising the difficulties for parents and how they have to cope with their situation and how they need more support.

A/A*: 7–8 marks
B/C: 5–6 marks
D/E: 3–4 marks
F/G: 1–2 marks

5 Answers likely to mention how she feels sympathy for parents, how they need support, 'compassion' and more 'common sense' from the state. Finally, more money needs to be invested.

A/A*: 7–8 marks
B/C: 5–6 marks
D/E: 3–4 marks
F/G: 1–2 marks

pages 130–131

1 'battled': Two from: a fighter/ he found it a struggle/ maybe heroic / or anything sensible

'collapsed': Two from: broke down / could not cope with pressure / maybe has a medical problem / not equal to the task / or anything sensible

2 Two marks for each idea plus analysis, e.g.

1 look on face / eyes closed (1): exhausted / devastated / can't believe what has happened / in pain…(1)

2 black background (1): sense of darkness / doom; as if he has fallen into darkness and disappointment / nothing else matters – just his pain…(1)

3 Some possible answers:

- **'The world of work and Higher Education is becoming more complicated and**

competitive': alliteration builds effect / 4-syllable words stress complexity …

- **'It is essential… to explore…': no apparent alternative/ inducement of 'exploration'**…
- **'opportunities'/'wealth of opportunities':** opening up the future / sounds exciting, full of possibilities / value…
- **'important'/'importance':** repeated/ stresses how vital it is…
- **'valuable'/'crucial':** building up effect / balance between reward and desperate need…

A/A*:	7–8 marks
B/C:	5–6 marks
D/E:	3–4 marks
F/G:	1–2 marks

Extract from a Grade C response

The school says that the students need to attend because the world is becoming 'more complicated and competitive'. It uses alliteration here, and the 'c's sound quite complicated, like what the students will have to face. The fact that it is competitive is another good reason why they need to be there. In a way, it is saying that if they do not go, they will miss out and others will have an advantage over them…

4

C/A*:	Analytical comment on 'wealth of opportunities' for: 'wealth' (value) and range of chances ('opportunities'); and perhaps on 'aimed' – precisely targeted, like a trained marksman (2)
D/G:	one comment on the phrase or paraphrase of statement (1)

pages 132–133

1 Possible comments, with support:

strange looking funny man, with elegant woman; she is glamorous and embarrassed by his behaviour; 'frequent' TV technique – attractive young woman and older less attractive man; fashionable woman and old-fashioned man

C/A*:	2 points with clear support from text (4 marks)
D:	2 points with some support (3 marks)
E/F:	2 points (2 marks)
G:	1 point (1 mark)

Extract from a Grade C response

The two presenters do not seem to go together at all. Tess Daly is tall and beautiful and looks like she has just stepped out of a fashion show. The small fat man with her must be there to make everyone laugh, because he looks old and is going bald. He might even be tumbling backwards and she is laughing at him and trying to rescue him. His trousers are the sort of thing a clown might wear…

2 Detail will depend on points made. However, likely to select the joke ('short'); Corbett's height; 'towered over'.

A/A*:	4 marks
B/C:	3 marks
D/E:	2 marks
F/G:	1 mark

3 Possible points:

'Squeezy living'; concept of 14 cheerleaders; 'stretches out'; 'sniff out'; 'only two wore seat belts'; 'no room for the pom-poms'; 'must have been bigger'; speed of getting into car; group of under 8s…

A/A*:	7–8 marks
B/C:	5–6 marks
D/E:	3–4 marks
F/G:	1–2 marks

pages 134–135

1 Likely details:

umbrella collapsed, steam coming out of ears, list of disasters, 'take five and nibble chocolate'. Answers might see this as serious or jokey, but should be supported with evidence and explained.

A/A*:	4 marks
B/C:	3 marks
D/E:	2 marks
F/G:	1 mark

2 Might say this is offering evidence, which convinces; might focus on apparently scientific interpretation of evidence. Better answers likely to question whether the interpretation can be believed when given by employee of a chocolate company.

A/A*:	4 marks
B/C:	3 marks
D/E:	2 marks
F/G:	1 mark

Extract from a Grade C response

The penultimate paragraph seems to be designed to convince us that eating chocolate is a good thing. We are told how much to eat and that if we do eat the right amount (40 grams over two weeks), our metabolism will be improved. We might believe this because a researcher tells us. However, the

Extract from a Grade C response

The review of 'Taken' uses language which will attract the sort of person who watches action movies. There are violent phrases like 'shoot-em-up' which take us back to cowboy days and 'deadbeat dad' which has alliteration and makes him sound low down and beaten. There is also language to appeal to young people, such as 'alienated sprog'. In contrast, 'Now that's poetry' is for a much more intellectual audience, so the language being used is much less harsh – it starts with the soft 'love story' and 'making verse captivating on screen'...

pages 150–152 Exam practice (Higher)

1 Appropriate details:

'award-winning escorted tour of your life'; 'expert tour managers'; 'quality hotels'; 'select excursions included'; 'head and shoulders above the rest'; 'over 30 years'; voted 'best tour operator'; 'topping consumer surveys'; 'best organisation, service, quality'; 'job is to make them perfect'; unique home departure service; '34 unbeatable itineraries'

A/A*:	7–8 marks
B/C:	5–6 marks
D/E:	3–4 marks
F/G:	1–2 marks

2 Possible presentational points:

Picture: links with text; gives impression of country and people; indigenous population happy; beauty of countryside

Headline: bold capitals, rhyme making things seem harmonious

Sub-heading: larger font to stand out; directs the reader to the picture; emotive approach – 'soaring', 'plunging', 'take your breath away'

Caption: sense of grandeur, reflected in picture; 'Highlight' – idea that there are particularly outstanding moments; also, the picture is from a high point

A/A*:	7–8 marks
B/C:	5–6 marks
D/E:	3–4 marks
F/G:	1–2 marks

3 Likely content:

liked it – 'This I cannot recommend highly enough'; amused – 'decorate the place'; mocks – 'such attractions as an altar made of rib cages' etc; fascinated – details such as the grim reaper; sarcastic – 'engagingly called...'; modern viewpoint – 'These guys must have been a barrel of laughs'; exaggeration – 'some guy coming along with a tape measure'; sees ridiculous side of it all – 'a half-mad monk with time on his hands'; cynical – 'nice little money-spinner'...

A/A*:	7–8 marks
B/C:	5–6 marks
D/E:	3–4 marks
F/G:	1–2 marks

Extract from a Grade C response

Bryson thinks the idea of the mausoleum is 'inspired' and has great fun telling the reader about all the items which are in it. He describes all the grim 'attractions' and there is so much detail that he must have enjoyed the visit. He also seems to find some of it funny, because he talks about the 'grim reaper' and the idea of 'cheery sentiments' which are not cheery at all. When he says 'These guys must have been a barrel of laughs to be around', he is actually thinking exactly the opposite...

4 Possible language points:

The True Peru: rhyme in headline; 'soaring condors' – assonance gives sense of space; 'plunging gorges' – dramatic adjectives; 'take your breath away' – emotive metaphor / cliché; 'Literally' – short sentence to stop you; 'hamlet' sounds rustic; 'higher than...the roof of Europe' – metaphor indicates height; 'lunar' – vivid metaphor/adjective; 'I tilt my head back...' – sentence stretches and captures desperation for air, etc.

America: positive vocabulary throughout; adjectives of excellence; hyperbole – 'tour of your life'; clichés – 'head and shoulders above the rest; description of destination – 'delightful', 'stunning sights'; list of three – 'organisation, quality and service'; suggests credibility / professionalism – 'philosophy', 'investments'; superlative – 'perfect'; personalised – 'your front door', etc

Bill Bryson: sarcasm / irony throughout; colloquial style – 'some monk', 'barrel of laughs', 'some guy'; unexpected vocabulary – 'decorate'; rhetoric – 'Is that rich enough?'; long sentence about bones to show how the decorations stretch out; humour in detail – 'trimmed', 'fashioned', 'chandeliers'; ridiculous images – 'grim reaper in his hooded robe', etc.

A/A*:	14–16 marks
B/C:	10–13 marks
D/E:	6–9 marks
F/G:	1–5 marks

pages 153–155 Exam Practice (Foundation)

1 Any four from:

sight seeing tours, possibility of extending stay, all the sights of America's West Coast, plenty of free time, Grand Canyon, Las Vegas, Palm Springs, Hollywood, Pacific Coast, San Francisco

C/A*: 4 attractions
D/E: 3 attractions
F: 2 attractions
G: 1 attraction

2 Sights visited, Tour Manager, chance to extend stay, 'great value', 'plenty of time to relax and make own discoveries', flights from local airports, etc.

A/A*: 4 marks
B/C: 3 marks
D/E: 2 marks
F/G: 1 mark

3 Hospital: different from UK; unclean; syringes and flies; staff just spoke Turkish; place where you get singing and food after course of treatment

People: doctor knew what he was doing; orderly kind; efficient nurse; all workers appear kind

A/A*: 7–8 marks
B/C: 5–6 marks
D/E: 3–4 marks
F/G: 1–2 marks

Extract from a Grade C response

It seems that the writer does not like Turkish hospitals. He says that there were lots of things wrong, like blood on the walls, so probably he and his wife were very disappointed. The doctor did not even speak English and that will have upset them. He suggests though that the people there were very nice. The nurse was 'efficient' and he gives her credit for that and the orderly was very unusual and stroked his wife's hair…

4 Answers might include:

Clear: 'This is what happens…', 'After a minute…', 'Then…' etc – told like a story

Feelings stated simply: 'the people of Paris want me dead'

Interesting: 'turn you into gooey crepe' – vivid metaphor; 'So you wait' – short sentence sounds antagonistic; 'a quarter of a mile away' – exaggeration to stress size of road; humour – 'to look at the fin-de-siècle lamppost; children 'herded' like cattle.

A/A*: 10–12 marks
B/C: 7–9 marks
D/E: 4–6 marks
F/G: 1–3 marks

5

	Discover America's Golden West	Holiday Disaster
pictures	Main picture: tram, palm trees set scene, looks exotic; sunny, attractive Man looks happy; bridge behind to show what visitors will see	Prominent cartoon exaggerates problems in the hospital – syringes all over the floor, flies buzzing Man and wife looking anxious, with man making vain attempt to be reassuring, while doctor looks evil and as if he's really rather enjoying himself
other presentational features	Name of firm prominent; 'Discover…' bold and highlights sense of discovery; text boxes to simplify the information; plane to draw attention to plane i nformation; phone number large at bottom and this text box has white on black to grab attention; cost of holiday highlighted, presumably to indicate it's cheap…	Bold text under the heading sets comic tone of article – Turkey is for Christmas, not holidays', with a play on the word 'Turkey' Skull and crossbones again emphasises the tone

A/A*: 10–12 marks
B/C: 7–9 marks
D/E: 4–6 marks
F/G: 1–3 marks

Producing non-fiction texts

No two people will write the same answer to the kind of tasks contained in this Exam Practice Workbook – or, indeed, in the exam itself. There is no such thing as a right or wrong answer when it comes to writing essays, but your examiner will expect you to demonstrate certain skills in your writing.

The following grid gives you an indication of the sort of grade your response is likely to achieve.

Grade	Skills required
A/A*	• content is detailed, well organised and convincing • totally suitable for the intended purpose and audience • likely to grab and hold the reader's interest • uses varied paragraphs which develop meaning • original and effective use of language • accurate spelling of an advanced but appropriate vocabulary • a wide range of accurate punctuation
B	• content is appropriate and well organised • appropriate for the intended purpose and audience • likely to hold the reader's interest • uses varied paragraphs • effective use of language • mostly accurate spelling of suitable vocabulary • a range of accurate punctuation
C	• content is appropriate for the task • clear understanding of the purpose and audience • interests the reader • uses well-structured paragraphs • uses language appropriately • mostly accurate spelling, with some more complex words • a range of punctuation
D	• content addresses the topic satisfactorily • some suitability for the purpose and audience • some interest for the reader • uses paragraphs, mostly of same length • language mostly used appropriately • generally accurate spelling • punctuation – mostly basic – used accurately
E	• content attempts to deal with the topic • attempts suitable style for purpose and audience • occasionally interesting • uses some paragraphs • language sometimes appropriate • uses some accurate spelling and punctuation
F/G	• content has some link with the topic • may not be a suitable style for purpose and audience • fails to interest the reader • might not use paragraphs • language might be inappropriate • some accurate spelling of simple words but often inaccurate punctuation

pages 162–163

1 and **2**

A/A*:	15–16 marks
B:	13–14 marks
C:	10–12 marks
D:	8--9 marks
E:	5–7 marks
F/G:	1-4 marks

page 165

Further practice:

A/A*:	6 marks
B:	5 marks
C:	4 marks
D:	3 marks
E:	2 marks
F/G:	1 mark

pages 166–167

1 Alternative versions are possible, e.g. the exclamation mark could be in a different place.

Why is it that some schools have some teachers that are far from perfect? Why is it that some students do not, as a consequence, reach the grades of which they should be capable? It simply is not fair. In my own case, the teachers in my school, most of whom have been here for many years, seem excellent. How lucky am I! What a relief it is to be here.

1 mark for each correct use:

A/A*:	8 marks
B:	7 marks
C:	6 marks
D:	5 marks
E:	4 marks
F/G:	1–3 marks

2 As soon as I walked into the classroom, Mrs Reynolds saw me.

"Just the young man I was looking for," she said. "I would like a word with you."

I immediately feared the worst.

"I don't think," I said, "that I have done anything wrong yet today."

"No. I just want some information," she said, smiling like a rattlesnake.

A/A*:	only one error (10 marks)
B:	2–3 errors (8–9 marks)
C:	4 errors (6–7 marks)
D:	5 errors (4–5 marks)
E:	6 errors (3 marks)
F/G:	more than 6 errors (1–2 marks)

3 Each of the schools in this area has been improved massively in the past few years: there are new buildings with state of the art computer facilities; two schools now have their own swimming pools; and in every school the libraries have been completely replaced.

A/A*:	correct (4 marks)
B/C:	1 error (3 marks)
D/E:	2 errors (1 mark)
F/G:	incorrect (0 marks)

5 The school's security measures weren't perfect, that's for sure. Some of the boys' lockers were ransacked and one girl's bag was stolen.

A/A*:	all correct (5 marks)
B:	1 error (4 marks)
C:	2 errors (3 marks)
D/F:	3 errors (2 marks)
G:	more than 3 errors (1 mark)

6

A/A*:	6 marks
B:	5 marks
C:	4 marks
D:	3 marks
E:	2 marks
F/G:	1 mark

pages 168–169

1 Extract will be more formal and sentences will be corrected.

A/A*:	6 marks
B:	5 marks
C:	4 marks
D:	3 marks
E:	2 marks
F/G:	1 mark

2 Two marks for each improved alternative.

3 Response will be in linked sentences, with a topic sentence, etc.

A/A*:	6 marks
B:	5 marks
C:	4 marks
D:	3 marks
E:	2 marks
F/G:	1 mark

4 Language will be formal and suitable for a public performance.

A/A*:	6 marks
B:	5 marks
C:	4 marks
D:	3 marks
E:	2 marks
F/G:	1 mark